Restoration Come

Restoration Comedy

Introduced by Duncan Wu

with texts taken from
Restoration Drama: An Anthology

edited by David Womersley

Blackwell
Publishing

Copyright © 2002 by Blackwell Publishers Ltd
a Blackwell Publishing company

Editorial matter, selection and arrangement copyright © Duncan Wu and David
Womersley 2002

Editorial Offices:
108 Cowley Road, Oxford OX4 1JF, UK
Tel: +44 (0)1865 791100
350 Main Street, Malden, MA 02148-5018, USA
Tel: +1 781 388 8250

The Blackwell Publishing logo is a trade mark of Blackwell Publishing Ltd.

First published 2002 by Blackwell Publishers Ltd, a Blackwell Publishing Company.

Library of Congress Cataloging-in-Publication Data has been applied for.

ISBN 0-631-23471-3 (hbk) ISBN 0-631-23472-1 (pbk)

A catalogue record for this title is available from the British Library

Set in 8/10pt Galliard
by Kolam Information Services Pvt. Ltd, Pondicherry, India

For further information on
Blackwell Publishers, visit our website:
www.blackwellpublishers.com

Contents

Series Editor's Preface

The Blackwell Essential Literature series offers readers the chance to possess authoritative texts of key poems (and in one case drama) across the standard periods and movements. Based on correspondent volumes in the Blackwell Anthologies series most of these volumes run to no more than 200 pages. The acknowledged virtues of the Blackwell Anthologies are range and variety; those of the Essential Literature series are authoritative selection, compactness and ease of use. They will be particularly helpful to students hard-pressed for time, who need a digest of the poetry of each historical period.

In selecting the contents of each volume particular attention has been given to major writers whose works are widely taught at most schools and universities. Each volume contains a general introduction designed to introduce the reader to those central works.

Together, these volumes comprise a crucial resource for anyone who reads or studies poetry.

Duncan Wu
St Catherine's College, Oxford

Introduction

Duncan Wu

England's great tradition of theatre-writing and performing came to an abrupt end when in 1642 the Puritans succeeded in making dramatic entertainments illegal. Despite frequent infractions of that ordinance over the years (masques were even performed at Cromwell's behest), it was not until Charles II restored the Stuart succession in 1660 that theatre found a new lease of life. He licensed two new companies: the King's company, managed by Thomas Killigrew, and the Duke's company, managed by William D'Avenant. (They were to join forces in 1682.) As an unashamed affront to Puritan delicacy, women were allowed to play female parts for the first time (as had been customary in France, where D'Avenant and Killigrew had been exiled with the court).

Restoration theatres were more sophisticated affairs than those in which Shakespeare and his contemporaries had worked at the beginning of the century. The new buildings were roofed, with backstage areas, a proscenium arch, areas for musicians (the equivalent of orchestra pits), thrust stages, scenery, and curtains in front of the stage. Proprietors were willing to invest considerable capital, ensuring that theatres had state of the art facilities for audience and actors alike. The first Theatre Royal in Drury Lane opened in 1663, the ancestor of the one that stands on the same site today. Nell Gwynne made her debut there in Dryden's *Indian Queen* in 1665. No less than Sir Christopher Wren designed the Dorset Garden Theatre that fronted the River Thames, which opened in 1671. It cost £9,000 to build – a fortune for those times.

The front of house was in many respects the most important feature of the new theatres. There were three main areas: galleries, boxes and the pit. The pit was the most fashionable place to be seen, as Horner indicates when in *The Country Wife* he remarks: 'I wou'd no more miss seeing a new Play the first day, than I wou'd miss sitting in the wits Row'. Horner's enthusiasm derives partly from the fact that making assignations, drinking and chatting was for many theatregoers the point of being there, and their inattentiveness is sometimes deplored in various prologues and epilogues.

The two plays in this volume span 25 years: *The Country Wife* (1675) and *The Way of the World* (1700). The catch-all handle 'Restoration comedy' is in this context rather misleading. It could be argued that the Restoration came to an end when Charles's brother James, who succeeded him in 1685, fled to France (on the second attempt) three years later. After his abdication parliament brought William of Orange to London from Holland, proclaimed king in what became known as the 'Glorious Revolution'. Thus, while Wycherley's play dates from the Restoration period proper, Congreve's is from that of the late Stuarts, having been first produced during the reign of William and Mary.[1]

The historical context in which each was written is reflected in their respective characters. There's no doubting that in which Wycherley's play is set, from the very first speech; Wycherley knew that the moment when the curtain went up on his actors offered his one opportunity (perhaps the last) to seize the audience's attention – and he did it, cleverly, with a dirty joke: 'A Quack is as fit for a Pimp, as a Midwife for a Bawd; they are still but in their way, both helpers of Nature'. This isn't just a joke; it contains the essence of what is to follow. The conceit of the play is that Horner's deception – that he claims to be rendered impotent by a cure for venereal disease – will enable him to make jealous husbands pimp their wives to him, even the tyrannical Pinchwife. Horner is the sexually voracious 'Quack' who will lead these husbands (and wives) to their doom. But the joke also alerts us to the milieu in which these characters live and breathe. It is, recognizably, the metropolitan London of Charles II's reign (one scene is even set in Covent Garden piazza), the city described by Rochester, who has a similar clear-sightedness as to its moral character.

Most of all, this is a world of infidelity and sexual license. When Harcourt tells Horner that 'your Sting is gone', the joke is on him; Horner's unimpaired virility is the secret that underpins the dramatic action. It means that there are two worlds in the play: one in which that secret is known and understood, another in which jealous husbands entrust their wives to someone they mistakenly regard as 'an errant French Capon'.[2] The viewing and buying of china, an innocent enough activity, becomes in this play a code for Horner's rampant cuckolding of other men's wives. (China-houses – specializing in oriental merchandise – were often used for assignations.) For sheer comic invention, Act IV, scene iii must be one of the most impressive things to come out of this phase of English drama. The tension generated from Horner's bedding of Lady Fidget is as tightly plotted, as ingenious and funny as Orton's *What the Butler Saw*. Orton once observed that 'Farce is higher than comedy in that it is very close to tragedy. You've only got to play some of Shakespeare's tragedies plain and they are nearly farcical.'[3] The tension in Wycherley's masterpiece (and kinship with Orton's work) derives from the darker elements in the plot. The most obvious manifestation of this is Jack Pinchwife, a thuggish ex-rake who forces his wife to cross-dress in order (so he believes) to conceal her attractiveness,[4] and then forces her to write a letter to Horner at his dictation, under the threat, 'Write as I bid you, or I

---

[1]   Expert opinion varies, but there is a growing consensus that for academic purposes Restoration drama can be considered as having begun in 1660 and ended in 1714.

[2]   A capon is a castrated cock.

[3]   As quoted, John Lahr, *Prick Up Your Ears: The Biography of Joe Orton* (Harmondsworth: Allen Lane, 1978), p. 225.

[4]   This is another irony, of course, because the actress playing Margery Pinchwife, like Elizabeth Boutell, is thereby given an opportunity to display her legs.

will write Whore with this Penknife in your Face'. Pinchwife's view of love and sex is riddled with violence. He says that Cupid 'gave women first their craft, their art of deluding', and he declares his wish to 'strangle that little Monster'. When he comes upon his wife's private correspondence with Horner he draws his sword on her with the intention of making 'an end of you thus, and all my plagues together'. He draws his sword on her again at the end of the play, saying 'I will never hear woman again, but make 'em all silent', and then threatens Horner with the same fate; it is, indeed, at that moment that this farcical 'comedy' most closely approaches tragedy.

Those darker elements arise largely out of male sexual anxiety and the moral emptiness of the city. If men are not motivated by lust, their interest in women stems from money or social gain (as with Sparkish's marriage to Alithea). Sir Jaspar's interest in his wife is little more than proprietorial. They seem to live in a state of constant agitation – 'Making you a Cuckold, 'tis that they all doe, as soon as they can'. Even the more relaxed Sparkish believes that 'if her constitution incline her to't, she'l have it sooner or later by the world'. The dramatic tension arising from this is fully articulated in the furtiveness with which Horner carries out his scheme, arranging to let Mrs Pinchwife out 'the back way'.

But the most telling indicator of the character of this play lies in its ending. In Shakespearean and Jonsonian comedy we measure the success of the drama by its ability to resolve moral ambiguity. *Measure for Measure* remains problematic because the Duke's trustworthiness is in question, and his idea of a satisfactory ending hardly accords with ours. *The Country Wife* is less obviously fraught, but its resolution hardly inspires confidence. Its plot is concluded only by a reassertion of the deception that caused the trouble in the first place, when the Quack doctor returns to abuse his integrity as a man of science, declaring that Horner is 'An Eunuch!' Can this lie be sustained indefinitely? Almost certainly not; it barely survives to the final moments of the play, threatened as it is by Mrs Pinchwife who is anxious to testify to Horner's potency: ''Tis false Sir, you shall not disparage poor Mr Horner, for to my certain knowledge –'. As usual, she is silenced, and the truth suppressed one last time. This is a world built on lies in which people are better off not knowing the truth, especially if it would realize their worst fears. The best that can be hoped for is a continuation of the duplicity that permits its inhabitants to continue fearing their wives' fidelity, while those wives secretly enjoy their lovers. Horner jokingly remarks that

> a silly Mistriss, is like a weak place, soon got, soon lost, a man has scarce time for plunder; she betrays her Husband, first to her Gallant, and then her Gallant, to her Husband.

It is no joke. The men of this play, be they husband or gallant, feel themselves to be the playthings of women, who control their well-being by dint of the power they exert within the relationship.

Congreve's *The Way of the World*, written a generation later, is a less threatened work, and the product of a less fragile environment. No less a critic than William Hazlitt described it as 'an essence almost too fine; and the sense of pleasure evaporates in an aspiration after something that seems too exquisite ever to have been realized'.[5] By the time it was written in 1700 unease over the Catholicizing tendencies of Charles and James had receded under the Protestant William III; peace had been established between France and Britain in 1697, and the Act of Settlement of 1700 consolidated the shift of power away from the monarch towards parliament. It would all make for a less volatile political regime. None of these events are specifically referred to in Congreve's play, but the greater certainty they generated is part of its character. For instance, where in Wycherley's play it is hard to find any evidence of mutual affection among the characters (and the insecurity of their world stems from that fact), the fundamental assumption of *The Way of the World* is that beneath the sparring, gossip and jockeying for position, its protagonists genuinely care for and even love each other. In his prefatory epistle Congreve states that his aim was to create characters who displayed 'an affected Wit; a Wit, which at the same time that it is affected, is also false'. His point is that beneath the surface relationships blossom and take their course. His characters are more persuasive than Wycherley's, partly because they have greater depth.

This is evident from the outset. In the first scene we encounter Fainall and Mirabell apparently swapping remarks about Mirabell's romantic life, while beneath the surface each attempts to fathom the other's partiality for Mrs Marwood. At the beginning of Act II (in St James's Park), Mrs Fainall and Mrs Marwood exchange a vituperative banter about their mutual hatred of men, while each attempts to work out the other's feelings for Mirabell. 'You change Colour', Mrs Fainall remarks, at the mention of his name. 'Because I hate him', lies Mrs Marwood – which Mrs Fainall compounds with a matching untruth: 'So do I; but I can hear him nam'd'. Congreve describes a world in which the feigning display of wit is preferable to – and more socially acceptable than – emotional disclosure. These characters prefer to baffle, to keep each other guessing, to masquerade, to banter, rather than speak the feelings they truly feel.

The play is full of satire, but Congreve's characters are not one-dimensional; they are at once figures in a comic portrayal of London life, and real people with an emotional and psychological investment in the relationships of which they are part. Like most London gentlemen, Mirabell seeks a secure income, and regards Millamant as a suitable match on that account; Millamant, for her part, treats her encounters with him largely as an ongoing game. But their conversations reveal a relationship in which there is real passion on both sides. The most obvious example of this is the famous proviso episode, Act IV, scene i, in which they barter, in satirical mode, the material circumstances of their marriage – at least, haggling over money and chattels is what we expect. But Mirabell and Millamant prove less concerned with wealth than with their future relationship. Millamant may be attempting to amuse when she speaks of being allowed to 'lie a Bed

[5]   William Hazlitt, *Lectures on the English Comic Writers*, Lecture IV.

in a morning as long as I please', but when she argues that they are 'as strange as if we had been married a great while; and as well bred as if we were not marri'd at all', she envisages a union she expects to last. And when Mirabell urges her not to wear a mask, or mix with gentlewomen at court, it is felt not to be a piece of masculine tyranny so much as an expression of genuine attachment to Millamant as she is. Astonishingly, Mirabell goes so far as to express concern for the children he expects her to have in the future. When he has left the room, Millamant reveals her true feelings: 'Well, If Mirabell shou'd not make a good Husband, I am a lost thing; – for I find I love him violently'.

The betrothed lovers provide the standard against which to measure such characters as Fainall and his mistress, Mrs Marwood. In their case the monetary incentive that seems initially to have drawn Mirabell to Millamant has not been displaced by emotion. Material considerations motivate them consistently throughout. 'I never lov'd her', Fainall says of the woman to whom he has long been married, and 'Jealous of her I cannot be'. Significantly, the only real violence in the play is that threatened by Fainall against his mistress when their conspiracy breaks down.

Fainall is detained from hurting anyone, and it is symptomatic of the play that even parents are in the end toothless, and even become co-operative. A tyrant in the dressing-room, Lady Wishfort could hardly be regarded as a real threat. This is clear from her first appearance, in a state of casual undress at her dressing-table, raging at her hapless servant. She is the forerunner of Lady Bracknell, and her blustering, like that of Wilde's character, is played mainly for laughs. Her fondness for ratifia (a fruit liqueur) her 'mortal Terror at the apprehension of offending against Decorums', her 'Olio of Affairs' – indeed, her entire vocabulary which includes such words as 'tatterdemalion' and 'Rantipole' (placing her one step away from Mrs Malaprop) – mark her out as a comic character, so that when she declares of Mirabell that 'I'll have him murder'd. I'll have him poyson'd', we do not detect the hint of psychological imbalance found in Mr Pinchwife, let alone evidence of serious intent. And who but a comic character would take as a compliment the remark that 'You are all Camphire and Frankincense, all Chastity and Odour'? That is why Congreve can turn her into a victim of others' deceptions; she is, in the end, too sympathetic to be an outright villain. All in all, Congreve's satire is gentler than that of Wycherley or Rochester. In his London, sexual license is not a matter of life and death, nor is it the excuse for psychological imbalance. When Witwoud says of Petulant that the drinks he has ordered are 'for two fasting Strumpets, and a Bawd troubl'd with Wind', we are on traditional British comic territory, where bodily functions are the occasion for laughter.

The way of the world, invoked by Fainall as justification for his misdeeds, is not in the end a likeable thing. The play's subtext is that although money does make the world go round, life is meaningless without an emotional existence, something to be found only by setting baser appetites aside and cultivating one's feelings, however unnatural or awkward it may be. In the final scene Mirabell does not approach Millamant as we might expect, prompting, for the last time, a shred of doubt as to his true intentions.

'Why do's not the man take me? wou'd you have me give my self to you over again.' 'Ay', he responds, 'and over and over again; for I wou'd have you as often as possibly I can.' It is an unabashed declaration of love, innocent of irony or cynicism. His final quip is a salute to the rakish manner he has abandoned: 'Well, heav'n grant I love you not too well, that's all my fear'.

There are many other Restoration comedies which deserve attention: Buckingham's *The Rehearsal* (1671), Wycherley's *The Plain Dealer* (1676), Etherege's *The Man of Mode* (1676), Congreve's *Love for Love* (1695), Cibber's *Love's Last Shift* (1696), Vanbrugh's *The Relapse* (1696), Farquhar's *The Recruiting Officer* (1706) and *The Beaux' Stratagem* (1707), and Susannah Centlivre's *The Busie Body* (1709). All can be found in David Womersley's exemplary *Restoration Drama: An Anthology*, to which I am deeply indebted as a source for this volume.

Further Reading

Owen, Sue (ed.) (2001) *A Companion to Restoration Drama* (Oxford: Blackwell).

Womersley, David (ed.) (2000) *A Companion to Literature from Milton to Blake* (Oxford: Blackwell).

Womersley, David (ed.) (2000) *Restoration Drama: An Anthology* (Oxford: Blackwell).

William Wycherley
(1641–1716)

The Country Wife (1675)

PROLOGUE, SPOKEN BY MR. HART

Poets like Cudgel'd Bullys, never do
At first, or second blow, submit to you;
But will provoke you still, and ne're have done,
Till you are weary first, with laying on:
The late so bafled Scribler of this day,   5
Though he stands trembling, bids me boldly say,
What we, before most Playes are us'd to do,
For Poets out of fear, first draw on you;
In a fierce Prologue, the still Pit defie,
And e're you speak, like Castril, *give the lye;*   10
But though our Bayses *Batles oft I've fought,*
And with bruis'd knuckles, their dear Conquests bought;
Nay, never yet fear'd Odds upon the Stage,
In Prologue dare not Hector with the Age,
But wou'd take Quarter from your saving hands,   15
Though Bayse *within all yielding Countermands,*
Says you Confed'rate Wits no Quarter give,
Ther'fore his Play shan't ask your leave to live:
Well, let the vain rash Fop, by huffing so,
Think to obtain the better terms of you;   20
But we the Actors humbly will submit,
Now, and at any time, to a full Pit;
Nay, often we anticipate your rage,
And murder Poets for you, on our Stage:
We set no Guards upon our Tyring-Room,   25
But when with flying Colours, there you come,
We patiently you see, give up to you,
Our Poets, Virgins, nay our Matrons too.

THE PERSONS

Mr. *Horner,*	Mr. *Hart.*
Mr. *Harcourt,*	Mr. *Kenaston.*
Mr. *Dorilant,*	Mr. *Lydal.*

Mr. *Pinchwife*,	Mr. *Mohun*.
Mr. *Sparkish*,	Mr. *Haynes*.
Sir. *Jaspar Fidget*,	Mr. *Cartwright*.
Mrs. *Margery Pinchwife*,	Mrs. *Bowtel*.
Mrs. *Alithea*,	Mrs. *James*.
My Lady *Fidget*,	Mrs. *Knep*.
Mrs. *Dainty Fidget*,	Mrs. *Corbet*.
Mrs. *Squeamish*,	Mrs. *Wyatt*.
Old Lady *Squeamish*,	Mrs. *Rutter*.
Waiters, Servants, *and* Attendants.	
A *Boy.*	
A *Quack*,	Mr. *Schotterel*.
Lucy, Alithea *'s Maid*,	Mrs. *Cory.*

The Scene, London.

Act I

Scene I

Enter Horner, *and* Quack *following him at a distance.*

Hor. A Quack is as fit for a Pimp, as a Midwife for a Bawd; they are still but in their way, both helpers of Nature. – [*aside.*] – Well, my dear Doctor, hast thou done what I desired.

Qu. I have undone you for ever with the Women, and reported you throughout the whole Town as bad as an *Eunuch*, with as much   5
trouble as if I had made you one in earnest.

Hor. But have you told all the Midwives you know, the Orange Wenches at the Play-houses, the City Husbands, and old Fumbling Keepers of this end of the Town, for they'l be the readiest to report it.

Qu. I have told all the Chamber-maids, Waiting women, Tyre   10
women, and Old women of my acquaintance; nay, and whisper'd it as a secret to'em, and to the Whisperers of *Whitehal*; so that you need not doubt 'twill spread, and you will be as odious to the handsome young Women, as –

Hor. As the small Pox. – Well –   15

Qu. And to the married Women of this end of the Town, as –

Hor. As the great ones; nay, as their own Husbands.

Qu. And to the City Dames as Annis-seed *Robin* of filthy and contemptible memory; and they will frighten their Children with your name, especially their Females.   20

Hor. And cry *Horner's* coming to carry you away: I am only afraid 'twill not be believ'd; you told'em 'twas by an *English-French* disaster, and an *English-French* Chirurgeon, who has given me at once, not only a Cure, but an Antidote for the future, against that damn'd malady, and that worse distemper, love, and all other Womens evils.   25

Qu. Your late journey into *France* has made it the more credible, and
your being here a fortnight before you appear'd in publick, looks as
if you apprehended the shame, which I wonder you do not: Well I
have been hired by young Gallants to bely'em t'other way; but you
are the first wou'd be thought a Man unfit for Women.   30
Hor. Dear Mr. Doctor, let vain Rogues be contented only to be
thought abler Men than they are, generally 'tis all the pleasure
they have, but mine lyes another way.
Qu. You take, methinks, a very preposterous way to it, and as ridiculous as if we Operators in Physick, shou'd put forth Bills to disparage   35
our Medicaments, with hopes to gain Customers.
Hor. Doctor, there are Quacks in love, as well as Physick, who get but
the fewer and worse Patients, for their boasting; a good name is
seldom got by giving it ones self, and Women no more than honour
are compass'd by bragging: Come, come Doctor, the wisest Lawyer   40
never discovers the merits of his cause till the tryal; the wealthiest
Man conceals his riches, and the cunning Gamster his play; Shy
Husbands and Keepers like old Rooks are not to be cheated, but by
a new unpractis'd trick; false friendship will pass now no more than
false dice upon'em, no, not in the City.   45

Enter Boy.

Boy. There are two Ladies and a Gentleman coming up.
Hor. A Pox, some unbelieving Sisters of my former acquaintance,
who I am afraid, expect their sense shou'd be satisfy'd of the falsity
of the report.

Enter Sir Jasp. Fidget, *Lady* Fidget, *and Mrs.* Dainty Fidget.

No – this formal Fool and Women!   50
Qu. His Wife and Sister.
Sr. Jas. My Coach breaking just now before your door Sir, I look upon
as an occasional reprimand to me Sir, for not kissing your hands Sir,
since your coming out of *France* Sir; and so my disaster Sir, has been
my good fortune Sir; and this is my Wife, and Sister Sir.   55
Hor. What then, Sir?
Sr. Jas. My Lady, and Sister, Sir. – Wife, this is Master *Horner.*
La. Fid. Master *Horner*, Husband!
Sr. Jas. My Lady, my Lady *Fidget*, Sir.
Hor. So, Sir.   60
Sr. Jas. Won't you be acquainted with her Sir? [So the report is true, I
find by his coldness or aversion to the Sex; but I'll play the wag with
him.]

Aside.

Pray salute my Wife, my Lady, Sir.
Hor. I will kiss no Mans Wife, Sir, for him, Sir; I have taken my eternal   65
leave, Sir, of the Sex already, Sir.
Sr. Jas. Hah, hah, hah; I'll plague him yet.

Aside.

Not know my Wife, Sir?

Hor. I do know your Wife, Sir, she's Woman, Sir, and consequently a
Monster, Sir, a greater Monster than a Husband, Sir.   70

Sr. Jas. A Husband; how, Sir?

Hor. So, Sir; but I make no more Cuckholds, Sir.

Makes horns.

Sr. Jas. Hah, hah, hah, *Mercury, Mercury.*

La. Fid. Pray, Sir *Jaspar*, let us be gone from this rude fellow.

Mrs. Daint. Who, by his breeding, wou'd think, he had ever been in   75
France?

La. Fid. Foh, he's but too much a French fellow, such as hate Women
of quality and virtue, for their love to their Husbands, Sr. *Jaspar*, a
Woman is hated by 'em as much for loving her Husband, as for
loving their Money: But pray, let's be gone.   80

Hor. You do well, Madam, for I have nothing that you came for: I
have brought over not so much as a Bawdy Picture, new Postures,
nor the second Part of the *Ecole de Filles*, Nor –

Qu. Hold for shame, Sir; what d'y mean? you'l ruine your self for ever
with the Sex –   85

Apart to Horner.

Sr. Jas. Hah, hah, hah, he hates Women perfectly I find.

Dain. What pitty 'tis he shou'd.

L. Fid. Ay, he's a base rude Fellow for't; but affectation makes not a
Woman more odious to them, than Virtue.

Hor. Because your Virtue is your greatest affectation, Madam.   90

Lad. Fid. How, you sawcy Fellow, wou'd you wrong my honour?

Hor. If I cou'd.

Lad. Fid. How d'y mean, Sir?

Sr. Jas. Hah, hah, hah, no he can't wrong your Ladyships honour, upon
my honour; he poor Man – hark you in your ear – a meer Eunuch.   95

Lad. O filthy French Beast, foh, foh; why do we stay? let's be gone; I
can't endure the sight of him.

Sr. Jas. Stay, but till the Chairs come, they'l be here presently.

Lad. No, no.

Sr. Jas. Nor can I stay longer; 'tis – let me see, a quarter and a half   100
quarter of a minute past eleven; the Council will be state, I must
away: business must be preferr'd always before Love and Ceremony
with the wise Mr. *Horner.*

Hor. And the Impotent Sir *Jaspar.*

Sr. Jas. Ay, ay, the impotent Master *Horner*, hah, ha, ha.   105

Lad. What leave us with a filthy Man alone in his lodgings?

Sr. Jas. He's an innocent Man now, you know; pray stay, I'll hasten
the Chaires to you. – Mr. *Horner* Your Servant, I shou'd be glad to
see you at my house; pray, come and dine with me, and play at Cards
with my Wife after dinner, you are fit for Women at that game yet;   110

hah, ha – ['Tis as much a Husbands prudence to provide innocent
diversion for a Wife, as to hinder her unlawful pleasures; and he had
better employ her, than let her employ her self.

Aside.

Farewel.

Exit Sir Jaspar.

Hor. Your Servant Sr. *Jaspar.*   115
Lad. I will not stay with him, foh –
Hor. Nay, Madam, I beseech you stay, if it be but to see, I can be as
    civil to Ladies yet, as they wou'd desire.
Lad. No, no, foh, you cannot be civil to Ladies.
Dain. You as civil as Ladies wou'd desire.   120
Lad. No, no, no, foh, foh, foh.

Exeunt Ladie Fid. *and* Dainty.

Qu. Now I think, I, or you your self rather, have done your business
    with the Women.
Hor. Thou art an Ass, don't you see already upon the report and my
    carriage, this grave Man of business leaves his Wife in my lodgings, 125
    invites me to his house and wife, who before wou'd not be ac-
    quainted with me out of jealousy.
Qu. Nay, by this means you may be the more acquainted with the
    Husbands, but the less with the Wives.
Hor. Let me alone, if I can but abuse the Husbands, I'll soon disabuse 130
    the Wives: Stay – I'll reckon you up the advantages, I am like to have
    by my Stratagem: First, I shall be rid of all my old Acquaintances,
    the most insatiable sorts of Duns, that invade our Lodgings in a
    morning: And next, to the pleasure of making a New Mistriss, is
    that of being rid of an old One, and of all old Debts Love when it 135
    comes to be so, is paid the most unwillingly.
Qu. Well, you may be so rid of your old Acquaintances; but how will
    you get any new Ones?
Hor. Doctor, thou wilt never make a good Chymist, thou art so
    incredulous and impatient; ask but all the young Fellows of the 140
    Town, if they do not loose more time like Huntsmen, in starting the
    game, than in running it down; one knows not where to find'em,
    who will, or will not; Women of Quality are so civil, you can hardly
    distinguish love from good breeding, and a Man is often mistaken;
    but now I can be sure, she that shews an aversion to me loves the 145
    sport, as those Women that are gone, whom I warrant to be right:
    And then the next thing, is your Women of Honour, as you call'em,
    are only chary of their reputations, not their Persons, and 'tis
    scandal they wou'd avoid, not Men: Now may I have, by the
    reputation of an Eunuch, the Priviledges of One; and be seen in a 150
    Ladies Chamber, in a morning as early as her Husband; kiss Virgins

before their Parents, or Lovers; and may be in short the *Pas par tout*
of the Town. Now Doctor.

Qu. Nay, now you shall be the Doctor; and your Process is so new,
that we do not know but it may succeed.   155

Hor. Not so new neither, *Probatum est* Doctor.

Qu. Well, I wish you luck and many Patients whil'st I go to mine.

Exit Quack.

Enter Harcourt, *and* Dorilant *to* Horner.

Har. Come, your appearance at the Play yesterday, has I hope
hardned you for the future against the Womens contempt, and
the Mens raillery; and now you'l abroad as you were wont.   160

Hor. Did I not bear it bravely?

Dor. With a most Theatrical impudence; nay more than the Orange-
wenches shew there, or a drunken vizard Mask, or a great belly'd
Actress; nay, or the most impudent of Creatures, an ill Poet; or what
is yet more impudent, a second-hand Critick.   165

Hor. But what say the Ladies, have they no pitty?

Har. What Ladies? the vizard Masques you know never pitty a Man
when all's gone, though in their Service.

Dor. And for the Women in the boxes, you'd never pitty them, when
'twas in your power.   170

Har. They say 'tis pitty, but all that deal with common Women
shou'd be serv'd so.

Dor. Nay, I dare swear, they won't admit you to play at Cards with
them, go to Plays with 'em, or do the little duties which other
Shadows of men, are wont to do for'em.   175

Hor. Who do you call Shadows of Men?

Dor. Half Men.

Hor. What Boyes?

Dor. Ay your old Boyes, old *beaux Garcons*, who like superannuated
Stallions are suffer'd to run, feed, and whinney with the Mares as 180
long as they live, though they can do nothing else.

Hor. Well a Pox on love and wenching, Women serve but to keep a
Man from better Company; though I can't enjoy them, I shall you
the more: good fellowship and friendship, are lasting, rational and
manly pleasures.   185

Har. For all that give me some of those pleasures, you call effeminate
too, they help to relish one another.

Hor. They disturb one another.

Har. No, Mistresses are like Books; if you pore upon them too much,
they doze you, and make you unfit for Company; but if us'd   190
discreetly, you are the fitter for conversation by'em.

Dor. A Mistress shou'd be like a little Country retreat near the Town,
not to dwell in constantly, but only for a night and away; to tast the
Town the better when a Man returns.

Hor. I tell you, 'tis as hard to be a good Fellow, a good Friend, and a 195
Lover of Women, as 'tis to be a good Fellow, a good Friend, and

a Lover of Money: You cannot follow both, then choose your side;
Wine gives you liberty, Love takes it away.

Dor. Gad, he's in the right on't.

Hor. Wine gives you joy, Love grief and tortures, besides the Chir- 200
urgeon's: Wine makes us witty, Love only Sots: Wine makes us
sleep, Love breaks it.

Dor. By the World he has reason, *Harcourt.*

Hor. Wine makes –

Dor. Ay, Wine makes us – makes us Princes, Love makes us Beggars, 205
poor Rogues, y gad – and Wine –

Hor. So, there's one converted. – No, no, Love and Wine, Oil and
Vinegar.

Har. I grant it; Love will still be uppermost.

Hor. Come, for my part I will have only those glorious, manly pleas- 210
ures of being very drunk, and very slovenly.

Enter Boy.

Boy. Mr. *Sparkish* is below, Sir.

Har. What, my dear Friend! a Rogue that is fond of me, only I think
for abusing him.

Dor. No, he can no more think the Men laugh at him, than that 215
Women jilt him, his opinion of himself is so good.

Hor. Well, there's another pleasure by drinking, I thought not of; I
shall loose his acquaintance, because he cannot drink; and you
know 'tis a very hard thing to be rid of him, for he's one of those
nauseous offerers at wit, who like the worst Fidlers run themselves 220
into all Companies.

Har. One, that by being in the Company of Men of sense wou'd pass
for one.

Hor. And may so to the short-sighted World, as a false Jewel
amongst true ones, is not discern'd at a distance; his Company is 225
as troublesome to us, as a Cuckolds, when you have a mind to his
Wife's.

Har. No, the Rogue will not let us enjoy one another, but ravishes
our conversation, though he signifies no more to't, than Sir *Martin
Mar-all*'s gaping, and auker'd thrumming upon the Lute, does to 230
his Man's Voice, and Musick.

Dor. And to pass for a wit in Town, shewes himself a fool every night
to us, that are guilty of the plot.

Hor. Such wits as he, are, to a Company of reasonable Men, like
Rooks to the Gamesters, who only fill a room at the Table, but 235
are so far from contributing to the play, that they only serve to spoil
the fancy of those that do.

Dor. Nay, they are us'd like Rooks too, snub'd, check'd, and abus'd;
yet the Rogues will hang on.

Hor. A Pox on'em, and all that force Nature, and wou'd be still what 240
she forbids'em; Affectation is her greatest Monster.

Har. Most Men are the contraries to that they wou'd seem; your
bully you see, is a Coward with a long Sword; the little humbly
fawning Physician with his Ebony cane, is he that destroys Men.

Dor. The Usurer, a poor Rogue, possess'd of moldy Bonds, and   245
Mortgages; and we they call Spend-thrifts, are only wealthy, who
lay out his money upon daily new purchases of pleasure.

Hor. Ay, your errantest cheat, is your Trustee, or Executor; your
jealous Man, the greatest Cuckhold; your Church-man, the greatest
Atheist; and your noisy pert Rogue of a wit, the greatest Fop,   250
dullest Ass, and worst Company as you shall see: For here he comes.

Enter Sparkish *to them.*

Spar. How is't, Sparks, how is't? Well Faith, *Harry*, I must railly thee a
little, ha, ha, ha, upon the report in Town of thee, ha, ha, ha, I can't
hold y Faith; shall I speak?

Hor. Yes, but you'l be so bitter then.   255

Spar. Honest *Dick* and *Franck* here shall answer for me, I will not be
extream bitter by the Univers.

Har. We will be bound in ten thousand pound Bond, he shall not be
bitter at all.

Dor. Nor sharp, nor sweet.   260

Hor. What, not down right insipid?

Spar. Nay then, since you are so brisk, and provoke me, take what
follows; you must know, I was discoursing and raillying with some
Ladies yesterday, and they hapned to talk of the fine new signes in
Town.   265

Hor. Very fine Ladies I believe.

Spar. Said I, I know where the best new sign is. Where, says one of
the Ladies? In *Covent-Garden*, I reply'd. Said another, In what
street? In *Russel-street*, answer'd I. Lord says another, I'm sure
there was ne're a fine new sign there yesterday. Yes, but there was,   270
said I again, and it came out of *France*, and has been there a
fortnight.

Dor. A Pox I can hear no more, prethee.

Hor. No hear him out; let him tune his crowd a while.

Har. The worst Musick the greatest preparation.   275

Spar. Nay faith, I'll make you laugh. It cannot be, says a third Lady.
Yes, yes, quoth I again. Says a fourth Lady,

Hor. Look to't, we'l have no more Ladies.

Spar. No. – then mark, mark, now, said I to the fourth, did you never
see Mr. *Horner*, he lodges in *Russel-street*, and he's a sign of a Man,   280
you know, since he came out of *France*, heh, hah, he.

Hor. But the Divel take me, if thine be the sign of a jest.

Spar. With that they all fell a laughing, till they bepiss'd themselves;
what, but it do's not move you, methinks? well I see one had as
good go to Law without a witness, as break a jest without a laugher   285
on ones side. – Come, come Sparks, but where do we dine, I have
left at *Whitehal* an Earl to dine with you.

Dor. Why, I thought thou hadst lov'd a Man with a title better, than a
 Suit with a French trimming to't.

Har. Go, to him again.   290

Spar. No, Sir, a wit to me is the greatest title in the World.

Hor. But go dine with your Earl, Sir, he may be exceptious; we are
 your Friends, and will not take it ill to be left, I do assure you.

Har. Nay, faith he shall go to him.

Spar. Nay, pray Gentlemen.   295

Dor. We'l thrust you out, if you wo'not, what disappoint any Body
 for us.

Spar. Nay, dear Gentlemen hear me.

Hor. No, no, Sir, by no means; pray go Sir.

Spar. Why, dear Rogues.   300

          They all thrust him out of the room.

Dor. No, no.

All. Ha, ha, ha.

              Spar. *returns.*

Spar. But, Sparks, pray hear me; what d'ye think I'll eat then with gay
 shallow Fops, and silent Coxcombs? I think wit as necessary at
 dinner as a glass of good wine, and that's the reason I never have   305
 any stomach when I eat alone. – Come, but where do we dine?

Hor. Ev'n where you will.

Spar. At *Chateline*'s.

Dor. Yes, if you will.

Spar. Or at the *Cock.*   310

Dor. Yes, if you please.

Spar. Or at the *Dog* and *Partridg.*

Hor. Ay, if you have mind to't, for we shall dine at neither.

Spar. Pshaw, with your fooling we shall loose the new Play; and I
 wou'd no more miss seeing a new Play the first day, than I wou'd   315
 miss setting in the wits Row; therefore I'll go fetch my Mistriss and
 away.

              Exit Sparkish.

     Manent Horner, Harcourt, Dorilant; *Enter to them*
         Mr. Pinchwife.

Hor. Who have we here, *Pinchwife*?

Mr. Pinc. Gentlemen, your humble Servant.

Hor. Well, *Jack*, by thy long absence from the Town, the grumness of   320
 thy countenance, and the slovenlyness of thy habit; I shou'd give
 thee joy, shou'd I not, of Marriage?

Mr. Pin. [Death does he know I'm married too? I thought to have
 conceal'd it from him at least.]

              Aside.

My long stay in the Country will excuse my dress, and I have a suit   325
of Law, that brings me up to Town, that puts me out of humour;
besides I must give *Sparkish* to morrow five thousand pound to lye
with my Sister.

Hor. Nay, you Country Gentlemen rather than not purchase, will buy
any thing, and he is a crackt title, if we may quibble: Well, but am I   330
to give thee joy, I heard thou wert marry'd.

Mr. Pin. What then?

Hor. Why, the next thing that is to be heard, is thou'rt a Cuckold.

Mr. Pin. Insupportable name.

Aside.

Hor. But I did not expect Marriage from such a Whoremaster as you,   335
one that knew the Town so much, and Women so well.

Mr. Pin. Why, I have marry'd no *London* Wife.

Hor. Pshaw, that's all one, that grave circumspection in marrying a
Country Wife, is like refusing a deceitful pamper'd *Smithfield* Jade,
to go and be cheated by a Friend in the Country.   340

Mr. Pin. A Pox on him and his Simile.

Aside.

At least we are a little surer of the breed there, know what her
keeping has been, whether foyl'd or unsound.

Hor. Come, come, I have known a clap gotten in *Wales*, and there are
Cozens, Justices, Clarks, and Chaplains in the Country, I won't say   345
Coach-men, but she's handsome and young.

Pin. I'll answer as I shou'd do.

Aside.

No, no, she has no beauty, but her youth; no attraction, but her
modesty, wholesome, homely, and huswifely, that's all.

Dor. He talks as like a Grasier as he looks.   350

Pin. She's too auker'd, ill favour'd, and silly to bring to Town.

Har. Then methinks you shou'd bring her, to be taught breeding.

Pin. To be taught; no, Sir, I thank you, good Wives, and private
Souldiers shou'd be ignorant. – [I'll keep her from your instructions, I warrant you.   355

Har. The Rogue is as jealous, as if his wife were not ignorant.

Aside.

Hor. Why, if she be ill favour'd, there will be less danger here for you,
than by leaving her in the Country; we have such variety of dainties,
that we are seldom hungry.

Dor. But they have alwayes coarse, constant, swinging stomachs in   360
the Country.

Har. Foul Feeders indeed.

Dor. And your Hospitality is great there.

Har. Open house, every Man's welcome.

Pin. So, so, Gentlemen. 365

Hor. But prethee, why woud'st thou marry her? if she be ugly, ill-bred, and silly, she must be rich then.

Pin. As rich as if she brought me twenty thousand pound out of this Town; for she'l be as sure not to spend her moderate portion, as a *London* Baggage wou'd be to spend hers, let it be what it wou'd; so 370 'tis all one: then because shes ugly, she's the likelyer to be my own; and being ill-bred, she'l hate conversation; and since silly and innocent, will not know the difference betwixt a 'Man of one and twenty, and one of forty –

Hor. Nine – to my knowledge; but if she be silly, she'l expect as much 375 from a Man of forty nine, as from him of one and twenty: But methinks wit is more necessary than beauty, and I think no young Woman ugly that has it, and no handsome Woman agreable without it.

Pin. 'Tis my maxime, he's a Fool that marrys, but he's a greater that does not marry a Fool; what is wit in a Wife good for, but to make a 380 Man a Cuckold?

Hor. Yes, to keep it from his knowledge.

Pin. A Fool cannot contrive to make her husband a Cuckold.

Hor. No, but she'l club with a Man that can; and what is worse, if she cannot make her Husband a Cuckold, she'l make him jealous, and 385 pass for one, and then 'tis all one.

Pin. Well, well, I'll take care for one, my Wife shall make me no Cuckold, though she had your help Mr. *Horner*, I understand the Town, Sir.

Dor. His help! 390

Aside.

Har. He's come newly to Town it seems, and has not heard how things are with him.

Aside.

Hor. But tell me, has Marriage cured thee of whoring, which it seldom does.

Har. 'Tis more than age can do. 395

Hor. No, the word is, I'll marry and live honest; but a Marriage vow is like a penitent Gamesters Oath, and entring into Bonds, and penalties to stint himself to such a particular small sum at play for the future, which makes him but the more eager, and not being able to hold out, looses his Money again, and his forfeit to boot. 400

Dor. Ay, ay, a Gamester will be a Gamester, whilst his Money lasts; and a Whoremaster, whilst his vigour.

Har. Nay, I have known'em, when they are broke and can loose no more, keep a fumbling with the Box in their hands to fool with only, and hinder other Gamesters. 405

Dor. That had wherewithal to make lusty stakes.

Pin. Well, Gentlemen, you may laugh at me, but you shall never lye with my Wife, I know the Town.

Hor. But prethee, was not the way you were in better, is not keeping
    better than Marriage?   410

Pin. A Pox on't, the Jades wou'd jilt me, I cou'd never keep a Whore
    to my self.

Hor. So then you only marry'd to keep a Whore to your self; well,
    but let me tell you, Women, as you say, are like Souldiers made
    constant and loyal by good pay, rather than by Oaths and Coven- 415
    ants, therefore I'd advise my Friends to keep rather than marry;
    since too I find by your example, it does not serve ones turn, for I
    saw you yesterday in the eighteen penny place with a pretty Coun-
    try-wench.

Pin. How the Divel, did he see my Wife then? I sate there that she 420
    might not be seen; but she shall never go to a play again.

                                             Aside.

Hor. What dost thou blush at nine and forty, for having been seen
    with a Wench?

Dor. No Faith, I warrant 'twas his Wife, which he seated there out of
    sight, for he's a cunning Rogue, and understands the Town.   425

Har. He blushes, then 'twas his Wife; for Men are now more ashamed
    to be seen with them in publick, than with a Wench.

Pin. Hell and damnation, I'm undone, since *Horner* has seen her, and
    they know 'twas she.

                                             Aside.

Hor. But prethee, was it thy Wife? she was exceedingly pretty; I was in 430
    love with her at that distance.

Pin. You are like never to be nearer to her. Your Servant Gentlemen.

                                      Offers to go.

Hor. Nay, prethee stay.

Pin. I cannot, I will not.

Hor. Come you shall dine with us.   435

Pin. I have din'd already.

Hor. Come, I know thou hast not; I'll treat thee dear Rogue, thou
    sha't spend none of thy *Hampshire* Money to day.

Pin. Treat me; so he uses me already like his Cuckold.

                                             Aside.

Hor. Nay, you shall not go.   440

Pin. I must, I have business at home.

                                      Exit Pinchwife.

Hor. To beat his Wife, he's as jealous of her, as a *Cheapside* Husband
    of a *Covent-garden* Wife.

Hor. Why, 'tis as hard to find an old Whoremaster without jealousy
    and the gout, as a young one without fear or the Pox.   445
As Gout in Age, from Pox in Youth proceeds;

So Wenching past, then jealousy succeeds:
The worst disease that Love and Wenching breeds.

Act II

Scene I

Mrs. Margery Pinchwife, *and* Alithea: *Mr.* Pinchwife *peeping behind at the door.*

Mrs. Pin. Pray, Sister, where are the best Fields and Woods, to walk in in *London*?

Alit. A pretty Question; why, Sister! *Mulberry Garden*, and St. *James's Park*; and for close walks the *New Exchange*.

Mrs. Pin. Pray, Sister, tell me why my Husband looks so grum here in   5
Town? and keeps me up so close, and will not let me go a walking, nor let me wear my best Gown yesterday?

Alith. O he's jealous, Sister.

Mrs. Pin. Jealous, what's that?

Alith. He's afraid you shou'd love another Man.   10

Mrs. Pin. How shou'd he be afraid of my loving another man, when he will not let me see any but himself.

Alith. Did he not carry you yesterday to a Play?

Mrs. Pin. Ay, but we sate amongst ugly People, he wou'd not let me come near the Gentry, who sate under us, so that I cou'd not   15
see'em: He told me, none but naughty Women sate there, whom they tous'd and mous'd; but I wou'd have ventur'd for all that.

Alith. But how did you like the Play?

Mrs. Pin. Indeed I was a weary of the Play, but I lik'd hugeously the Actors; they are the goodlyest proper'st Men, Sister.   20

Alith. O but you must not like the Actors, Sister.

Mrs. Pin. Ay, how shou'd I help it, Sister? Pray, Sister, when my Husband comes in, will you ask leave for me to go a walking?

Alith. A walking, hah, ha; Lord, a Country Gentlewomans leasure is the drudgery of a foot-post; and she requires as much airing as her   25
Husbands Horses.

Aside.

Enter Mr. Pinchwife *to them.*

But here comes your Husband; I'll ask, though I'm sure he'l not grant it.

Mrs. Pin. He says he won't let me go abroad, for fear of catching the Pox.   30

Alith. Fye, the small Pox you shou'd say.

Mrs. Pin. Oh my dear, dear Bud, welcome home; why dost thou look so fropish, who has nanger'd thee?

Mr. Pin. You're a Fool.

Mrs. Pinch. *goes aside, & cryes.*

Alith. Faith so she is, for crying for no fault, poor tender Creature!   35

Mr. Pin. What you wou'd have her as impudent as yourself, as errant a Jilflirt, a gadder, a Magpy, and to say all a meer notorious Town-Woman?

Alit. Brother, you are my only Censurer; and the honour of your Family shall sooner suffer in your Wife there, than in me, though I   40
take the innocent liberty of the Town.

Mr. Pin. Hark you Mistriss, do not talk so before my Wife, the innocent liberty of the Town!

Alith. Why, pray, who boasts of any intrigue with me? what Lampoon has made my name notorious? what ill Women frequent my   45
Lodgings? I keep no Company with any Women of scandalous reputations.

Mr. Pin. No, you keep the Men of scandalous reputations Company.

Alith. Where? wou'd you not have me civil? answer 'em in a Box at the Plays? in the drawing room at *Whitehal*? in St. *James's Park? Mul-*   50
berry-garden? or –

Mr. Pin. Hold, hold, do not teach my Wife, where the Men are to be found; I believe she's the worse for your Town documents already; I bid you keep her in ignorance as I do.

Mrs. Pin. Indeed be not angry with her Bud, she will tell me nothing   55
of the Town, though I ask her a thousand times a day.

Mr. Pin. Then you are very inquisitive to know, I find?

Mrs. Pin. Not I indeed, Dear, I hate *London*; our Place-house in the Country is worth a thousand of 't, wou'd I were there again.

Mr. Pin. So you shall I warrant; but were you not talking of Plays,   60
and Players, when I came in? you are her encourager in such discourses.

Mrs. Pin. No indeed, Dear, she chid me just now for liking the Player Men.

Mr. Pin. Nay, if she be so innocent as to own to me her likeing them,   65
there is no hurt in 't –

Aside.

Come my poor Rogue, but thou lik'st none better then me?

Mrs. Pin. Yes indeed, but I do, the Player Men are finer Folks.

Mr. Pin. But you love none better then me?

Mrs. Pin. You are mine own Dear Bud, and I know you, I hate a   70
Stranger.

Mr. Pin. Ay, my Dear, you must love me only, and not be like the naughty Town Women, who only hate their Husbands, and love every Man else, love Plays, Visits, fine Coaches, fine Cloaths, Fidles, Balls, Treates, and so lead a wicked Town-life.   75

Mrs. Pin. Nay, if to enjoy all these things be a Town-life, *London* is not so bad a place, Dear.

Mr. Pin. How! if you love me, you must hate *London.*

Ali. The Fool has forbid me discovering to her the pleasures of the Town, and he is now setting her a gog upon them himself.   80

Mrs. Pin. But, Husband, do the Town-women love the Player Men too?

Mr. Pin. Yes, I warrant you.

Mrs. Pin. Ay, I warrant you.

Mr. Pin. Why, you do not, I hope?   85

Mrs. Pin. No, no, Bud; but why have we no Player-men in the Country?

Mr. Pin. Ha – Mrs. Minx, ask me no more to go to a Play.

Mrs. Pin. Nay, why, Love? I did not care for going; but when you forbid me, you make me as't were desire it.   90

Alith. So 'twill be in other things, I warrant.

                                                                                                          Aside.

Mrs. Pin. Pray, let me go to a Play, Dear.

Mr. Pin. Hold your Peace, I wo'not.

Mrs. Pin. Why, Love?

Mr. Pin. Why, I'll tell you.   95

Alith. Nay, if he tell her, she'l give him more cause to forbid her that place.

                                                                                                          Aside.

Mrs. Pin. Pray, why, Dear?

Mr. Pin. First, you like the Actors, and the Gallants may like you.

Mrs. Pin. What, a homely Country Girl? no Bud, no body will like me.   100

Mr. Pin. I tell you, yes, they may.

Mrs. Pin. No, no, you jest – I won't believe you, I will go.

Mr. Pin. I tell you then, that one of the lewdest Fellows in Town, who saw you there, told me he was in love with you.

Mrs. Pin. Indeed! who, who, pray who wast?   105

Mr. Pin. I've gone too far, and slipt before I was aware; how overjoy'd she is!

                                                                                                          Aside.

Mrs. Pin. Was it any *Hampshire* Gallant, any of our Neighbours? I promise you, I am beholding to him.

Mr. Pin. I promise you, you lye; for he wou'd but ruin you, as he has   110
done hundreds: he has no other love for Women, but that, such as he, look upon Women like Basilicks, but to destroy'em.

Mrs. Pin. Ay, but if he loves me, why shou'd he ruin me? answer me to that: methinks he shou'd not, I wou'd do him no harm.

Alith. Hah, ha, ha.   115

Mr. Pin. 'Tis very well; but I'll keep him from doing you any harm, or me either.

                                  Enter Sparkish *and* Harcourt.

But here comes Company, get you in, get you in.

Mrs. Pin. But pray, Husband, is he a pretty Gentleman, that loves me?
Mr. Pin. In baggage, in.   120

Thrusts her in: shuts the door.

What all the lewd Libertines of the Town brought to my Lodging,
by this easie Coxcomb! S'death I'll not suffer it.
Spar. Here *Harcourt*, do you approve my choice? Dear, little Rogue, I
told you, I'd bring you acquainted with all my Friends, the wits, and –

Harcourt *salutes her.*

Mr. Pin. Ay, they shall know her, as well as you your self will, I warrant   125
you.
Spar. This is one of those, my pretty Rogue, that are to dance at your
Wedding to morrow; and him you must bid welcome ever, to what
you and I have.
Mr. Pin. Monstrous! –   130

Aside.

Spar. Harcourt how dost thou like her, Faith? Nay, Dear, do not look
down; I should hate to have a Wife of mine out of countenance at
any thing.
Mr. Pin. Wonderful!
Spar. Tell me, I say, *Harcourt*, how dost thou like her? thou hast   135
star'd upon her enough, to resolve me.
Har. So infinitely well, that I cou'd wish I had a Mistriss too, that might
differ from her in nothing, but her love and engagement to you.
Alith. Sir, Master *Sparkish* has often told me, that his Acquaintance
were all Wits and Raillieurs, and now I find it.   140
Spar. No, by the Universe, Madam, he does not railly now; you may
believe him: I do assure you, he is the honestest, worthyest, true
hearted Gentleman – A man of such perfect honour, he wou'd say
nothing to a Lady, he does not mean.
Mr. Pin. Praising another Man to his Mistriss!   145
Har. Sir, you are so beyond expectation obliging, that –
Spar. Nay, I gad, I am sure you do admire her extreamly, I see't in
your eyes. – He does admire you Madam. – By the World, don't
you?
Har. Yes, above the World, or, the most glorious part of it, her whole   150
Sex; and till now I never thought I shou'd have envy'd you, or any
Man about to marry, but you have the best excuse for Marriage I
ever knew.
Alith. Nay, now, Sir, I'm satisfied you are of the Society of the Wits,
and Raillieurs, since you cannot spare your Friend, even when he   155
is but too civil to you; but the surest sign is, since you are an Enemy
to Marriage, for that I hear you hate as much as business or bad
Wine.
Har. Truly, Madam, I never was an Enemy to Marriage, till now,
because Marriage was never an Enemy to me before.   160

Alith. But why, Sir, is Marriage an Enemy to you now? Because it robs you of your Friend here; for you look upon a Friend married, as one gone into a Monastery, that is dead to the World.

Har. 'Tis indeed, because you marry him; I see Madam, you can guess my meaning: I do confess heartily and openly, I wish it were 165 in my power to break the Match, by Heavens I wou'd.

Spar. Poor *Franck*!

Alith. Wou'd you be so unkind to me?

Har. No, no, 'tis not because I wou'd be unkind to you.

Spar. Poor *Franck*, no gad, 'tis only his kindness to me. 170

Pin. Great kindness to you indeed; insensible Fop, let a Man make love to his Wife to his face.

Aside.

Spar. Come dear *Franck*, for all my Wife there that shall be, thou shalt enjoy me sometimes dear Rogue; by my honour, we Men of wit condole for our deceased Brother in Marriage, as much as for one 175 dead in earnest: I think that was prettily said of me, ha *Harcourt*? – But come *Franck*, be not melancholy for me.

Har. No, I assure you I am not melancholy for you.

Spar. Prethee, *Frank*, dost think my Wife that shall be there a fine Person? 180

Har. I cou'd gaze upon her, till I became as blind as you are.

Spar. How, as I am! how!

Har. Because you are a Lover, and true Lovers are blind, stockblind.

Spar. True, true; but by the World, she has wit too, as well as beauty: go, go with her into a corner, and trye if she has wit, talk to her any 185 thing, she's bashful before me.

Har. Indeed if a Woman wants wit in a corner, she has it no where.

Alith. Sir, you dispose of me a little before your time. –

Aside to Sparkish.

Spar. Nay, nay, Madam let me have an earnest of your obedience, or – go, go, Madam – 190

Harcourt *courts* Alithea *aside.*

Pin. How, Sir, if you are not concern'd for the honour of a Wife, I am for that of a Sister; he shall not debauch her: be a Pander to your own Wife, bring Men to her, let'em make love before your face, thrust'em into a corner together, then leav'em in private! is this your Town wit and conduct? 195

Spar. Hah, ha, ha, a silly wise Rogue, wou'd make one laugh more then a stark Fool, hah, ha: I shall burst. Nay, you shall not disturb'em; I'll vex thee, by the World.

Struggles with Pinch. *to keep him from* Harc. *and* Alith.

Alith. The writings are drawn, Sir, settlements made; 'tis too late, Sir, and past all revocation. 200

Har. Then so is my death.

Alith. I wou'd not be unjust to him.

Har. Then why to me so?

Alith. I have no obligation to you.

Har. My love. 205

Alith. I had his before.

Har. You never had it; he wants you see jealousie, the only infallible
sign of it.

Alith. Love proceeds from esteem; he cannot distrust my virtue,
besides he loves me, or he wou'd not marry me. 210

Har. Marrying you, is no more sign of his love, then bribing your
Woman, that he may marry you, is a sign of his generosity: Marriage
is rather a sign of interest, then love; and he that marries a fortune,
covets a Mistress, not loves her: But if you take Marriage for a sign
of love, take it from me immediately. 215

Alith. No, now you have put a scruple in my head; but in short, Sir, to
end our dispute, I must marry him, my reputation wou'd suffer in the
World else.

Har. No, if you do marry him, with your pardon, Madam, your
reputation suffers in the World, and you wou'd be thought in 220
necessity for a cloak.

Alith. Nay, now you are rude, Sir. – Mr. *Sparkish*, pray come hither,
your Friend here is very troublesom, and very loving.

Har. Hold, hold –

Aside to Alithea.

Mr. Pin. D'ye hear that? 225

Spar. Why, d'ye think I'll seem to be jealous, like a Country Bumpkin?

Mr. Pin. No, rather be a Cuckold, like a credulous Cit.

Har. Madam, you wou'd not have been so little generous as to have
told him.

Alith. Yes, since you cou'd be so little generous, as to wrong him. 230

Har. Wrong him, no Man can do't, he's beneath an injury; a Bubble,
a Coward, a sensless Idiot, a Wretch so contemptible to all the
World but you, that –

Alith. Hold, do not rail at him, for since he is like to be my Husband,
I am resolv'd to like him: Nay, I think I am oblig'd to tell him, you 235
are not his Friend. – Master *Sparkish*, Master *Sparkish*.

Spar. What, what; now dear Rogue, has not she wit?

Har. Not so much as I thought, and hoped she had.

Speaks surlily.

Alith. Mr. *Sparkish*, do you bring People to rail at you?

Har. Madam – 240

Spar. How! no, but if he does rail at me, 'tis but in jest I warrant; what
we wits do for one another; and never take any notice of it.

Alith. He spoke so scurrilously of you, I had no patience to hear him;
besides he has been making love to me.

Har. True damn'd tell-tale-Woman.   245

Aside.

Spar. Pshaw, to shew his parts – we wits rail and make love often, but
to shew our parts; as we have no affections, so we have no malice,
we –

Alith. He said, you were a Wretch, below an injury.

Spar. Pshaw.   250

Har. Damn'd, sensless, impudent, virtuous Jade; well since she won't
let me have her, she'l do as good, she'l make me hate her.

Alith. A Common Bubble.

Spar. Pshaw.

Alith. A Coward.   255

Spar. Pshaw, pshaw.

Alith. A sensless driveling Idiot.

Spar. How, did he disparage my parts? Nay, then my honour's concern'd, I can't put up that, Sir; by the World, Brother help me to kill
him; [I may draw now, since we have the odds of him: – 'tis a good,   260
occasion too before my Mistriss] –

Aside.
Offers to draw.

Alith. Hold, hold.

Spar. What, what.

Alith. I must not let'em kill the Gentleman neither, for his kindness
to me; I am so far from hating him, that I wish my Gallant had his   265
person and understanding: – Nay if my honour –

Aside.

Spar. I'll be thy death.

Alith. Hold, hold, indeed to tell the truth, the Gentleman said after
all, that what he spoke, was but out of friendship to you.

Spar. How! say, I am, I am a Fool, that is no wit, out of friendship to   270
me.

Alith. Yes, to try whether I was concern'd enough for you, and made
love to me only to be satisfy'd of my virtue, for your sake.

Har. Kind however –

Aside.

Spar. Nay, if it were so, my dear Rogue, I ask thee pardon; but why   275
wou'd not you tell me so, faith.

Har. Because I did not think on't, faith.

Spar. Come, *Horner* does not come, *Harcourt*, let's be gone to the
new Play. – Come Madam.

Alith. I will not go, if you intend to leave me alone in the Box, and   280
run into the pit, as you use to do.

Spar. Pshaw, I'll leave *Harcourt* with you in the Box, to entertain
you, and that's as good; if I sate in the Box, I shou'd be thought

no Judge, but of trimmings. – Come away *Harcourt*, lead her
down.   285

> *Exeunt* Sparkish, Harcourt, *and* Alithea.

Pin. Well, go thy wayes, for the flower of the true Town Fops, such as
spend their Estates, before they come to'em, and are Cuckolds
before they'r married. But let me go look to my own Free-hold –
How –

> *Enter my Lady* Fidget, *Mistriss* Dainty Fidget, *and*
> *Mistriss* Squeamish.

Lad. Your Servant, Sir, where is your Lady? we are come to wait upon   290
her to the new Play.
Pin. New Play!
Lad. And my Husband will wait upon you presently.
Pin. Damn your civility –

> *Aside.*

Madam, by no means, I will not see Sir *Jaspar* here, till I have waited   295
upon him at home; nor shall my Wife see you, till she has waited
upon your Ladyship at your lodgings.
Lad. Now we are here, Sir –
Pin. No, Madam.
Dain. Pray, let us see her.   300
Squeam. We will not stir, till we see her.
Pin. A Pox on you all –

> *Aside.*
> *Goes to the door, and returns.*

she has lock'd the door, and is gone abroad.
Lad. No, you have lock'd the door, and she's within.
Dain. They told us below, she was here.   305
Pin. [Will nothing do?] – Well it must out then, to tell you the truth,
Ladies, which I was afraid to let you know before, least it might
endanger your lives, my Wife has just now the Small Pox come out
upon her, do not be frighten'd; but pray, be gone Ladies, you shall
not stay here in danger of your lives; pray get you gone Ladies.   310
Lad. No, no, we have all had'em.
Squeam. Alack, alack.
Dain. Come, come, we must see how it goes with her, I understand
the disease.
Lad. Come.   315
Pin. Well, there is no being too hard for Women at their own weapon,
lying, therefore I'll quit the Field.

> *Aside.*
> *Exit* Pinchwife.

Squeam. Here's an example of jealousy.

Lad. Indeed as the World goes, I wonder there are no more jealous, since Wives are so neglected.   320

Dain. Pshaw, as the World goes, to what end shou'd they be jealous.

Lad. Foh, 'tis a nasty World.

Squeam. That Men of parts, great acquaintance, and quality shou'd take up with, and spend themselves and fortunes, in keeping little Play-house Creatures, foh.   325

Lad. Nay, that Women of understanding, great acquaintance, and good quality, shou'd fall a keeping too of little Creatures, foh.

Squeam. Why, 'tis the Men of qualities fault, they never visit Women of honour, and reputation, as they us'd to do; and have not so much as common civility, for Ladies of our rank, but use us with the same   330
indifferency, and ill breeding, as if we were all marry'd to'em.

Lad. She says true, 'tis an errant shame Women of quality shou'd be so slighted; methinks, birth, birth, shou'd go for something; I have known Men admired, courted, and followed for their titles only.

Squeam. Ay, one wou'd think Men of honour shou'd not love no   335
more, than marry out of their own rank.

Dain. Fye, fye upon'em, they are come to think cross breeding for themselves best, as well as for their Dogs, and Horses.

Lad. They are Dogs, and Horses for't.

Squeam. One wou'd think if not for love, for vanity a little.   340

Dain. Nay, they do satisfy their vanity upon us sometimes; and are kind to us in their report, tell all the World they lye with us.

Lad. Damn'd Rascals, that we shou'd be only wrong'd by'em; to report a Man has had a Person, when he has not had a Person, is the greatest wrong in the whole World, that can be done to a person.   345

Squeam. Well, 'tis an errant shame, Noble Persons shou'd be so wrong'd, and neglected.

Lad. But still 'tis an erranter shame for a Noble Person, to neglect her own honour, and defame her own Noble Person, with little inconsiderable Fellows, foh! –   350

Dain. I suppose the crime against our honour, is the same with a Man of quality as with another.

Lad. How! no sure the Man of quality is likest one's Husband, and therefore the fault shou'd be the less.

Dain. But then the pleasure shou'd be the less.   355

Lad. Fye, fye, fye, for shame Sister, whither shall we ramble? be continent in your discourse, or I shall hate you.

Dain. Besides an intrigue is so much the more notorious for the man's quality.

Squeam. 'Tis true, no body takes notice of a private Man, and there-   360
fore with him, 'tis more secret, and the crime's the less, when 'tis not known.

Lad. You say true; y faith I think you are in the right on't: 'tis not an injury to a Husband, till it be an injury to our honours; so that a Woman of honour looses no honour with a private Person; and to   365
say truth –

Dain. So the little Fellow is grown a private Person – with her –

Apart to Squeamish.

Lad. But still my dear, dear Honour.

Enter Sir Jaspar, Horner, Dorilant.

Sr. Jas. Ay, my dear, dear of honour, thou hast still so much honour in
thy mouth –   370
Hor. That she has none elsewhere –

Aside.

Lad. Oh, what d'ye mean to bring in these upon us?
Dain. Foh, these are as bad as Wits.
Squeam. Foh!
Lad. Let us leave the Room.   375
Sr. Jas. Stay, stay, faith to tell you the naked truth.
Lad. Fye, Sir *Jaspar*, do not use that word naked.
Sr. Jas. Well, well, in short I have business at *Whitehal*, and cannot go
to the play with you, therefore wou'd have you go –
Lad. With those two to a Play?   380
Sr. Jas. No, not with t'other, but with Mr. *Horner*, there can be no
more scandal to go with him, than with Mr. *Tatle*, or Master
Limberham.
Lad. With that nasty Fellow! no – no.
Sr. Jas. Nay, prethee Dear, hear me.   385

Whispers to Lady Fid.

Hor. Ladies.

Horner, Dorilant *drawing near*
Squeamish, *and* Daint.

Dain. Stand off.
Squeam. Do not approach us.
Dain. You heard with the wits, you are obscenity all over.
Squeam. And I wou'd as soon look upon a Picture of *Adam* and *Eve*, 390
without fig leaves, as any of you, if I cou'd help it, therefore keep
off, and do not make us sick.
Dor. What a Divel are these?
Hor. Why, these are pretenders to honour, as criticks to wit, only by
censuring others; and as every raw peevish, out-of-humour'd,   395
affected, dull, Tea-drinking, Arithmetical Fop sets up for a wit, by
railing at men of sence, so these for honour, by railing at the Court,
and Ladies of as great honour, as quality.
Sr. Jas. Come, Mr. *Horner*, I must desire you to go with these Ladies
to the Play, Sir.   400
Hor. I! Sir.
Sr. Jas. Ay, ay, come, Sir.
Hor. I must beg your pardon, Sir, and theirs, I will not be seen in
Womens Company in publick again for the World.

Sr. Jas. Ha, ha, strange Aversion!   405

Squeam. No, he's for Womens company in private.

Sr. Jas. He – poor Man – he! hah, ha, ha.

Dain. 'Tis a greater shame amongst lew'd fellows to be seen in
virtuous Womens company, than for the Women to be seen with
them.   410

Hor. Indeed, Madam, the time was I only hated virtuous Women, but
now I hate the other too; I beg your pardon Ladies.

Lad. You are very obliging, Sir, because we wou'd not be troubled
with you.

Sr. Jas. In sober sadness he shall go.   415

Dor. Nay, if he wo'not, I am ready to wait upon the Ladies; and I
think I am the fitter Man.

Sr. Jas. You, Sir, no I thank you for that – Master Horner is a
privileg'd Man amongst the virtuous Ladies, 'twill be a great
while before you are so; heh, he, he, he's my Wive's Gallant, heh,   420
he, he; no pray withdraw, Sir, for as I take it, the virtuous Ladies
have no business with you.

Dor. And I am sure, he can have none with them: 'tis strange a Man
can't come amongst virtuous Women now, but upon the same
terms, as Men are admitted into the great Turks Seraglio; but   425
Heavens keep me, from being an hombre Player with'em: but
where is *Pinchwife* –

Exit Dorilant.

Sr. Jas. Come, come, Man; what avoid the sweet society of Woman-
kind? that sweet, soft, gentle, tame, noble Creature Woman, made
for Man's Companion –   430

Hor. So is that soft, gentle, tame, and more noble Creature a Spaniel,
and has all their tricks, can fawn, lye down, suffer beating, and fawn
the more; barks at your Friends, when they come to see you; makes
your bed hard, gives you Fleas, and the mange sometimes: and all
the difference is, the Spaniel's the more faithful Animal, and fawns   435
but upon one Master.

Sr. Jas. Heh, he, he.

Squeam. O the rude Beast.

Dain. Insolent brute.

Lad. Brute! stinking mortify'd rotten French Weather, to dare –   440

Sr. Jas. Hold, an't please your Ladyship; for shame Master *Horner*,
your Mother was a Woman – [Now shall I never reconcile'em]

Aside.

Hark you, Madam, take my advice in your anger; you know you
often want one to make up your droling pack of hombre Players;
and you may cheat him easily, for he's an ill Gamester, and conse-   445
quently loves play: Besides you know, you have but two old civil
Gentlemen (with stinking breaths too) to wait upon you abroad,
take in the third, into your service; the other are but crazy: and a

Lady shou'd have a supernumerary Gentleman-Usher, as a supernumerary Coach-horse, least sometimes you shou'd be forc'd to   450
stay at home.

Lad. But are you sure he loves play, and has money?

Sr. Jas. He loves play as much as you, and has money as much as I.

Lad. Then I am contented to make him pay for his scurrillity; money
makes up in a measure all other wants in Men. – Those whom we   455
cannot make hold for Gallants, we make fine.

Aside.

Sr. Jas. So, so; now to mollify, to wheedle him, –

Aside.

Master *Horner* will you never keep civil Company, methinks 'tis time
now, since you are only fit for them: Come, come, Man you must e'en
fall to visiting our Wives, eating at our Tables, drinking Tea with our   460
virtuous Relations after dinner, dealing Cards to'em, reading Plays,
and Gazets to'em, picking Fleas out of their shocks for'em, collecting
Receipts, New Songs, Women, Pages, and Footmen for'em.

Hor. I hope they'l afford me better employment, Sir.

Sr. Jas. Heh, he, he, 'tis fit you know your work before you come into   465
your place; and since you are unprovided of a Lady to flatter, and a
good house to eat at, pray frequent mine, and call my Wife Mistriss,
and she shall call you Gallant, according to the custom.

Hor. Who I? –

Sr. Jas. Faith, thou sha't for my sake, come for my sake only.   470

Hor. For your sake –

Sr. Jas. Come, come, here's a Gamester for you, let him be a little
familiar sometimes; nay, what if a little rude; Gamesters may be rude
with Ladies, you know.

Lad. Yes, losing Gamesters have a privilege with Women.   475

Hor. I alwayes thought the contrary, that the winning Gamester had
most privilege with Women, for when you have lost your money to
a Man, you'l loose any thing you have, all you have, they say, and he
may use you as he pleases.

Sr. Jas. Heh, he, he, well, win or loose you shall have your liberty with   480
her.

Lad. As he behaves himself; and for your sake I'll give him admittance
and freedom.

Hor. All sorts of freedom, Madam?

Sr. Jas. Ay, ay, ay, all sorts of freedom thou can'st take, and so go to   485
her, begin thy new employment; wheedle her, jest with her, and be
better acquainted one with another.

Hor. I think I know her already, therefore may venter with her, my
secret for hers. –

Aside.
Horner, *and Lady* Fidget *whisper.*

Sr. Jas. Sister *Cuz*, I have provided an innocent Play-fellow for you 490
  there.
Dain. Who he!
Squeam. There's a Play-fellow indeed.
Sr. Jas. Yes sure, what he is good enough to play at Cards, Blind-mans
  buff, or the fool with sometimes. 495
Squeam. Foh, we'l have no such Play-fellows.
Dain. No, Sir, you shan't choose Play-fellows for us, we thank you.
Sr. Jas. Nay, pray hear me.

Whispering to them.

Lad. But, poor Gentleman, cou'd you be so generous? so truly a Man
  of honour, as for the sakes of us Women of honour, to cause your 500
  self to be reported no Man? No Man! and to suffer your self the
  greatest shame that cou'd fall upon a Man, that none might fall
  upon us Women by your conversation; but indeed, Sir, as perfectly,
  perfectly, the same Man as before your going into *France*, Sir; as
  perfectly, perfectly, Sir. 505
Hor. As perfectly, perfectly, Madam; nay, I scorn you shou'd take my
  word; I desire to be try'd only, Madam.
Lad. Well, that's spoken again like a Man of honour, all Men of
  honour desire to come to the test: But indeed, generally you Men
  report such things of your selves, one does not know how, or whom 510
  to believe; and it is come to that pass, we dare not take your words,
  no more than your Taylors, without some staid Servant of yours be
  bound with you; but I have so strong a faith in your honour, dear,
  dear, noble Sir, that I'd forfeit mine for yours at any time, dear Sir.
Hor. No, Madam, you shou'd not need to forfeit it for me, I have 515
  given you security already to save you harmless, my late reputation
  being so well known in the World, Madam.
Lady. But if upon any future falling out, or upon a suspition of my
  taking the trust out of your hands, to employ some other, you your
  self shou'd betray your trust, dear Sir; I mean, if you'l give me leave 520
  to speak obscenely, you might tell, dear Sir.
Hor. If I did, no body wou'd believe me; the reputation of impotency
  is as hardly recover'd again in the World, as that of cowardise, dear
  Madam.
Lad. Nay then, as one may say, you may do your worst, dear, dear, Sir. 525
Sr. Jas. Come, is your Ladyship reconciled to him yet? have you
  agreed on matters? for I must be gone to *Whitehal.*
Lad. Why, indeed, Sir *Jaspar*, Master *Horner* is a thousand, thousand
  times a better Man, than I thought him: Cosen *Squeamish*, Sister
  Dainty, I can name him now, truly not long ago you know, I 530
  thought his very name obscenity, and I wou'd as soon have lain
  with him, as have nam'd him.
Sr. Jas. Very likely, poor Madam.
Dain. I believe it.
Squeam. No doubt on't. 535

Sr. Jas. Well, well – that your Ladyship is as virtuous as any she, – I
know, and him all the Town knows – heh, he, he; therefore now you
like him, get you gone to your business together; go, go, to your
business, I say, pleasure, whilst I go to my pleasure, business.

Lad. Come then dear Gallant.   540

Hor. Come away, my dearest Mistriss.

Sr. Jas. So, so, why 'tis as I'd have it.

Exist Sr. Jaspar.

Hor. And as I'd have it.

Lad. Who for his business, from his Wife will run; Takes the best care,
to have her bus'ness done.   545

Exeunt omnes.

Act III

Scene I

Alithea, *and Mrs.* Pinchwife.

Alith. Sister, what ailes you, you are grown melancholy?

Mrs. Pin. Wou'd it not make any one melancholy, to see you go every
day fluttering about abroad, whil'st I must stay at home like a poor
lonely, sullen Bird in a cage?

Alit. Ay, Sister, but you came young, and just from the nest to your   5
cage, so that I thought you lik'd it; and cou'd be as chearful in't, as
others that took their flight themselves early, and are hopping
abroad in the open Air.

Mrs. Pin. Nay, I confess I was quiet enough, till my Husband told me,
what pure lives, the *London* Ladies live abroad, with their dancing,   10
meetings, and junketings, and drest every day in their best gowns;
and I warrant you, play at nine Pins every day of the week, so they do.

Enter Mr. Pinchwife.

Mr. Pin. Come, what's here to do? you are putting the Town pleasures in her head, and setting her a longing.

Alit. Yes, after Nine-pins; you suffer none to give her those longings,   15
you mean, but your self.

Mr. Pin. I tell her of the vanities of the Town like a Confessor.

Alith. A Confessor! just such a Confessor, as he that by forbidding a
silly Oastler to grease the Horses teeth, taught him to do't.

Mr. Pin. Come Mistriss *Flippant*, good Precepts are lost, when bad   20
Examples are still before us; the liberty you take abroad makes her
hanker after it; and out of humour at home, poor. Wretch! she
desired not to come to *London*, I wou'd bring her.

Alith. Very well.

Mr. Pin. She has been this week in Town, and never desired, till this   25
    afternoon, to go abroad.

Alith. Was she not at a Play yesterday?

Mr. Pin. Yes, but she ne'er ask'd me; I was my self the cause of her
    going.

Alith. Then if she ask you again, you are the cause of her asking, and   30
    not my example.

Mr. Pin. Well, to morrow night I shall be rid of you; and the next day
    before 'tis light, she and I'll be rid of the Town, and my dreadful
    apprehensions: Come, be not melancholly, for thou sha't go into
    the Country after to morrow, Dearest.   35

Alith. Great comfort.

Mrs. Pin. Pish, what d'ye tell me of the Country for?

Mr. Pin. How's this! what, pish at the Country?

Mrs. Pin. Let me alone, I am not well.

Mr. Pin. O, if that be all – what ailes my dearest?   40

Mrs. Pin. Truly I don't know; but I have not been well, since you told
    me there was a Gallant at the Play in love with me.

Mr. Pin. Ha –

Alith. That's by my example too.

Mr. Pin. Nay, if you are not well, but are so concern'd, because a   45
    lew'd Fellow, chanc'd to lye, and say he lik'd you, you'l make me
    sick too.

Mrs. Pin. Of what sickness?

Mr. Pin. O, of that which is worse than the Plague, Jealousy.

Mrs. Pin. Pish, you jear, I'm sure there's no such disease in our   50
    Receipt-book at home.

Mr. Pin. No, thou never met'st with it, poor Innocent – well, if thou
    Cuckold me, 'twill be my own fault – for Cuckolds and Bastards, are
    generally makers of their own fortune.

Aside.

Mrs. Pin. Well, but pray Bud, let's go to a Play to night.   55

Mr. Pin. 'Tis just done, she comes from it; but why are you so eager
    to see a Play?

Mrs. Pin. Faith Dear, not that I care one pin for their talk there; but I
    like to look upon the Player-men, and wou'd see, if I cou'd, the
    Gallant you say loves me; that's all dear Bud.   60

Mr. Pin. Is that all dear Bud?

Alith. This proceeds from my example.

Mr. Pin. But if the Play be done, let's go abroad however, dear Bud.

Mr. Pin. Come have a little patience, and thou shalt go into the
    Country on Friday.   65

Mrs. Pin. Therefore I wou'd see first some sights, to tell my Neigh-
    bours of. Nay, I will go abroad, that's once.

Alith. I'm the cause of this desire too.

Mr. Pin. But now I think on't, who was the cause of *Horners* coming
    to my Lodging to day? that was you.   70

Alith. No, you, because you wou'd not let him see your handsome
Wife out of your Lodging.

Mrs. Pin. Why, O Lord! did the Gentleman come hither to see me
indeed?

Mr. Pin. No, no; – You are not cause of that damn'd question too,   75
Mistriss *Alithea*? – [Well she's in the right of it; he is in love with my
Wife – and comes after her – 'tis so – but I'll nip his love in the bud;
least he should follow us into the Country, and break his Chariot-
wheel near our house, on purpose for an excuse to come to't; but I
think I know the Town.   80

Aside.

Mrs. Pin. Come, pray Bud, let's go abroad before 'tis late; for I will
go, that's flat and plain.

Mr. Pin. So! the obstinacy already of a Town-wife, and I must, whilst
she's here, humour her like one.

Aside.

Sister, how shall we do, that she may not be seen, or known?   85

Alith. Let her put on her Mask.

Mr. Pin. Pshaw, a Mask makes People but the more inquisitive, and is
as ridiculous a disguise, as a stage- beard; her shape, stature, habit will
be known: and if we shou'd meet with *Horner*, he wou'd be sure to
take acquaintance with us, must wish her joy, kiss her, talk to her, leer   90
upon her, and the Devil and all; no I'll not use her to a Mask, 'tis
dangerous; for Masks have made more Cuckolds, than the best faces
that ever were known.

Alith. How will you do then?

Mrs. Pin. Nay, shall we go? the *Exchange* will be shut, and I have a   95
mind to see that.

Mr. Pin. So – I have it – I'll dress her up in the Suit, we are to carry
down to her Brother, little Sir *James*; nay, I understand the Town
tricks: Come let's go dress her; a Mask! no – a Woman mask'd, like a
cover'd Dish, gives a Man curiosity, and appetite, when, it may be,   100
uncover'd, 'twou'd turn his stomack; no, no.

Alith. Indeed your comparison is something a greasie one: but I had a
gentle Gallant, us'd to say, a Beauty mask'd, like the Sun in Eclipse,
gathers together more gazers, than if it shin'd out.

Exeunt.

Scene II

The Scene changes to the new Exchange: *Enter* Horner,
Harcourt, Dorilant.

Dor. Engag'd to Women, and not Sup with us?

Hor. Ay, a Pox on'em all.

Har. You were much a more reasonable Man in the morning, and had
as noble resolutions against'em, as a Widdower of a weeks liberty.

Dor. Did I ever think, to see you keep company with Women in vain. 5

Hor. In vain! no – 'tis, since I can't love'em, to be reveng'd on'em.

Har. Now your Sting is gone, you look'd in the Box amongst all
those Women, like a drone in the hive, all upon you; shov'd and ill-
us'd by'em all, and thrust from one side to t'other.

Dor. Yet he must be buzzing amongst'em still, like other old beetle- 10
headed, lycorish drones; avoid'em, and hate'm as they hate you.

Hor. Because I do hate'em, and wou'd hate'em yet more, I'll frequent'em; you may see by Marriage, nothing makes a Man hate a
Woman more, than her constant conversation: In short, I converse
with'em, as you do with rich Fools, to laugh at'em, and use'em ill. 15

Dor. But I wou'd no more Sup with Women, unless I cou'd lye
with'em, than Sup with a rich Coxcomb, unless I cou'd cheat him.

Hor. Yes, I have known thee Sup with a Fool, for his drinking, if he
cou'd set out your hand that way only, you were satisfy'd; and if
he were a Wine-swallowing mouth 'twas enough. 20

Har. Yes, a Man drink's often with a Fool, as he tosses with a Marker,
only to keep his hand in Ure; but do the Ladies drink?

Hor. Yes, Sir, and I shall have the pleasure at least of laying'em flat
with a Bottle; and bring as much scandal that way upon'em, as
formerly t'other. 25

Har. Perhaps you may prove as weak a Brother amongst'em that way,
as t'other.

Dor. Foh, drinking with Women, is as unnatural, as scolding with'em;
but 'tis a pleasure of decay'd Fornicators, and the basest way of
quenching Love. 30

Har. Nay, 'tis drowning Love, instead of quenching it; but leave us
for civil Women too!

Dor. Ay, when he can't be the better for'em; we hardly pardon a Man,
that leaves his Friend for a Wench, and that's a pretty lawful call.

Hor. Faith, I wou'd not leave you for'em, if they wou'd not drink. 35

Dor. Who wou'd disappoint his Company at *Lewis*'s, for a Gossiping?

Har. Foh, Wine and Women good apart, together as nauseous as
Sack and Sugar: But hark you, Sir, before you go, a little of your
advice, an old maim'd General, when unfit for action is fittest for
Counsel; I have other designs upon Women, than eating and drink- 40
ing with them: I am in love with *Sparkish*'s Mistriss, whom he is to
marry to morrow, now how shall I get her?

Enter Sparkish, *looking about.*

Hor. Why, here comes one will help you to her.

Har. He! he, I tell you, is my Rival, and will hinder my love.

Hor. No, a foolish Rival, and a jealous Husband assist their Rivals 45
designs; for they are sure to make their Women hate them, which is
the first step to their love, for another Man.

Har. But I cannot come near his Mistriss, but in his company.

Hor. Still the better for you, for Fools are most easily cheated, when
   they themselves are accessaries; and he is to be bubled of his Mistriss,   50
   as of his Money, the common Mistriss, by keeping him company.
Spar. Who is that, that is to be bubled? Faith let me snack, I han't met
   with a buble since Christmas: gad; I think bubles are like their
   Brother Woodcocks, go out with the cold weather.
Har. A Pox, he did not hear all I hope.   55

Apart to Horner.

Spar. Come, you bubling Rogues you, where do we sup – Oh,
   Harcourt, my Mistriss tells me, you have been making fierce love
   to her all the Play long, hah, ha – but I –
Har. I make love to her?
Spar. Nay, I forgive thee; for I think I know thee, and I know her, but   60
   I am sure I know my self.
Har. Did she tell you so? I see all Women are like these of the
   Exchange, who to enhance the price of their commodities, report
   to their fond Customers offers which were never made'em.
Hor. Ay, Women are as apt to tell before the intrigue, as Men after it,   65
   and so shew themselves the vainer Sex; but hast thou a Mistriss,
   Sparkish? 'tis as hard for me to believe it, as that thou ever hadst a
   buble, as you brag'd just now.
Spar. O your Servant, Sir; are you at your raillery, Sir? but we were
   some of us beforehand with you to day at the Play: the Wits were   70
   something bold with you, Sir; did you not hear us laugh?
Har. Yes, But I thought you had gone to Plays, to laugh at the Poets
   wit, not at your own.
Spar. Your Servant, Sir, no I thank you; gad I go to a Play as to a
   Country-treat, I carry my own wine to one, and my own wit to   75
   t'other, or else I'm sure I shou'd not be merry at either; and the
   reason why we are so often lowder, than the Players, is, because we
   think we speak more wit, and so become the Poets Rivals in his
   audience: for to tell you the truth, we hate the silly Rogues; nay, so
   much that we find fault even with their Bawdy upon the Stage,   80
   whilst we talk nothing else in the Pit as lowd.
Hor. But, why should'st thou hate the silly Poets, thou hast too much
   wit to be one, and they like Whores are only hated by each other;
   and thou dost scorn writing, I'am sure.
Spar. Yes, I'd have you to know, I scorn writing; but Women,   85
   Women, that make Men do all foolish things, make'em write
   Songs too; every body does it: 'tis ev'n as common with Lovers,
   as playing with fans; and you can no more help Rhyming to your
   Phyllis, than drinking to your *Phyllis.*
Har. Nay, Poetry in love is no more to be avoided, than jealousy.   90
Dor. But the Poets damn'd your Songs, did they?
Spar. Damn the Poets, they turn'd'em into Burlesque, as they call it;
   that Burlesque is a *Hocus-Pocus*-trick, they have got, which by the
   virtue of *Hictius doctius, topsey turvey,* they make a wise and witty

Man in the World, a Fool upon the Stage you know not how; and   95
'tis therefore I hate'em too, for I know not but it may be my own
case; for they'l put a Man into a Play for looking a Squint: Their
Predecessors were contented to make Serving-men only their
Stage-Fools, but these Rogues must have Gentlemen, with a Pox
to'em, nay Knights: and indeed you shall hardly see a Fool upon the   100
Stage, but he's a Knight; and to tell you the truth, they have kept
me these six years from being a Knight in earnest, for fear of being
knighted in a Play, and dubb'd a Fool.

Dor. Blame'em not, they must follow their Copy, the Age.

Har. But why should'st thou be afraid of being in a Play, who expose   105
your self every day in the Play- houses, and as publick Places.

Hor. 'Tis but being on the Stage, instead of standing on a Bench in
the Pit.

Dor. Don't you give money to Painters to draw you like? and are you
afraid of your Pictures, at length in a Play-house, where all your   110
Mistresses may see you.

Spar. A Pox, Painters don't draw the Small Pox, or Pimples in ones
face; come damn all your silly Authors whatever, all Books and
Booksellers, by the World, and all Readers, courteous or uncour-
teous.   115

Har. But, who comes here, *Sparkish*?

       Enter Mr. Pinchwife, *and his Wife in Mans Cloaths*,
           Alithea, Lucy *her Maid.*

Spar. Oh hide me, there's my Mistriss too.

           Sparkish *hides himself behind* Harcourt.

Har. She sees you.

Spar. But I will not see her, 'tis time to go to *Whitehal*, and I must not
fail the drawing Room.   120

Har. Pray, first carry me, and reconcile me to her.

Spar. Another time, faith the King will have sup't.

Har. Not with the worse stomach for thy absence; thou art one of
those Fools, that think their attendance at the King's Meals, as
necessary as his Physicians, when you are more troublesom to   125
him, than his Doctors, or his Dogs.

Spar. Pshaw, I know my interest, Sir, prethee hide me.

Hor. Your Servant, *Pinchwife*, – what he knows us not –

Mr. Pin. Come along.

                  To his Wife aside.

Mrs. Pin. Pray, have you any Ballads, give me sixpenny worth?   130

Clasp. We have no Ballads.

Mrs. Pin. Then give me *Covent-garden*-Drollery, and a Play or two –
Oh here's *Tarugos* Wiles, and the Slighted Maiden, I'll have them.

Mr. Pin. No, Playes are not for your reading; come along, will you discover your self?   135

Apart to her.

Hor. Who is that pretty Youth with him, *Sparkish?*

Spar. I believe his Wife's Brother, because he's something like her, but I never saw her but once.

Hor. Extremly handsome, I have seen a face like it too; let us follow'em.

Exeunt Pinchwife, *Mistriss* Pinchwife.
Alithea, Lucy, Horner, Dorilant *following them.*

Har. Come, *Sparkish*, your Mistriss saw you, and will be angry you go   140
not to her; besides I wou'd fain be reconcil'd to her, which none but you can do, dear Friend.

Spar. Well that's a better reason, dear Friend; I wou'd not go near her now, for her's, or my sake, but I can deny you nothing; for though I have known thee a great while, never go, if I do not love thee, as   145
well as a new Acquaintance.

Har. I am oblig'd to you indeed, dear Friend, I wou'd be well with her only, to be well with thee still; for these tyes to Wives usually dissolve all tyes to Friends: I wou'd be contended, she shou'd enjoy you a nights, but I wou'd have you to my self a dayes, as I have had,   150
dear Friend.

Spar. And thou shalt enjoy me a dayes, dear, dear Friend, never stir; and I'll be divorced from her, sooner than from thee; come along –

Har. So we are hard put to't, when we make our Rival our Procurer;   155
but neither she, nor her Brother, wou'd let me come near her now: when all's done, a Rival is the best cloak to steal to a Mistress under, without suspicion; and when we have once got to her as we desire, we throw him off like other Cloaks.

Aside.
[*Exit* Sparkish, *and* Harcourt *following him. Re-enter*
Mr. Pinchwife, *Mistress* Pinchwife *in Man's Cloaths.*

Mr. Pin. Sister, if you will not go, we must leave you –   160

To Alithea.

The Fool her Gallant, and she, will muster up all the young santerers of this place, and they will leave their dear Seamstresses to follow us; what a swarm of Cuckolds, and Cuckold-makers are here?

Aside.

Come let's be gone Mistriss *Margery.*

Mrs. Pin. Don't you believe that, I han't half my belly full of sights yet.   165

Mr. Pin. Then walk this way.

Mrs. Pin. Lord, what a power of brave signs are here! stay – the Bull's-head, the Rams-head, and the Stags-head, Dear –

Mr. Pin. Nay, if every Husbands proper sign here were visible, they
wou'd be all alike.   170
Mr. Pin. What d'ye mean by that, Bud?
Mr. Pin. 'Tis no matter – no matter, Bud.
Mrs. Pin. Pray tell me; nay, I will know.
Mr. Pin. They wou'd be all Bulls, Stags, and Rams heads.

Exeunt Mr. Pinchwife, *Mrs.* Pinchwife.

Re-enter Sparkish, Harcourt, Alithea, Lucy, *at t'other door.*

Spar. Come, dear Madam, for my sake you shall be reconciled to him.   175
Alith. For your sake I hate him.
Har. That's something too cruel, Madam, to hate me for his sake.
Spar. Ay indeed, Madam, too, too cruel to me, to hate my Friend for
my sake.
Alith. I hate him because he is your Enemy; and you ought to hate   180
him too, for making love to me, if you love me.
Spar. That's a good one, I hate a Man for loving you; if he did love
you, 'tis but what he can't help, and 'tis your fault not his, if he
admires you: I hate a Man for being of my opinion, I'll ne'er do't,
by the World.   185
Alith. Is it for your honour or mine, to suffer a Man to make love to
me, who am to marry you to morrow?
Spar. Is it for your honour or mine, to have me jealous? That he
makes love to you, is a sign you are handsome; and that I am not
jealous, is a sign you are virtuous, that I think is for your honour.   190
Alith. But 'tis your honour too, I am concerned for.
Har. But why, dearest Madam, will you be more concern'd for his
honour, than he is himself; let his honour alone for my sake, and his.
He, he, has no honour –
Spar. How's that?   195
Har. But what, my dear Friend can guard himself.
Spar. O ho – that's right again.
Har. Your care of his honour argues his neglect of it, which is no
honour to my dear Friend here; therefore once more, let his honour
go which way it will, dear Madam.   200
Spar. Ay, ay, were it for my honour to marry a Woman, whose virtue I
suspected, and cou'd not trust her in a Friends hands?
Alith. Are you not afraid to loose me?
Har. He afraid to loose you, Madam! No, no – you may see how the
most estimable, and most glorious Creature in the World, is valued   205
by him; will you not see it?
Spar. Right, honest *Franck*, I have that noble value for her, that I
cannot be jealous of her.
Spar. You mistake him, he means you care not for me, nor who has me.
Spar. Lord, Madam, I see you are jealous; will you wrest a poor Mans 210
meaning from his words?
Alith. You astonish me, Sir, with your want of jealousie.

Spar. And you make me guiddy, Madam, with your jealousie, and
fears, and virtue, and honour; gad, I see virtue makes a Woman as
troublesome, as a little reading, or learning.   215
Alith. Monstrous!
Lucy. [Well to see what easie Husbands these Women of quality can
meet with, a poor Chamber-maid can never have such Lady-like
luck; besides he's thrown away upon her, she'l make no use of her
fortune, her blessing, none to a Gentleman, for a pure Cuckold, for 220
it requires good breeding to be a Cuckold.

Behind.

Alith. I tell you then plainly, he pursues me to marry me.
Spar. Pshaw –
Har. Come, Madam, you see you strive in vain to make him jealous of
me; my dear Friend is the kindest Creature in the World to me.   225
Spar. Poor fellow.
Har. But his kindness only is not enough for me, without your
favour; your good opinion, dear Madam, 'tis that must perfect my
happiness: good Gentleman he believes all I say, wou'd you wou'd
do so, jealous of me! I wou'd not wrong him nor you for the World. 230
Spar. Look you there; hear him, hear him, and do not walk away so.

Alithea *walks carelessly, to and fro.*

Har. I love you, Madam, so –
Spar. How's that! Nay – now you begin to go too far indeed.
Har. So much I confess, I say I love you, that I wou'd not have you
miserable, and cast your self away upon so unworthy, and inconsid- 235
erable a thing, as what you see here.

Clapping his hand on his breast, points at Sparkish.

Spar. No faith, I believe thou woud'st not, now his meaning is plain:
but I knew before thou woud'st not wrong me nor her.
Har. No, no, Heavens forbid, the glory of her Sex shou'd fall so low
as into the embraces of such a contemptible Wretch, the last of 240
Mankind – my dear Friend here – I injure him.

Embracing Sparkish.

Alith. Very well.
Spar. No, no, dear Friend, I knew it Madam, you see he will rather
wrong himself than me, in giving himself such names.
Alith. Do not you understand him yet?   245
Spar. Yes, how modestly he speaks of himself, poor Fellow.
Alith. Methinks he speaks impudently of your self, since – before your
self too, insomuch that I can no longer suffer his scurrilous abu-
siveness to you, no more than his love to me.

offers to go.

Spar. Nay, nay, Madam, pray stay, his love to you: Lord, Madam, has 250
he not spoke yet plain enough?

Alith. Yes indeed, I shou'd think so.

Spar. Well then, by the World, a Man can't speak civilly to a Woman now, but presently she says, he makes love to her: Nay, Madam, you shall stay, with your pardon, since you have not yet understood him, 255 till he has made an eclaircisment of his love to you, that is what kind of love it is; answer to thy Catechisme: Friend, do you love my Mistriss here?

Har. Yes, I wish she wou'd not doubt it.

Spar. But how do you love her? 260

Har. With all my Soul.

Alith. I thank him, methinks he speaks plain enough now.

Spar. You are out still.

To Alithea.

But with what kind of love, *Harcourt?*

Har. With the best, and truest love in the World. 265

Spar. Look you there then, that is with no matrimonial love, I'm sure.

Alith. How's that, do you say matrimonial love is not best?

Spar. Gad, I went too far e're I was aware: But speak for thy self *Harcourt*, you said you wou'd not wrong me, nor her.

Har. No, no, Madam, e'n take him for Heaven's sake. 270

Spar. Look you there, Madam.

Har. Who shou'd in all justice be yours, he that loves you most.

Claps his hand on his breast.

Alith. Look you there, Mr. *Sparkish*, who's that?

Spar. Who shou'd it be? go on *Harcourt.*

Har. Who loves you more than Women, Titles, or fortune Fools. 275

Points at Sparkish.

Spar. Look you there, he means me stil, for he points at me.

Alith. Ridiculous!

Har. Who can only match your Faith, and constancy in love.

Spar. Ay.

Har. Who knows, if it be possible, how to value so much beauty and 280 virtue.

Spar. Ay.

Har. Whose love can no more be equall'd in the world, than that Heavenly form of yours.

Spar. No – 285

Har. Who cou'd no more suffer a Rival, than your absence, and yet cou'd no more suspect your virtue, than his own constancy in his love to you.

Spar. No –

Har. Who in fine loves you better than his eyes, that first made him 290 love you.

Spar. Ay – nay, Madam, faith you shan't go, till –

Alith. Have a care, lest you make me stay too long –

Spar. But till he has saluted you; that I may be assur'd you are friends, after his honest advice and declaration: Come pray, Madam, be   295
friends with him.

Enter Master Pinchwife, *Mistriss* Pinchwife.

Alith. You must pardon me, Sir, that I am not yet so obedient to you.

Mr. Pin. What, invite your Wife to kiss Men? Monstrous, are you not asham'd? I will never forgive you.

Spar. Are you not asham'd, that I shou'd have more confidence in the   300
chastity of your Family, than you have; you must not teach me, I am a man of honour, Sir, though I am frank and free; I am frank, Sir –

Mr. Pin. Very frank, Sir, to share your Wife with your friends.

Spar. He is an humble, menial Friend, such as reconciles the differences of the Marriage-bed; you know Man and Wife do not alwayes   305
agree, I design him for that use, therefore wou'd have him well with my Wife.

Mr. Pin. A menial Friend – you will get a great many menial Friends, by shewing your Wife as you do.

Spar. What then, it may be I have a pleasure in't, as I have to shew fine   310
Clothes, at a Play-house the first day, and count money before poor Rogues.

Mr. Pin. He that shews his wife, or money will be in danger of having them borrowed sometimes.

Spar. I love to be envy'd, and wou'd not marry a Wife, that I alone   315
cou'd love; loving alone is as dull, as eating alone; is it not a frank age, and I am a frank Person? and to tell you the truth, it may be I love to have Rivals in a Wife, they make her seem to a Man still, but as a kept Mistriss; and so good night, for I must to *Whitehal.* Madam, I hope you are now reconcil'd to my Friend; and so I wish you a good night,   320
Madam, and sleep if you can, for tomorrow you know I must visit you early with a Canonical Gentleman. Good night dear *Harcourt.*

Exit Sparkish.

Har. Madam, I hope you will not refuse my visit to morrow, if it shou'd be earlyer, with a Canonical Gentleman, than Mr. *Sparkish*'s.

Mr. Pin. This Gentle-woman is yet under my care, therefore you must   325
yet forbear your freedom with her, Sir.

Coming between Alithea *and* Harcourt.

Har. Must, Sir –

Mr. Pin. Yes, Sir, she is my Sister.

Har. 'Tis well she is, Sir – for I must be her Servant, Sir. Madam –

Mr. Pin. Come away Sister, we had been gone, if it had not been for   330
you, and so avoided these lewd Rakehells, who seem to haunt us.

Enter Horner, Dorilant *to them.*

Hor. How now *Pinchwife?*

Mr. Pin. Your Servant.

Hor. What, I see a little time in the Country makes a Man turn wild
and unsociable, and only fit to converse with his Horses, Dogs, and 335
his Herds.

Mr. Pin. I have business, Sir, and must mind it; your business is
pleasure, therefore you and I must go different wayes.

Hor. Well, you may go on, but this pretty young Gentleman –

Takes hold of Mrs. Pinchwife.

Har. The Lady – 340
Dor. And the Maid –
Hor. Shall stay with us, for I suppose their business is the same with
ours, pleasure.

Mr. Pin. 'Sdeath he knows her, she carries it so sillily, yet if he does
not, I shou'd be more silly to discover it first. 345

Aside.

Alith. Pray, let us go, Sir.
Mr. Pin. Come, come –
Hor. Had you not rather stay with us?

To Mrs. Pinchwife.

Prethee *Pinchwife*, who is this pretty young Gentleman?
Mr. Pin. One to whom I'm a guardian. 350
[I wish I cou'd keep her out of your hands –

Aside.

Hor. Who is he? I never saw any thing so pretty in all my life.
Mr. Pin. Pshaw, do not look upon him so much, he's a poor
bashful youth, you'l put him out of countenance. Come away
Brother. 355

Offers to take her away.

Hor. O your Brother!
Mr. Pin. Yes, my Wifes Brother; come, come, she'l stay supper for us.
Hor. I thought so, for he is very like her I saw you at the Play with,
whom I told you, I was in love with.
Mr. Pin. O Jeminy! is this he that was in love with me, I am glad on't 360
I vow, for he's a curious fine Gentleman, and I love him already
too.

Aside.

Is this he Bud?

To Mr. Pinchwife.

Mr. Pin. Come away, come away.

To his Wife.

Hor. Why, what haste are you in? why wont you let me talk with him? 365

Mr. Pin. Because you'l debauch him, he's yet young and innocent,
and I wou'd not have him debauch'd for any thing in the World.
How she gazes on him! the Divel –

Aside.

Hor. Harcourt, Dorilant, look you here, this is the likeness of that
Dowdey he told us of, his Wife, did you ever see a lovelyer Creature?   370
the Rogue has reason to be jealous of his Wife, since she is like him,
for she wou'd make all that see her, in love with her.
Har. And as I remember now, she is as like him here as can be.
Dor. She is indeed very pretty, if she be like him.
Hor. Very pretty, a very pretty commendation – she is a glorious   375
Creature, beautiful beyond all things I ever beheld.
Mr. Pin. So, so.
Har. More beautiful than a Poets first Mistriss of Imagination.
Hor. Or another Mans last Mistriss of flesh and blood.
Mr. Pin. Nay, now you jeer, Sir; pray don't jeer me –   380
Mr. Pin. Come, come. [By Heavens she'l discover her self.

Aside.

Hor. I speak of your Sister, Sir.
Mr. Pin. Ay, but saying she was handsome, if like him, made him
blush. [I am upon a wrack –

Aside.

Hor. Methinks he is so handsome, he shou'd not be a Man.   385
Mr. Pin. O there 'tis out, he has discovered her, I am not able to
suffer any longer.
[Come, come away, I say –

To his Wife.

Hor. Nay, by your leave, Sir, he shall not go yet –
Harcourt, Dorilant, let us torment this jealous Rogue a little.   390

To them.

Hor. ⎱
Dor. ⎰ How?
Hor. I'll shew you.
Mr. Pin. Come, pray let him go, I cannot stay fooling any longer; I
tell you his Sister stays supper for us.
Hor. Do's she, come then we'l all go sup with her and thee.   395
Mr. Pin. No, now I think on't, having staid so long for us, I warrant
she's gone to bed – [I wish she and I were well out of their hands –

Aside.

Come, I must rise early to morrow, come.
Hor. Well then, if she be gone to bed, I wish her and you a good night.
But pray, young Gentleman, present my humble service to her.   400

Mrs. Pin. Thank you heartily, Sir.

Mr. Pin. S'death, she will discover her self yet in spight of me.

Aside.

He is something more civil to you, for your kindness to his Sister, than I am, it seems.

Hor. Tell her, dear sweet little Gentleman, for all your Brother there,   405
that you have reviv'd the love, I had for her at first sight in the Playhouse.

Mrs. Pin. But did you love her indeed, and indeed?

Mr. Pin. So, so.

Aside.

Away, I say.   410

Hor. Nay stay; yes indeed, and indeed, pray do you tell her so, and give her this kiss from me.

Kisses her.

Mr. Pin. O Heavens! what do I suffer; now 'tis too plain he knows her, and yet –

Aside.

Hor. And this, and this –   415

Kisses her again.

Mrs. Pin. What do you kiss me for, I am no Woman.

Mr. Pin. So – there 'tis out.

Aside.

Come, I cannot, nor will stay any longer.

Hor. Nay, they shall send your Lady a kiss too; here *Harcourt, Dorilant*, will you not?   420

They kiss her.

Mr. Pin. How, do I suffer this? was I not accusing another just now, for this rascally patience, in permitting his Wife to be kiss'd before his face? ten thousand ulcers gnaw away their lips.

Aside.

Come, come.

Hor. Good night dear little Gentleman; Madam good-night; farewel   425
Pinchwife. [Did not I tell you, I wou'd raise his jealous gall.

Apart to Harcourt *and* Dorilant.
Exeunt Horner, Harcourt, *and* Dorilant.

Mr. Pin. So they are gone at last; stay, let me see first if the Coach be at this door.

Exit.

Hor. What not gone yet? will you be sure to do as I desired you, sweet
Sir? 430

                Horner, Harcourt, Dorilant *return.*

Mrs. Pin. Sweet Sir, but what will you give me then?
Hor. Any thing, come away into the next walk.

         Exit Horner, *haling away Mrs.* Pinchwife.

Alith. Hold, hold, – what d'ye do?
Lucy. Stay, stay, hold –
Har. Hold Madam, hold, let him present him, he'l come presently; 435
nay, I will never let you go, till you answer my question.

       Alithea, Lucy *strugling with* Harcourt, *and* Dorilant.

Lucy. For God's sake, Sir, I must follow'em.
Dor. No, I have something to present you with too, you shan't follow
them.

              Pinchwife *returns.*

Mr. Pin. Where? – how? – what's become of? gone – whither? 440
Lucy. He's only gone with the Gentleman, who will give him some-
thing, an't please your Worship.
Mr. Pin. Something – give him something, with a Pox – where are
they?
Alith. In the next walk only, Brother. 445
Mr. Pin. Only, only; where, where?

     Exit Pinchwife, *and returns presently, then goes out again.*

Har. What's the matter with him? why so much concern'd? but
dearest Madam –
Alith. Pray, let me go, Sir, I have said, and suffer'd enough already.
Har. Then you will not look upon, nor pitty my sufferings? 450
Alith. To look upon'em, when I cannot help'em, were cruelty, not
pitty, therefore I will never see you more.
Har. Let me then, Madam, have my priviledge of a banished Lover,
complaining or railing, and giving you but a farewell reason; why, if
you cannot condescend to marry me, you shou'd not take that 455
wretch my Rival.
Alith. He only, not you, since my honour is engag'd so far to him, can
give me a reason, why I shou'd not marry him; but if he be true, and
what I think him to me, I must be so to him; your Servant, Sir.
Har. Have Women only constancy when 'tis a vice, and like fortune 460
only true to fools?
Dor. Thou sha't not stir thou robust Creature, you see I can deal with
you, therefore you shou'd stay the rather, and be kind.

          To Lucy, *who struggles to get from him.*
                Enter Pinchwife.

Mr. Pin. Gone, gone, not to be found; quite gone, ten thousand
plagues go with'em; which way went they? 465
Alith. But into t'other walk, Brother.
Lucy. Their business will be done presently sure, an't please your
Worship, it can't be long in doing I'm sure on't.
Alith. Are they not there?
Mr. Pin. No, you know where they are, you infamous Wretch, Eternal 470
shame of your Family, which you do not dishonour enough your
self, you think, but you must help her to do it too, thou legion of
Bawds.
Alith. Good Brother.
Mr. Pin. Damn'd, damn'd Sister. 475
Alith. Look you here, she's coming.

Enter Mistriss Pinchwife *in Mans cloaths, running with her hat under
her arm, full of Oranges and dried fruit,* Horner *following.*

Mrs. Pin. O dear Bud, look you here what I have got, see.
Mr. Pin. And what I have got here too, which you can't see.

Aside rubbing his forehead.

Mrs. Pin. The fine Gentleman has given me better things yet.
Mr. Pin. Ha's he so? [Out of breath and colour'd – I must hold yet. 480

Aside.

Hor. I have only given your little Brother an Orange, Sir.
Mr. Pin. Thank you, Sir.

To Horner.

You have only squeez'd my Orange, I suppose, and given it me
again; yet I must have a City-patience.

Aside.

Come, come away – 485

To his Wife.

Mrs. Pin. Stay, till I have put up my fine things, Bud.

Enter Sir Jaspar Fidget.

Sr. Jas. O Master *Horner*, come, come, the Ladies stay for you; your
Mistriss, my Wife, wonders you make not more hast to her.
Hor. I have staid this half hour for you here, and 'tis your fault I am
not now with your Wife. 490
Sr. Jas. But pray, don't let her know so much, the truth on't is, I was
advancing a certain Project to his Majesty, about – I'll tell you.
Hor. No, let's go, and hear it at your house: Good night sweet little
Gentleman; one kiss more, you'l remember me now I hope.

Kisses her.

Dor. What, Sir *Jaspar*, will you separate Friends? he promis'd to sup   495
   with us; and if you take him to your house, you'l be in danger of our
   company too.

Sr. Jas. Alas Gentlemen my house is not fit for you, there are none but
   civil Women there, which are not for your turn; he you know can
   bear with the society of civil Women, now, ha, ha, ha; besides he's   500
   one of my Family; – he's – heh, heh, heh.

Dor. What is he?

Sr. Jas. Faith my Eunuch, since you'l have it, heh, he, he.

> *Exit Sir* Jaspar Fidget, *and* Horner.

Dor. I rather wish thou wert his, or my Cuckold: *Harcourt*, what a
   good Cuckold is lost there, for want of a Man to make him one;   505
   thee and I cannot have *Horners* privilege, who can make use of it.

Har. Ay, to poor *Horner* 'tis like coming to an estate at threescore,
   when a Man can't be the better for't.

Mr. Pin. Come.

Mrs. Pin. Presently Bud.   510

Dor. Come let us go too: Madam, your Servant.

> *To* Alith.

Good night Strapper. –

> *To* Lucy.

Har. Madam, though you will not let me have a good day, or night, I
   wish you one; but dare not name the other half of my wish.

Alith. Good night, Sir, for ever.   515

Mrs. Pin. I don't know where to put this here, dear Bud, you shall eat
   it; nay, you shall have part of the fine Gentlemans good things, or
   treat as you call it, when we come home.

Mr. Pin. Indeed I deserve it, since I furnish'd the best part of it.

> *Strikes away the Orange.*

The Gallant treates, presents, and gives the Ball;   520
But 'tis the absent Cuckold, pays for all.

Act IV

Scene I

In Pinchwife'*s house in the morning.*

Lucy, Alithea *dress'd in new Cloths.*

Lucy. Well – Madam, now have I dress'd you, and set you out with so
   many ornaments, and spent upon you ounces of essence, and
   pulvilio; and all this for no other purpose, but as People adorn,

and perfume a Corps, for a stinking second-hand-grave, such or as
bad I think Master *Sparkish*'s bed.   5
Alith. Hold your peace.
Lucy. Nay, Madam, I will ask you the reason, why you wou'd banish
poor Master *Harcourt* for ever from your sight? how cou'd you be
so hard-hearted?
Alith. 'Twas because I was not hard-hearted.   10
Lucy. No, no; 'twas stark love and kindness, I warrant.
Alith. It was so; I wou'd see him no more, because I love him.
Lucy. Hey day, a very pretty reason.
Alith. You do not understand me.
Lucy. I wish you may your self.   15
Alith. I was engag'd to marry, you see, another man, whom my
justice will not suffer me to deceive, or injure.
Lucy. Can there be a greater cheat, or wrong done to a Man, than to
give him your person, without your heart, I shou'd make a con-
science of it.   20
Alith. I'll retrieve it for him after I am married a while.
Lucy. The Woman that marries to love better, will be as much mistaken, as the Wencher that marries to live better. No, Madam,
marrying to encrease love, is like gaming to become rich; alas you
only loose, what little stock you had before.   25
Alith. I find by your Rhetorick you have been brib'd to betray me.
Lucy. Only by his merit, that has brib'd your heart you see against your
word, and rigid honour; but what a Divel is this honour? 'tis sure a
disease in the head, like the Megrim, or Falling-sickness, that always
hurries People away to do themselves mischief; Men loose their lives   30
by it: Women what's dearer to'em, their love, the life of life.
Alith. Come, pray talk you no more of honour, nor Master *Harcourt*;
I wish the other wou'd come, to secure my fidelity to him, and his
right in me.
Lucy. You will marry him then?   35
Alith. Certainly, I have given him already my word, and will my hand
too, to make it good when he comes.
Lucy. Well, I wish I may never stick pin more, if he be not an errant
Natural, to t'other fine Gentleman.
Alith. I own he wants the wit of *Harcourt*, which I will dispense   40
withal, for another want he has, which is want of jealousie, which
men of wit seldom want.
Lucy. Lord, Madam, what shou'd you do with a fool to your Husband, you intend to be honest don't you? then that husbandly
virtue, credulity, is thrown away upon you.   45
Alith. He only that could suspect my virtue, shou'd have cause to do
it; 'tis *Sparkish*'s confidence in my truth, that obliges me to be so
faithful to him.
Lucy. You are not sure his opinion may last.
Alith. I am satisfied, 'tis impossible for him to be jealous, after the   50
proofs I have had of him: Jealousie in a Husband, Heaven defend

me from it, it begets a thousand plagues to a poor Woman, the loss
of her honour, her quiet, and her –

Lucy. And her pleasure.

Alith. What d'ye mean, Impertinent?   55

Lucy. Liberty is a great pleasure, Madam.

Alith. I say loss of her honour, her quiet, nay, her life sometimes; and
what's as bad almost, the loss of this Town, that is, she is sent into the
Country, which is the last ill usage of a Husband to a Wife, I think.

Lucy. O do's the wind lye there?   60

Aside.

Then of necessity, Madam, you think a man must carry his Wife into
the Country, if he be wise; the Country is as terrible I find to our
young English Ladies, as a Monastery to those abroad: and on my
Virginity, I think they wou'd rather marry a *London*-Goaler, than a
high Sheriff of a Country, since neither can stir from his employ-   65
ment: formerly Women of wit married Fools, for a great Estate, a
fine seat, or the like; but now 'tis for a pretty seat only in *Lincoln's
Inn-fields*, St. *James's-fields*, or the *Pall-mall*.

Enter to them Sparkish, *and* Harcourt *dress'd like a Parson*.

Spar. Madam, your humble Servant, a happy day to you, and to us all.

Har. Amen. –   70

Alith. Who have we here?

Spar. My Chaplain faith – O Madam, poor *Harcourt* remembers his
humble service to you; and in obedience to your last commands,
refrains coming into your sight.

Alith. Is not that he?   75

Spar. No, fye no; but to shew that he ne're intended to hinder our
Match has sent his Brother here to joyn our hands: when I get me a
Wife, I must get her a Chaplain, according to the Custom; this is his
Brother, and my Chaplain.

Alith. His Brother?   80

Lucy. And your Chaplain, to preach in your Pulpit then –

Aside.

Alith. His Brother!

Spar. Nay, I knew you wou'd not believe it; I told you, Sir, she wou'd
take you for your Brother *Frank*.

Alith. Believe it!   85

Lucy. His Brother! hah, ha, he, he has a trick left still it seems –

Aside.

Spar. Come my dearest, pray let us go to Church before the Canonical hour is past.

Alith. For shame you are abus'd still.

Spar. By the World 'tis strange now you are so incredulous.   90

Alith. 'Tis strange you are so credulous.

Spar. Dearest of my life, hear me, I tell you this is *Ned Harcourt* of *Cambridge*, by the world, you see he has a sneaking Colledg look; 'tis true he's something like his Brother *Frank*, and they differ from each other no more than in their age, for they were Twins.   95

Lucy. Hah, ha, he.

Alith. Your Servant, Sir, I cannot be so deceiv'd, though you are; but come let's hear, how do you know what you affirm so confidently?

Spar. Why, I'll tell you all; *Frank Harcourt* coming to me this morning, to wish me joy and present his service to you: I ask'd him, if he   100
cou'd help me to a Parson; whereupon he told me, he had a Brother in Town who was in Orders, and he went straight away, and sent him, you see there, to me.

Alith. Yes, *Frank* goes, and puts on a black-coat, then tell's you, he is *Ned*, that's all you have for't.   105

Spar. Pshaw, pshaw, I tell you by the same token, the Midwife put her Garter about *Frank*'s neck, to know'em asunder, they were so like.

Alith. *Frank* tell's you this too.

Spar. Ay, and *Ned* there too; nay, they are both in a Story.

Alith. So, so, very foolish.   110

Spar. Lord, if you won't believe one, you had best trye him by your Chamber-maid there; for Chamber-maids must needs know Chaplains from other Men, they are so us'd to 'em.

Lucy. Let's see; nay, I'll be sworn he has the Canonical smirk, and the filthy, clammy palm of a Chaplain.   115

Alith. Well, most reverend Doctor, pray let us make an end of this fooling.

Har. With all my soul, Divine, Heavenly Creature, when you please.

Alith. He speaks like a Chaplain indeed.

Spar. Why, was there not, soul, Divine, Heavenly, in what he said.   120

Alith. Once more, most impertinent Black-coat, cease your persecution, and let us have a Conclusion of this ridiculous love.

Har. I had forgot, I must sute my Stile to my Coat, or I wear it in vain.

Aside.

Alith. I have no more patience left, let us make once an end of this troublesome Love, I say.   125

Har. So be it, Seraphick Lady, when your Honour shall think it meet, and convenient so to do.

Spar. Gad I'm sure none but a Chaplain cou'd speak so, I think.

Alith. Let me tell you Sir, this dull trick will not serve your turn, though you delay our marriage, you shall not hinder it.   130

Har. Far be it from me, Munificent Patroness, to delay your Marriage, I desire nothing more than to marry you presently, which I might do, if you your self wou'd; for my Noble, Good-natur'd and thrice Generous Patron here wou'd not hinder it.

Spar. No, poor man, not I faith.   135

Har. And now, Madam, let me tell you plainly, no body else shall marry you by Heavens, I'l die first, for I'm sure I shou'd die after it.

Lucy. How his Love has made him forget his Function, as I have seen
it in real Parsons.

Alith. That was spoken like a Chaplain too, now you understand him,   140
I hope.

Spar. Poor man, he takes it hainously to be refus'd; I can't blame him,
'tis putting an indignity upon him not to be suffer'd, but you'l
pardon me Madam, it shan't be, he shall marry us, come away, pray
Madam.   145

Lucy. Hah, ha, he, more ado! 'tis late.

Alith. Invincible stupidity, I tell you he wou'd marry me, as your
Rival, not as your Chaplain.

Spar. Come, come Madam.

Pulling her away.

Lucy. I pray Madam, do not refuse this Reverend Divine, the honour   150
and satisfaction of marrying you; for I dare say, he has set his heart
upon't, good Doctor.

Alith. What can you hope, or design by this?

Har. I cou'd answer her, a reprieve for a day only, often revokes a
hasty doom; at worst, if she will not take mercy on me, and let me   155
marry her, I have at least the Lovers second pleasure, hindring my
Rivals enjoyment, though but for a time.

Spar. Come Madam, 'tis e'ne twelve a clock, and my Mother charg'd
me never to be married out of the Canonical hours; come, come,
Lord here's such a deal of modesty, I warrant the first day.   160

Lucy. Yes, an't please your Worship, married women shew all their
Modesty the first day, because married men shew all their love the
first day.

Exeunt Sparkish, Alithea, Harcourt, *and* Lucy.

Scene II

The Scene changes to a Bed-chamber, where appear Pinchwife,
Mrs. Pinchwife.

Mr. Pinch. Come tell me, I say.

Mrs. Pinch. Lord, han't I told it an hundred times over.

Mr. Pinch. I wou'd try, if in the repetition of the ungrateful tale, I
cou'd find her altering it in the least circumstance, for if her story be
false, she is so too.   5

Aside.

Come how was't Baggage?

Mrs. Pinch. Lord, what pleasure you take to hear it sure!

Mr. Pinch. No, you take more in telling it I find, but speak how was't?

Mrs. Pinch. He carried me up into the house, next to the Exchange.

Mr. Pin. So, and you two were only in the room.   10

Mrs. Pin. Yes, for he sent away a youth that was there, for some dryed fruit, and China Oranges.

Mr. Pin. Did he so? Damn him for it – and for –

Mrs. Pin. But presently came up the Gentlewoman of the house.

Mr. Pin. O 'twas well she did, but what did he do whilest the fruit 15 came?

Mrs. Pin. He kiss'd me an hundred times, and told me he fancied he kiss'd my fine Sister, meaning me you know, whom he said he lov'd with all his Soul, and bid me be sure to tell her so, and to desire her to be at her window, by eleven of the clock this morning, and he wou'd 20 walk under it at that time.

Mr. Pin. And he was as good as his word, very punctual, a pox reward him for't.

Aside.

Mrs. Pin. Well, and he said if you were not within, he wou'd come up to her, meaning me you know, Bud, still. 25

Mr. Pin. So – he knew her certainly, but for this confession, I am oblig'd to her simplicity.

Aside.

But what you stood very still, when he kiss'd you?

Mrs. Pin. Yes I warrant you, wou'd you have had me discover'd my self? 30

Mr. Pin. But you told me, he did some beastliness to you, as you call'd it, what was't?

Mrs. Pin. Why, he put –

Mr. Pin. What?

Mrs. Pin. Why he put the tip of his tongue between my lips, and so 35 musl'd me – and I said, I'd bite it.

Mr. Pin. An eternal canker seize it, for a dog.

Mrs. Pin. Nay, you need not be so angry with him neither, for to say truth, he has the sweetest breath I ever knew.

Mr. Pin. The Devil – you were satisfied with it then, and wou'd do it 40 again.

Mrs. Pin. Not unless he shou'd force me.

Mr. Pin. Force you, changeling! I tell you no woman can be forced.

Mrs. Pin. Yes, but she may sure, by such a one as he, for he's a proper, goodly strong man, 'tis hard, let me tell you, to resist him. 45

Mr. Pin. So, 'tis plain she loves him, yet she has not love enough to make her conceal it from me, but the sight of him will increase her aversion for me, and love for him; and that love instruct how to deceive me, and satisfie him, all Ideot as she is: Love, 'twas he gave women first their craft, their art of deluding; out of natures hands, 50 they came plain, open, silly and fit for slaves, as she and Heaven intended 'em; but damn'd Love – Well – I must strangle that little Monster, whilest I can deal with him.

Go fetch Pen, Ink and Paper out of the next room.

Mrs. Pin. Yes Bud.   55

                                            Exit Mrs. Pinchwife.

Mr. Pin. Why should Women have more invention in love than men?
It can only be, because they have more desires, more solliciting
passions, more lust, and more of the Devil.

                                                            Aside.

                    Mistriss Pinchwife *returns.*

Come, Minks, sit down and write.
Mrs. Pin. Ay, dear Bud, but I can't do't very well.   60
Mr. Pin. I wish you cou'd not at all.
Mrs. Pin. But what shou'd I write for?
Mr. Pin. I'll have you write a Letter to your Lover.
Mrs. Pin. O Lord, to the fine Gentleman a Letter!
Mr. Pin. Yes, to the fine Gentleman.   65
Mrs. Pin. Lord, you do but jeer; sure you jest.
Mr. Pin. I am not so merry, come write as I bid you.
Mrs. Pin. What, do you think I am a fool?
Mr. Pin. She's afraid I would not dictate any love to him, therefore
she's unwilling; but you had best begin.   70
Mrs. Pin. Indeed, and indeed, but I won't, so I won't.
Mr. Pin. Why?
Mrs. Pin. Because he's in Town, you may send for him if you will.
Mr. Pin. Very well, you wou'd have him brought to you; is it come to
this? I say take the pen and write, or you'll provoke me.   75
Mrs. Pin. Lord, what d'ye make a fool of me for? Don't I know that
Letters are never writ, but from the Countrey to *London*, and from
London into the Countrey; now he's in Town, and I am in Town
too; therefore I can't write to him you know.
Mr. Pin. So I am glad it is no worse, she is innocent enough yet.   80

                                                            Aside.

Yes you may when your Husband bids you write Letters to people
that are in Town.
Mrs. Pin. O may I so! Then I'm satisfied.
Mr. Pin. Come begin – Sir –

                                                          Dictates.

Mrs. Pin. Shan't I say, Dear Sir? You know one says always something   85
more than bare Sir.
Mr. Pin. Write as I bid you, or I will write Whore with this Penknife in
your Face.
Mrs. Pin. Nay good Bud – Sir –

                                                          She writes.

Mr. Pin. Though I suffer'd last night your nauseous, loath'd Kisses   90
and Embraces – Write.

Mrs. Pin. Nay, why shou'd I say so, you know I told you, he had a sweet breath.

Mr. Pin. Write.

Mrs. Pin. Let me but put out, loath'd. 95

Mr. Pin. Write I say.

Mrs. Pin. Well then.

Writes.

Mr. Pin. Let's see what have you writ?
Though I suffer'd last night your kisses and embraces –

Takes the paper, and reads.

Thou impudent creature, where is nauseous and loath'd? 100

Mrs. Pin. I can't abide to write such filthy words.

Mr. Pin. Once more write as I'd have you, and question it not, or I will spoil thy writing with this, I will stab out those eyes that cause my mischief.

Holds up the penknife.

Mrs. Pin. O Lord, I will. 105

Mr. Pin. So – so – Let's see now!

Reads.

Though I suffer'd last night your nauseous, loath'd kisses, and embraces; Go on – Yet I would not have you presume that you shall ever repeat them – So –

She writes.

Mrs. Pin. I have writ it. 110

Mr. Pin. On then – I then conceal'd my self from your knowledge, to avoid your insolencies –

She writes.

Mrs. Pin. So –

Mr. Pin. The same reason now I am out of your hands –

She writes.

Mrs. Pin. So – 115

Mr. Pin. Makes me own to you my unfortunate, though innocent frolick, of being in man's cloths.

She writes.

Mrs. Pin. So –

Mr. Pin. That you may for ever more cease to pursue her, who hates and detests you – 120

She writes on.

Mrs. Pin. So – h –

Sighs.

Mr. Pin. What do you sigh? – detests you – as much as she loves her
Husband and her Honour –

Mrs. Pin. I vow Husband he'll ne'er believe, I shou'd write such a
Letter.   125

Mr. Pin. What he'd expect a kinder from you? come now your name
only.

Mrs. Pin. What, shan't I say your most faithful, humble Servant till
death?

Mr. Pin. No, tormenting Fiend; her stile I find wou'd be very soft.   130

Aside.

Come wrap it up now, whilest I go fetch wax and a candle; and write
on the back side, for Mr. *Horner.*

Exit Pinchwife.

Mrs. Pin. For Mr. *Horner* – So, I am glad he has told me his name;
Dear Mr. *Horner,* but why should I send thee such a Letter, that will
vex thee, and make thee angry with me; – well I will not send it – Ay   135
but then my husband will kill me – for I see plainly, he won't let me
love Mr. *Horner* – but what care I for my Husband – I won't so I
won't send poor Mr. *Horner* such a Letter – but then my Husband
– But oh – what if I writ at bottom, my Husband made me write it –
Ay but then my Husband wou'd see't – Can one have no shift, ah, a   140
London woman wou'd have had a hundred presently; stay – what if I
shou'd write a Letter, and wrap it up like this, and write upon't too;
ay but then my Husband wou'd see't – I don't know what to do –
But yet y vads I'll try, so I will – for I will not send this Letter to
poor Mr. *Horner,* come what will on't.   145

She writes, and repeats what she hath writ.

Dear, Sweet Mr. *Horner* – So – my Husband wou'd have me send
you a base, rude, unmannerly Letter – but I won't – *so* – and wou'd
have me forbid you loving me – but I wont – *so* – and wou'd have
me say to you, I hate you poor Mr. *Horner* – but I won't tell a lye for
him – *there* – for I'm sure if you and I were in the Countrey at cards 150
together, – *so* – I cou'd not help treading on your Toe under the
Table – *so* – or rubbing knees with you, and staring in your face, 'till
you saw me – *very well* – and then looking down, and blushing for
an hour together – *so* – but I must make haste before my Husband
come; and now he has taught me to write Letters: You shall have   155
longer ones from me, who am

Dear, dear, poor dear Mr. *Horner,* your most Humble Friend, and Servant
to command 'till death, *Margery Pinchwife.*

Stay I must give him a hint at bottom – *so* – now wrap it up just like
t'other – *so* – now write for Mr. *Horner,* – But oh now what shall I
do with it? for here comes my Husband.

Enter Pinchwife.

Mr. Pin. I have been detained by a Sparkish Coxcomb, who pre-   160
tended a visit to me; but I fear 'twas to my Wife.

> *Aside.*

What, have you done?
Mrs. Pin. Ay, ay Bud, just, now.
Mr. Pin. Let's see't, what d'ye tremble for; what, you wou'd not have
it go?   165
Mrs. Pin. Here – No I must not give him that, so I had been served if
I had given him this.

> *He opens, and reads the first Letter.*
> *Aside.*

Mr. Pin. Come, where's the Wax and Seal?
Mrs. Pin. Lord, what shall I do now? Nay then I have it –

> *Aside.*
> *Snatches the Letter from him, changes it for the*
> *other, seals it, and delivers it to him.*

Pray let me see't, Lord you think me so errand a fool, I cannot seal a   170
Letter, I will do't, so I will.
Mr. Pin. Nay, I believe you will learn that, and other things too,
which I wou'd not have you.
Mrs. Pin. So, han't I done it curiously?
I think I have, there's my Letter going to Mr. *Horner*, since he'll   175
needs have me send Letters to Folks.

> *Aside.*

Mr. Pin. 'Tis very well, but I warrant, you wou'd not have it go now?
Mrs. Pin. Yes indeed, but I wou'd, Bud, now.
Mr. Pin. Well you are a good Girl then, come let me lock you up in
your chamber, 'till I come back; and be sure you come not within   180
three strides of the window, when I am gone; for I have a spye in the
street.

> *Exit Mrs.* Pin.
> Pinchwife *locks the door.*

At least, 'tis fit she think so, if we do not cheat women, they'll cheat
us; and fraud may be justly used with secret enemies, of which a
Wife is the most dangerous; and he that has a handsome one to   185
keep, and a Frontier Town, must provide against treachery, rather
than open Force – Now I have secur'd all within, I'll deal with the
Foe without with false intelligence.

> *Holds up the Letter.*
> *Exit* Pinchwife.

Scene III

The Scene changes to Horner's *Lodging.*

Quack *and* Horner.

Quack. Well Sir, how fadges the new design; have you not the luck of
all your brother Projectors, to deceive only your self at last.

Hor. No, good *Domine* Doctor, I deceive you it seems, and others
too; for the grave Matrons, and old ridgid Husbands think me as
unfit for love, as they are; but their Wives, Sisters and Daughters,   5
know some of'em better things already.

Quack. Already!

Hor. Already, I say; last night I was drunk with half a dozen of your
civil persons, as you call 'em, and people of Honour, and so was
made free of their Society, and dressing rooms for ever hereafter;   10
and am already come to the privileges of sleeping upon their Pallats,
warming Smocks, tying Shooes and Garters, and the like Doctor,
already, already Doctor.

Quack. You have made use of your time, Sir.

Hor. I tell thee, I am now no more interruption to 'em, when they   15
sing, or talk bawdy, than a little squab French Page, who speaks no
English.

Quack. But do civil persons, and women of Honour drink, and sing
bawdy Songs?

Hor. O amongst Friends, amongst Friends; for your Bigots in   20
Honour, are just like those in Religion; they fear the eye of the
world, more than the eye of Heaven, and think there is no virtue,
but railing at vice; and no sin, but giving scandal: They rail at a poor,
little, kept Player, and keep themselves some young, modest Pulpit
Comedian to be privy to their sins in their Closets, not to tell 'em of   25
them in their Chappels.

Quack. Nay, the truth on't is, Priests amongst the women now, have
quite got the better of us Lay Confessors, Physicians.

Hor. And they are rather their Patients, but –

Enter my Lady Fidget, *looking about her.*

Now we talk of women of Honour, here comes one, step   30
behind the Screen there, and but observe; if I have not particular privileges, with the women of reputation already, Doctor,
already.

La. Fid. Well *Horner*, am not I a woman of Honour? you see I'm as
good as my word.   35

Hor. And you shall see Madam, I'll not be behind hand with you in
honour; and I'll be as good as my word too, if you please but to
withdraw into the next room.

La. Fid. But first, my dear Sir, you must promise to have a care of my
dear Honour.   40

Hor. If you talk a word more of your Honour, you'll make me incapable to wrong it; to talk of Honour in the mysteries of Love, is like talking of Heaven, or the Deity in an operation of Witchcraft, just when you are employing the Devil, it makes the charm impotent.

La. Fid. Nay, fie, let us not be smooty; but you talk of mysteries, and bewitching to me, I don't understand you.　45

Hor. I tell you Madam, the word money in a Mistresses mouth, at such a nick of time, is not a more disheartning sound to a younger Brother, than that of Honour to an eager Lover like myself.

La. Fid. But you can't blame a Lady of my reputation to be chary.　50

Hor. Chary – I have been chary of it already, by the report I have caus'd of my self.

La. Fid. Ay, but if you shou'd ever let other women know that dear secret, it would come out; nay, you must have a great care of your conduct; for my acquaintance are so censorious, (oh 'tis a wicked 　55 censorious world, Mr. *Horner*) I say, are so censorious, and detracting, that perhaps they'll talk to the prejudice of my Honour, though you shou'd not let them know the dear secret.

Hor. Nay Madam, rather than they shall prejudice your Honour, I'll prejudice theirs; and to serve you, I'll lye with 'em all, make the secret 　60 their own, and then they'll keep it: I am a *Machiavel* in love Madam.

La. Fid. O, no Sir, not that way.

Hor. Nay, the Devil take me, if censorious women are to be silenc'd any other way.

La. Fid. A secret is better kept I hope, by a single person, than a 　65 multitude; therefore pray do not trust any body else with it, dear, dear Mr. *Horner.*

Embracing him.

Enter Sir Jaspar Fidget.

Sir Jas. How now!

La. Fid. O my Husband – prevented – and what's almost as bad, found with my arms about another man – that will appear too much 　70 – what shall I say?

Aside.

Sir *Jaspar* come hither, I am trying if Mr. *Horner* were ticklish, and he's as ticklish as can be, I love to torment the confounded Toad; let you and I tickle him.

Sir Jas. No, your Ladyship will tickle him better without me, I 　75 suppose, but is this your buying China, I thought you had been at the China House?

Hor. China-House, that's my Cue, I must take it.

Aside.

A Pox, can't you keep your impertinent Wives at home? some men are troubled with the Husbands, but I with the Wives; but I'd have 　80

you to know, since I cannot be your Journey-man by night, I will
not be your drudge by day, to squire your wife about, and be your
man of straw, or scare-crow only to Pyes and Jays, that would be
nibling at your forbidden fruit; I shall be shortly the Hackney
Gentleman-Usher of the Town.   85

Sir Jas. Heh, heh, he, poor fellow he's in the right on't faith, to squire
women about for other folks, is as ungrateful an employment, as to
tell money for other folks;

Aside.

heh, he, he, ben't angry *Horner* –

La. Fid. No, 'tis I have more reason to be angry, who am left by you,   90
to go abroad indecently alone; or, what is more indecent, to pin my
self upon such ill bred people of your acquaintance, as this is.

Sir Jas. Nay, pr'ythee what has he done?

La. Fid. Nay, he has done nothing.

Sir Jas. But what d'ye take ill, if he has done nothing?   95

La. Fid. Hah, hah, hah, Faith, I can't but laugh however; why d'ye
think the unmannerly toad wou'd not come down to me to
the Coach, I was fain to come up to fetch him, or go without
him, which I was resolved not to do; for he knows China very
well, and has himself very good, but will not let me see it, lest I 100
should beg some; but I will find it out, and have what I came for
yet.

Exit Lady Fidget, *and locks the door,,*
followed by Horner *to the door.*

Hor. Lock the door Madam –

Apart to Lady Fidget.

So, she has got into my chamber, and lock'd me out; oh the
impertinency of woman-kind! Well Sir *Jaspar*, plain dealing is a 105
Jewel; if ever you suffer your Wife to trouble me again here,
she shall carry you home a pair of Horns, by my Lord Major she
shall; though I cannot furnish you my self, you are sure, yet I'll find
a way.

Sir Jas. Hah, ha, he, at my first coming in, and finding her arms about 110
him, tickling him it seems, I was half jealous, but now I see my
folly.

Aside.

Heh, he, he, poor *Horner.*

Hor. Nay, though you laugh now, 'twill be my turn e're long: Oh
women, more impertinent, more cunning, and more mischievous 115
than their Monkeys, and to me almost as ugly – now is she throwing
my things about, and rifling all I have, but I'll get into her the back
way, and so rifle her for it –

Sir Jas. Hah, ha, ha, poor angry *Horner.*

Hor. Stay here a little, I'll ferret her out to you presently, I warrant.   120

Exit Horner *at t'other door.*
Sir Jaspar *calls through the door to his Wife,*
she answers from within.

Sir Jas. Wife, my Lady *Fidget*, Wife, he is coming into you the back way.

La. Fid. Let him come, and welcome, which way he will.

Sir Jas. He'll catch you, and use you roughly, and be too strong for you.   125

La. Fid. Don't you trouble your self, let him if he can.

Quack. [*Behind*] This indeed, I cou'd not have believ'd from him, nor any but my own eyes.

Enter Mistriss Squeamish.

Squeam. Where's this Woman-hater, this Toad, this ugly, greasie, dirty Sloven?   130

Sir Jas. So the women all will have him ugly, methinks he is a comely person; but his wants make his form contemptible to 'em; and 'tis e'en as my Wife said yesterday, talking of him, that a proper hand-some Eunuch, was as ridiculous a thing, as a Gigantick Coward.

Squeam. Sir *Jaspar*, your Servant, where is the odious Beast?   135

Sir Jas. He's within in his chamber, with my Wife; she's playing the wag with him.

Squeam. Is she so, and he's a clownish beast, he'll give her no quarter, he'll play the wag with her again, let me tell you; come, let's go help her – What, the door's lock't?   140

Sir Jas. Ay, my Wife lock't it –

Squeam. Did she so, let us break it open then?

Sir Jas. No, no, he'll do her no hurt.

Squeam. No – But is there no other way to get into 'em, whither goes this? I will disturb 'em.   145

Aside.
Exit Squeamish *at another door.*

Enter old Lady Squeamish.

Old L. Squeam. Where is this Harlotry, this Impudent Baggage, this rambling Tomrigg? O Sir *Jaspar*, I'm glad to see you here, did you not see my vil'd Grandchild come in hither just now?

Sir Jas. Yes.

Old L. Squeam. Ay, but where is she then? where is she? Lord Sir *Jaspar*   150
I have e'ne ratled my self to pieces in pursuit of her, but can you tell what she makes here, they say below, no woman lodges here.

Sir Jas. No.

Old L. Squeam. No – What does she here then? say if it be not a womans lodging, what makes she here? but are you sure no woman   155
lodges here?

Sir Jas. No, nor no man neither, this is Mr. *Horners* Lodging.
Old L. Squeam. Is it so are you sure?
Sir Jas. Yes, yes.
Old L. Squeam. So then there's no hurt in't I hope, but where is he?   160
Sir Jas. He's in the next room with my Wife.
Old L. Squeam. Nay if you trust him with your wife, I may with my
    Biddy, they say he's a merry harmless man now, e'ne as harmless a
    man as ever came out of *Italy* with a good voice, and as pretty
    harmless company for a Lady, as a Snake without his teeth.   165
Sir Jas. Ay, ay poor man.

Enter Mrs. Squeamish.

Squeam. I can't find 'em – Oh are you here, Grandmother, I follow'd
    you must know my Lady *Fidget* hither, 'tis the prettyest lodging,
    and I have been staring on the prettyest Pictures.

Enter Lady Fidget with a piece of China in her hand, and
Horner following.

La. Fid. And I have been toyling and moyling, for the pretti'st piece   170
    of China, my Dear.
Hor. Nay she has been too hard for me do what I cou'd.
Squeam. Oh Lord I'le have some China too, good Mr. *Horner*, don't
    think to give other people China, and me none, come in with me
    too.   175
Hor. Upon my honour I have none left now.
Squeam. Nay, nay I have known you deny your China before now, but
    you shan't put me off so, come –
Hor. This Lady had the last there.
La. Fid. Yes indeed Madam, to my certain knowledge he has no more   180
    left.
Squeam. O but it may be he may have some you could not find.
La. Fid. What d'y think if he had had any left, I would not have had it
    too, for we women of quality never think we have China enough.
Hor. Do not take it ill, I cannot make China for you all, but I will have   185
    a Rol-waggon for you too, another time.
Squeam. Thank you dear Toad.
La. Fid. What do you mean by that promise?

To Horn. aside.

Hor. Alas she has an innocent, literal understanding.

Apart to Lady Fidget.

Old L. Squeam. Poor Mr. *Horner*, he has enough to doe to please you   190
    all, I see.
Hor. Ay Madam, you see how they use me.
Old L. Squeam. Poor Gentleman I pitty you.
Hor. I thank you Madam, I could never find pitty, but from such
    reverend Ladies as you are, the young ones will never spare a man.   195

Squeam. Come come, Beast, and go dine with us, for we shall want a
man at Hombre after dinner.
Hor. That's all their use of me Madam you see.
Squeam. Come Sloven, I'le lead you to be sure of you.

Pulls him by the Crevat.

Old L. Squeam. Alas poor man how she tuggs him, kiss, kiss her,   200
that's the way to make such nice women quiet.
Hor. No Madam, that Remedy is worse than the Torment, they know
I dare suffer any thing rather than do it.
Old La. Squeam. Prythee kiss her, and I'le give you her Picture in
little, that you admir'd you so last night, prythee do.   205
Hor. Well nothing but that could bribe me, I love a woman only in
Effigie, and good Painting as much as I hate them – I'le do't, for I
cou'd adore the Devil well painted.

Kisses Mrs. Squeam.

Squeam. Foh, you filthy Toad, nay now I've done jesting.
Old L. Squeam. Ha, ha, ha, I told you so.   210
Squeam. Foh a kiss of his –
Sir Jas. Has no more hurt in't, than one of my Spaniels.
Squeam. Nor no more good neither.
Quack. I will now believe any thing he tells me.

Behind.

Enter Mr. Pinchwife.

La. Fid. O Lord here's a man, Sir *Jaspar,* my Mask, my Mask, I would   215
not be seen here for the world.
Sir Jas. What not when I am with you.
La. Fid. No, no my honour – let's be gone.
Squeam. Oh Grandmother, let us be gone, make hast, make hast, I
know not how he may censure us.   220
La. Fid. Be found in the lodging of any thing like a man, away.

Exeunt Sir Jas. La. Fid. Old La. Squeam.
Mrs. Squeamish.

Quack. What's here another Cuckold – he looks like one, and none
else sure have any business with him.

Behind.

Hor. Well what brings my dear friend hither?
Mr. Pinch. Your impertinency.   225
Hor. My impertinency – why you Gentlemen that have got handsome
Wives, think you have a privilege of saying any thing to your friends,
and are as brutish, as if you were our Creditors.
Mr. Pinch. No Sir, I'le ne're trust you any way.
Hor. But why not, dear *Jack,* why diffide in me, thou knowst so well.   230

Mr. Pin. Because I do know you so well.

Hor. Han't I been always thy friend honest *Jack*, always ready to serve thee, in love, or battle, before thou wert married, and am so still.

Mr. Pin. I believe so you wou'd be my second now indeed.

Hor. Well then dear *Jack*, why so unkind, so grum, so strange to me,   235
come prythee kiss me deare Rogue, gad I was always I say, and am
still as much thy Servant as –

Mr. Pin. As I am yours Sir. What you wou'd send a kiss to my Wife, is
that it?

Hor. So there 'tis – a man can't shew his friendship to a married man,   240
but presently he talks of his wife to you, prythee let thy Wife alone,
and let thee and I be all one, as we were wont, what thou art as shye
of my kindness, as a Lumbard-street Alderman of a Courtiers
civility at Lockets.

Mr. Pin. But you are over kind to me, as kind, as if I were your   245
Cuckold already, yet I must confess you ought to be kind and civil
to me, since I am so kind, so civil to you, as to bring you this, look
you there Sir.

Delivers him a Letter.

Hor. What is't?

Mr. Pinch. Only a Love Letter Sir.   250

Hor. From whom – how, this is from your Wife – hum – and hum –

Reads.

Mr. Pin. Even from my Wife Sir, am I not wondrous kind and civil to
you, now too?
But you'l not think her so.

Aside.

Hor. Ha, is this a trick of his or hers?   255

Aside.

Mr. Pin. The Gentleman's surpriz'd I find, what you expected a
kinder Letter?

Hor. No faith not I, how cou'd I.

Mr. Pin. Yes yes, I'm sure you did, a man so well made as you are must
needs be disappointed, if the women declare not their passion at   260
first sight or opportunity.

Hor. But what should this mean? stay the Postscript.
Be sure you love me whatsoever my husband says to the contrary,
and let him not see this, lest he should come home, and pinch me,
or kill my Squirrel.   265

Reads aside.

It seems he knows not what the Letter contains.

Aside.

Mr. Pin. Come ne're wonder at it so much.

Hor. Faith I can't help it.

Mr. Pin. Now I think I have deserv'd your infinite friendship, and kindness, and have shewed my self sufficiently an obliging, kind   270
friend and husband, am I not so, to bring a Letter from my Wife to her Gallant?

Hor. Ay, the Devil take me, art thou, the most obliging, kind friend and husband in the world, ha, ha.

Mr. Pin. Well you may be merry Sir, but in short I must tell you Sir,   275
my honour will suffer no jesting.

Hor. What do'st thou mean?

Mr. Pin. Does the Letter want a Comment? then know Sir, though I have been so civil a husband, as to bring you a Letter from my Wife, to let you kiss and court her to my face, I will not be a Cuckold Sir,   280
I will not.

Hor. Thou art mad with jealousie, I never saw thy Wife in my life, but at the Play yesterday, and I know not if it were she or no, I court her, kiss her!

Mr. Pin. I will not be a Cuckold I say, there will be danger in making   285
me a Cuckold.

Hor. Why, wert thou not well cur'd of thy last clap?

Mr. Pin. I weare a Sword.

Hor. It should be taken from thee, lest thou should'st do thy self a mischiefe with it, thou art mad, Man.   290

Mr. Pin. As mad as I am, and as merry as you are, I must have more reason from you e're we part, I say again though you kiss'd, and courted last night my Wife in man's clothes, as she confesses in her Letter.

Hor. Ha –   295

Aside.

Mr. Pin. Both she and I say you must not design it again, for you have mistaken you woman, as you have done your man.

Hor. Oh – I understand something now –

Aside.

Was that thy Wife? why would'st thou not tell me 'twas she? faith my freedome with her was your fault, not mine.   300

Mr. Pin. Faith so 'twas –

Aside.

Hor. Fye, I'de never do't to a woman before her husbands face, sure.

Mr. Pin. But I had rather you should do't to my wife before my face, than behind my back, and that you shall never doe.

Hor. No – you will hinder me.   305

Mr. Pin. If I would not hinder you, you see by her Letter, she wou'd.

Hor. Well, I must e'ne acquiess then, and be contented with what she writes.

Mr. Pin. I'le assure you 'twas voluntarily writ, I had no hand in't you
  may believe me.   310

Hor. I do believe thee, faith.

Mr. Pin. And believe her too, for she's an innocent creature, has no
  dissembling in her, and so fare you well Sir.

Hor. Pray however present my humble service to her, and tell her I
  will obey her Letter to a title, and fulfill her desires be what they   315
  will, or with what difficulty soever I do't, and you shall be no more
  jealous of me, I warrant her, and you –

Mr. Pin. Well then fare you well, and play with any mans honour but
  mine, kiss any mans wife but mine, and welcome –

                                                Exit Mr. Pinch.

Hor. Ha, ha, ha, Doctor.   320

Quack. It seems he has not heard the report of you, or does not
  believe it.

Hor. Ha, ha, now Doctor what think you?

Quack. Pray let's see the Letter – hum – for – deare – love you –

                                                Reads the Letter.

Hor. I wonder how she cou'd contrive it! what say'st thou to't, 'tis an   325
  Original.

Quack. So are your Cuckolds too Originals: for they are like no other
  common Cuckolds, and I will henceforth believe it not impossible
  for you to Cuckold the Grand Signior amidst his Guards of
  Eunuchs, that I say –   330

Hor. And I say for the Letter, 'tis the first love Letter that ever was
  without Flames, Darts, Fates, Destinies, Lying and Dissembling in't.

             Enter Sparkish *pulling in Mr.* Pinchwife.

Spar. Come back, you are a pretty Brother-in-law, neither go to
  Church, nor to dinner with your Sister Bride.

Mr. Pin. My Sister denies her marriage, and you see is gone away   335
  from you dissatisfy'd.

Spar. Pshaw, upon a foolish scruple, that our Parson was not in lawful
  Orders, and did not say all the Common Prayer, but 'tis her
  modesty only I believe, but let women be never so modest the
  first day, they'l be sure to come to themselves by night, and I shall   340
  have enough of her then; in the mean time, *Harry Horner*, you
  must dine with me, I keep my wedding at my Aunts in the Piazza.

Hor. Thy wedding, what stale Maid has liv'd to despaire of a husband,
  or what young one of a Gallant?

Spar. O your Servant Sir – this Gentlemans Sister then – No stale   345
  Maid.

Hor. I'm sorry for't.

Mr. Pin. How comes he so concern'd for her –

                                                    Aside.

Spar. You sorry for't, why do you know any ill by her?

Hor. No, I know none but by thee, 'tis for her sake, not yours, and   350
another mans sake that might have hop'd, I thought –

Spar. Another Man, another man, what is his Name?

Hor. Nay since 'tis past he shall be nameless. Poor *Harcourt* I am
sorry thou hast mist her –

Aside.

Mr. Pin. He seems to be much troubled at the match –   355

Aside.

Spar. Prythee tell me – nay you shan't go Brother.

Mr. Pin. I must of necessity, but I'le come to you to dinner.

Exit Pinchwife.

Spar. But *Harry*, what have I a Rival in my Wife already? but with all
my heart, for he may be of use to me hereafter, for though my
hunger is now my sawce, and I can fall on heartily without, but the   360
time will come, when a Rival will be as good sawce for a married
man to a wife, as an Orange to Veale.

Hor. O thou damn'd Rogue, thou hast set my teeth on edge with thy
Orange.

Spar. Then let's to dinner, there I was with you againe, come.   365

Hor. But who dines with thee?

Spar. My Friends and Relations, my Brother *Pinchwife* you see of
your acquaintance.

Hor. And his Wife.

Spar. No gad, he'l nere let her come amongst us good fellows,   370
your stingy country Coxcomb keeps his wife from his friends, as
he does his little Firkin of Ale, for his own drinking, and a Gentleman can't get a smack on't, but his servants, when his back is turn'd
broach it at their pleasures, and dust it away, ha, ha, ha, gad I am
witty, I think, considering I was married to day, by the world, but   375
come –

Hor. No, I will not dine with you, unless you can fetch her too.

Spar. Pshaw what pleasure can'st thou have with women now,
Harry?

Hor. My eyes are not gone, I love a good prospect yet, and will not   380
dine with you, unless she does too, go fetch her therefore, but do
not tell her husband, 'tis for my sake.

Spar. Well I'le go try what I can do, in the mean time come away to
my Aunts lodging, 'tis in the way to *Pinchwifes*.

Hor. The poor woman has call'd for aid, and stretch'd forth her   385
hand Doctor, I cannot but help her over the Pale out of the
Bryars.

Exeunt Sparkish, Horner, Quack.

Scene IV

The Scene changes to Pinchwifes *house.*

Mrs. Pinchwife *alone leaning on her elbow.*

A Table, Pen, Ink, and Paper.

Mrs. Pin. Well 'tis even so, I have got the *London* disease, they call
Love, I am sick of my Husband, and for my Gallant; I have heard
this distemper, call'd a Feaver, but methinks 'tis liker an Ague, for
when I think of my Husband, I tremble and am in a cold sweat, and
have inclinations to vomit, but when I think of my Gallant, dear Mr.   5
Horner, my hot fit comes, and I am all in a Feaver, indeed, & as in
other Feavers, my own Chamber is tedious to me, and I would fain
be remov'd to his, and then methinks I shou'd be well; ah poor Mr.
Horner, well I cannot, will not stay here, therefore I'le make an end
of my Letter to him, which shall be a finer Letter than my last,   10
because I have studied it like any thing; O Sick, Sick!

Takes the Pen and writes.

Enter Mr. Pinchwife *who seeing her writing steales softly behind her,
and looking over her shoulder, snatches the paper from her.*

Mr. Pin. What writing more Letters?
Mrs. Pin. O Lord Budd, why d'ye fright me so?

She offers to run out: he stops her, and reads.

Mr. Pin. How's this! nay you shall not stir Madam. Deare, Deare,
deare, Mr *Horner* – very well – I have taught you to write Letters to   15
good purpose – but let's see't.
First I am to beg your pardon for my boldness in writing to you,
which I'de have you to know, I would not have done, had not you
said first you lov'd me so extreamly, which if you doe, you will never
suffer me to lye in the arms of another man, whom I loathe, nauseate,   20
and detest – [Now you can write these filthy words] but what follows
– Therefore I hope you will speedily find some way to free me from
this unfortunate match, which was never, I assure you, of my choice,
but I'm afraid 'tis already too far gone; however if you love me, as I do
you, you will try what you can do, but you must help me away before   25
to morrow, or else alass I shall be for ever out of your reach, for I can
defer no longer our – our – what is to follow our – speak what?

The Letter concludes.

our Journey into the Country I suppose – Oh Woman, damn'd
Woman, and Love, damn'd Love, their old Tempter, for this is one
of his miracles, in a moment, he can make those blind that cou'd   30
see, and those see that were blind, those dumb that could speak,
and those prattle who were dumb before, nay what is more than all,

make these dow-bak'd, sensless, indocile animals, Women, too hard
for us their Politick Lords and Rulers in a moment; But make an
end of your Letter, and then I'le make an end of you thus, and all   35
my plagues together.

Draws his Sword.

Mr. Pin. O Lord, O Lord you are such a Passionate Man, Budd.

Enter Sparkish.

Spar. How now what's here to doe.

Mr. Pin. This Fool here now!

Spar. What drawn upon your Wife? you shou'd never do that but at   40
night in the dark when you can't hurt her, this is my Sister in Law is
it not? ay faith e'ne our Country *Margery*, one may know her, come
she and you must go dine with me, dinner's ready, come, but
where's my Wife, is she not come home yet, where is she?

Pulls aside her Handkercheife.

Mr. Pin. Making you a Cuckold, 'tis that they all doe, as soon as they   45
can.

Spar. What the Wedding day? no, a Wife that designs to make a Cully
of her Husband, will be sure to let him win the first stake of love, by
the world, but come they stay dinner for us, come I'le lead down
our *Margery*.   50

Mrs. Pin. No – Sir go we'l follow you.

Spar. I will not wag without you.

Mr. Pin. This Coxcomb is a sensible torment to me amidst the
greatest in the world.

Spar. Come, come Madam *Margery*.   55

Mr. Pin. No I'le lead her my way, what wou'd you treat your friends
with mine, for want of your own Wife?

Leads her to t'other door, and locks her in and returns.

I am contented my rage shou'd take breath – ·

Aside.

Spar. I told *Horner* this.

Mr. Pin. Come now.   60

Spar. Lord, how shye you are of your Wife, but let me tell you
Brother, we men of wit have amongst us a saying, that Cuckolding
like the small Pox comes with a fear, and you may keep your Wife as
much as you will out of danger of infection, but if her constitution
incline her to't, she'l have it sooner or later by the world, say they.   65

Mr. Pin. What a thing is a Cuckold, that every fool can make him
ridiculous –

Aside.

Well Sir – But let me advise you, now you are come to be concern'd,
because you suspect the danger, not to neglect the means to prevent

it, especially when the greatest share of the Malady will light upon   70
your own head, for –

> Hows'ere the kind Wife's Belly comes to swell,
> The Husband breeds for her, and first is ill.

Act V

Scene I

Mr. Pinchwifes *House.*

Enter Mr. Pinchwife *and Mrs.* Pinchwife, *a Table and Candle.*

Mr. Pin. Come take the Pen and make an end of the Letter, just as you
intended, if you are false in a tittle, I shall soon perceive it, and punish
you with this as you deserve, write what was to follow – let's see –

Lays his hand on his Sword.

[You must make haste and help me away before to morrow, or else I
shall be for ever out of your reach, for I can defer no longer our –]   5
What follows our? –

Mrs. Pin. Must all out then Budd? –

Mrs. Pin. *takes the Pen and writes.*

Look you there then.

Mr. Pin. Let's see – [For I can defer no longer our – Wedding – Your
slighted *Alithea*] What's the meaning of this, my Sisters name to't,   10
speak, unriddle?

Mrs. Pin. Yes indeed Budd.

Mr. Pin. But why her name to't speak – speak I say?

Mrs. Pin. Ay but you'l tell her then again, if you wou'd not tell her
again.   15

Mr. Pin. I will not, I am stunn'd, my head turns round, speak.

Mrs. Pin. Won't you tell her indeed, and indeed.

Mr. Pin. No, speak I say.

Mrs. Pin. She'l be angry with me, but I had rather she should be
angry with me than you Budd; and to tell you the truth, 'twas she   20
made me write the Letter, and taught me what I should write.

Mr. Pin. Ha – I thought the stile was somewhat better than her own,
but how cou'd she come to you to teach you, since I had lock'd you
up alone.

Mrs. Pin. O through the key hole Budd.   25

Mr. Pin. But why should she make you write a Letter for her to him,
since she can write her self?

Mrs. Pin. Why she said because – for I was unwilling to do it.

Mr. Pin. Because what – because.

Mrs. Pin. Because lest Mr. *Horner* should be cruel, and refuse her, or 30
vaine afterwards, and shew the Letter, she might disown it, the
hand not being hers.

Mr. Pin. How's this? ha – then I think I shall come to my self again –
This changeling cou'd not invent this lye, but if she cou'd, why
should she? she might think I should soon discover it – stay – now I 35
think on't too, *Horner* said he was sorry she had married *Sparkish*,
and her disowning her marriage to me, makes me think she has
evaded it, for *Horner*'s sake, yet why should she take this course,
but men in love are fools, women may well be so. –

Aside.

But hark you Madam, your Sister went out in the morning, and I 40
have not seen her within since.

Mrs. Pin. A lack a day she has been crying all day above it seems in a
corner.

Mr. Pin. Where is she, let me speak with her.

Mrs. Pin. O Lord then he'l discover all – 45

Aside.

Pray hold Budd, what d'y mean to discover me, she'l know I have
told you then, pray Budd let me talk with her first –

Mr. Pin. I must speak with her to know whether *Horner* ever made
her any promise; and whether she be married to *Sparkish* or no.

Mrs. Pin. Pray dear Budd don't, till I have spoken with her and told 50
her that I have told you all, for she'll kill me else.

Mr. Pin. Go then and bid her come out to me.

Mrs. Pin. Yes, yes Budd –

Mr. Pin. Let me see –

Mrs. Pin. I'le go, but she is not within to come to him, I have just got 55
time to know of *Lucy* her Maid, who first set me on work, what lye I
shall tell next, for I am e'ne at my wits end –

Exit Mrs. Pinchwife.

Mr. Pin. Well I resolve it, *Horner* shall have her, I'd rather give him
my Sister than lend him my Wife, and such an alliance will prevent
his pretensions to my Wife sure, – I'le make him of kinn to her, and 60
then he won't care for her.

Mrs. Pin. *returns.*

Mrs. Pin. O Lord Budd I told you what anger you would make me
with my Sister.

Mr. Pin. Won't she come hither?

Mrs. Pin. No no, alack a day, she's asham'd to look you in the face, 65
and she says if you go in to her, she'l run away down stairs,
and shamefully go her self to Mr. *Horner*, who has promis'd
her marriage she says, and she will have no other, so she
won't –

Mr. Pin. Did he so – promise her marriage – then she shall have no   70
other, go tell her so, and if she will come and discourse with me a
little concerning the means, I will about it immediately, go –

Exit Mrs. Pin.

His estate is equal to *Sparkish*'s, and his extraction as much better
than his, as his parts are, but my chief reason is, I'd rather be of kin
to him by the name of Brother-in-law, than that of Cuckold – Well   75
what says she now?

Enter Mrs. Pin.

Mrs. Pin. Why she says she would only have you lead her to *Horners*
lodging – with whom she first will discourse the matter before she
talk with you, which yet she cannot doe; for alack poor creature, she
says she can't so much as look you in the face, therefore she'l come   80
to you in a mask, and you must excuse her if she make you no
answer to any question of yours, till you have brought her to Mr.
Horner, and if you will not chide her, nor question her, she'l come
out to you immediately.

Mr. Pin. Let her come I will not speak a word to her, nor require a   85
word from her.

Mrs. Pin. Oh I forgot, besides she says, she cannot look you in the
face, though through a mask, therefore wou'd desire you to put out
the Candle.

Exit Mrs. Pin. *puts out the Candle.*

Mr. Pin. I agree to all, let her make haste – there 'tis out – My case is   90
something better, I'd rather fight with *Horner* for not lying with
my Sister, than for lying with my Wife, and of the two I had rather
find my Sister too forward than my Wife; I expected no other from
her free education, as she calls it, and her passion for the Town –
well – Wife and Sister are names which make us expect Love and   95
duty, pleasure and comfort, but we find 'em plagues and torments,
and are equally, though differently troublesome to their keeper; for
we have as much a doe to get people to lye with our Sisters, as to
keep 'em from lying with our Wives.

Enter Mrs. Pinchwife *Masked, and in Hoods and Scarves, and a night
Gown and Petticoat of* Alitheas *in the dark.*

What are you come Sister? let us go then – but first let me lock up   100
my Wife, Mrs. *Margery* where are you?

Mrs. Pin. Here Budd.

Mr. Pin. Come hither, that I may lock you up, get you in, Come
Sister where are you now?

Locks the door.

Mrs. Pin. *gives him her hand, but when he lets her go, she steals softly on
t'other side of him, and is lead away by him for his Sister* Alithea.

Scene II

The Scene changes to Horners *Lodging.*

Quack, Horner.

Quack. What all alone, not so much as one of your Cuckolds here, nor one of their Wives! they use to take their turns with you, as if they were to watch you.

Hor. Yes it often happens, that a Cuckold is but his Wifes spye, and is more upon family duty, when he is with her gallant abroad hindring 5 his pleasure, than when he is at home with her playing the Gallant, but the hardest duty a married woman imposes upon a lover is, keeping her husband company always.

Quack. And his fondness wearies you almost as soon as hers.

Hor. A Pox, keeping a Cuckold company after you have had his Wife, 10 is as tiresome as the company of a Country Squire to a witty fellow of the Town, when he has got all his Mony.

Quack. And as at first a man makes a friend of the Husband to get the Wife, so at last you are faine to fall out with the Wife to be rid of the Husband. 15

Hor. Ay, most Cuckold-makers are true Courtiers, when once a poor man has crack'd his credit for 'em, they can't abide to come neer him.

Quack. But at first to draw him in are so sweet, so kind, so dear, just as you are to *Pinchwife*, but what becomes of that intrigue with his Wife? 20

Hor. A Pox he's as surly as an Alderman that has been bit, and since he's so coy, his Wife's kindness is in vain, for she's a silly innocent.

Quack. Did she not send you a Letter by him?

Hor. Yes, but that's a riddle I have not yet solv'd – allow the poor creature to be willing, she is silly too, and he keeps her up so close – 25

Quack. Yes, so close that he makes her but the more willing, and adds but revenge to her love, which two when met seldome faile of satisfying each other one way or other.

Hor. What here's the man we are talking of I think.

Enter Mr. Pinchwife *leading in his Wife Masqued, Muffled, and in her Sisters Gown.*

Hor. Pshaw. 30

Quack. Bringing his Wife to you is the next thing to bringing a Love Letter from her.

Hor. What means this?

Mr. Pin. The last time you know Sir I brought you a love Letter, now you see a Mistress, I think you'l say I am a civil man to you. 35

Hor. Ay the Devil take me will I say thou art the civillest man I ever met with, and I have known some; I fancy, I understand thee now, better than I did the Letter, but hark thee in thy eare –

Mr. Pin. What?

Hor. Nothing but the usual question man, is she sound on thy word?   40
Mr. Pin. What you take her for a Wench and me for a Pimp?
Hor. Pshaw, wench and Pimp, paw words, I know thou art an honest
    fellow, and hast a great acquaintance among the Ladies, and perhaps
    hast made love for me rather than let me make love to thy Wife –
Mr. Pin. Come Sir, in short, I am for no fooling.   45
Hor. Nor I neither, therefore prythee let's see her face presently, make
    her show man, art thou sure I don't know her?
Mr. Pin. I am sure you doe know her.
Hor. A Pox why dost thou bring her to me then?
Mr. Pin. Because she's Relation of mine.   50
Hor. Is she faith man, then thou art still more civil and obliging, dear
    Rogue.
Mr. Pin. Who desir'd me to bring her to you.
Hor. Then she is obliging, dear Rogue.
Mr. Pin. You'l make her welcome for my sake I hope.   55
Hor. I hope she is handsome enough to make her self wellcome;
    prythee let her unmask.
Mr. Pin. Do you speak to her, she wou'd never be rul'd by me.
Hor. Madam –

Mrs. Pin. whispers to Hor.

She says she must speak with me in private, withdraw prythee.   60
Mr. Pin. She's unwilling it seems I shou'd know all her undecent
    conduct in this business –

Aside.

Well then Ile leave you together, and hope when I am gone you'l
    agree, if not you and I shan't agree Sir. –
Hor. What means the Fool? – if she and I agree 'tis no matter what   65
    you and I do.

Whispers to Mrs Pin, who makes signs with her hand for him to be gone.

Mr. Pin. In the mean time I'le fetch a Parson, and find out *Sparkish*
    and disabuse him. You wou'd have me fetch a Parson, would you
    not, well then – Now I think I am rid of her, and shall have no more
    trouble with her – Our Sisters and Daughters like Usurers money,   70
    are safest, when put out; but our Wifes, like their writings, never
    safe, but in our Closets under Lock and Key.

Exit Mr. Pin.

Enter Boy.

Boy. Sir *Jaspar Fidget* Sir is coming up.
Hor. Here's the trouble of a Cuckold, now we are talking of, a pox on
    him, has he not enough to doe to hinder his Wifes sport, but he   75
    must other women's too. – Step in here Madam.

Exit Mrs. Pin.

Enter Sir Jaspar.

Sir Jas. My best and dearest Friend.

Hor. The old stile Doctor – Well be short, for I am busie, what would
your impertinent Wife have now?

Sir Jas. Well guess'd y'faith, for I do come from her. 80

Hor. To invite me to supper, tell her I can't come, go.

Sir Jas. Nay, now you are out faith, for my Lady and the whole knot of
the virtuous gang, as they call themselves, are resolv'd upon a frolick
of coming to you to night in a Masquerade, and are all drest already.

Hor. I shan't be at home. 85

Sir Jas. Lord how churlish he is to women – nay prythee don't
disappoint 'em, they'l think 'tis my fault, prythee don't, I'le send
in the Banquet and the Fiddles, but make no noise on't, for the
poor virtuous Rogues would not have it known for the world, that
they go a Masquerading, and they would come to no mans Ball, but 90
yours.

Hor. Well, well – get you gone, and tell 'em if they come, 'twill be at
the peril of their honour and yours.

Sir Jas. Heh, he, he – we'l trust you for that, farewell –

Exit Sir Jaspar.

Hor. Doctor anon you too shall be my guest. But now I'm going to a 95
private feast.

Scene III

The Scene changes to the Piazza of Covent Garden.

Sparkish, Pinchwife.

Spar. But who would have thought a woman could have been false to
me, by the world, I could not have thought it.

Spar. *with the Letter in his hand.*

Mr. Pin. You were for giving and taking liberty, she has taken it only
Sir, now you find in that Letter, you are a frank person, and so is she
you see there. 5

Spar. Nay if this be her hand – for I never saw it.

Mr. Pin. 'Tis no matter whether that be her hand or no, I am sure this
hand at her desire lead her to Mr. *Horner*, with whom I left her just
now, to go fetch a Parson to 'em at their desire too, to deprive you
of her for ever, for it seems yours was but a mock marriage. 10

Spar. Indeed she wou'd needs have it that 'twas *Harcourt* himself in a
Parsons habit, that married us, but I'm sure he told me 'twas his
Brother Ned.

Mr. Pin. O there 'tis out and you were deceiv'd not she, for you are
such a frank person – but I must be gone – you'l find her at Mr.   15
Horners, goe and believe your eyes.

Exit Mr. Pin.

Spar. Nay I'le to her, and call her as many Crocodiles, Syrens, Har-
pies, and other heathenish names, as a Poet would do a Mistress,
who had refus'd to heare his suit, nay more his Verses on her.
But stay, is not that she following a Torch at t'other end of the   20
Piazza, and from *Horners* certainly – 'tis so –

Enter Alithea *following a Torch, and* Lucy *behind.*

You are well met Madam though you don't think so; what you have
made a short visit to Mr. *Horner,* but I suppose you'l return to him
presently, by that time the Parson can be with him.
Ali. Mr. *Horner,* and the Parson Sir –   25
Spar. Come Madam no more dissembling, no more jilting for I am no
more a frank person.
Alith. How's this.
Lucy. So 'twill work I see –

Aside.

Spar. Cou'd you find out no easie Country Fool to abuse? none but   30
me, a Gentleman of wit and pleasure about the Town, but it was
your pride to be too hard for a man of parts, unworthy false woman,
false as a friend that lends a man mony to lose, false as dice, who
undoe those that trust all they have to 'em.
Lucy. He has been a great bubble by his similes as they say –   35

Aside.

Ali. You have been too merry Sir at your wedding dinner sure.
Spar. What d'y mock me too?
Ali. Or you have been deluded.
Spar. By you.
Ali. Let me understand you.   40
Spar. Have you the confidence, I should call it something else, since
you know your guilt, to stand my just reproaches? you did not write
an impudent Letter to Mr. *Horner,* who I find now has club'd with
you in deluding me with his aversion for women, that I might not
forsooth suspect him for my Rival.   45
Lucy. D'y think the Gentleman can be jealous now Madam –

Aside.

Ali. I write a Letter to Mr. *Horner!*
Spar. Nay Madam, do not deny it, your Brother shew'd it me just
now, and told me likewise he left you at *Horners* lodging to fetch a
Parson to marry you to him, and I wish you joy Madam, joy, joy, and   50
to him too much joy, and to my self more joy for not marrying you.

Ali. So I find my Brother would break off the match, and I can consent to't, since I see this Gentleman can be made jealous.

Aside.

O *Lucy*, by his rude usage and jealousie, he makes me almost afraid I am married to him, art thou sure 'twas *Harcourt* himself and no 55
Parson that married us.

Spar. No Madam I thank you, I suppose that was a contrivance too of Mr. *Horners* and yours, to make *Harcourt* play the Parson, but I would as little as you have him one now, no not for the world, for shall I tell you another truth, I never had any passion for you, 'till 60
now, for now I hate you, 'tis true I might have married your portion, as other men of parts of the Town do sometimes, and so your Servant, and to shew my unconcernedness, I'le come to your wedding, and resign you with as much joy as I would a stale wench to a new Cully, nay with as much joy as I would after the first night, if I had been 65
married to you, there's for you, and so your Servant, Servant.

Exit Spar.

Ali. How was I deceiv'd in a man!

Lucy. You'l believe then a fool may be made jealous now? for that easiness in him that suffers him to be led by a Wife, will likewise permit him to be perswaded against her by others. 70

Ali. But marry Mr. *Horner*, my brother does not intend it sure; if I thought he did, I would take thy advice, and Mr. *Harcourt* for my Husband, and now I wish, that if there be any over-wise woman of the Town, who like me would marry a fool, for fortune, liberty, or title, first that her husband may love Play, and be a Cully to all the 75
Town, but her, and suffer none but fortune to be mistress of his purse, then if for liberty, that he may send her into the Country under the conduct of some housewifely mother-in law; and if for title, may the world give 'em none but that of Cuckold.

Lucy. And for her greater curse Madam, may he not deserve it. 80

Ali. Away impertinent – is not this my old Lady *Lanterlus*?

Lucy. Yes Madam. [and here I hope we shall find Mr. *Harcourt* –

Aside.
Exeunt Ali. Lucy.

Scene IV

The Scene changes again to Horner's *Lodging.*

Horner, Lady Fidget, *Mrs.* Daynty Fidget, *Mrs.* Squeamish,
a Table, Banquet, and Bottles.

Hor. A Pox they are come too soon – before I have sent back my new – Mistress, all I have now to do, is to lock her in, that they may not see her –

Aside.

La. Fid. That we may be sure of our wellcome, we have brought our
entertainment with us, and are resolv'd to treat thee, dear Toad.   5

Dayn. And that we may be merry to purpose, have left Sir *Jaspar* and
my old Lady *Squeamish* quarrelling at home at Baggammon.

Squeam. Therefore let us make use of our time, lest they should
chance to interrupt us.

La. Fid. Let us sit then.   10

Hor. First that you may be private, let me lock this door, and that, and
I'le wait upon you presently.

La. Fid. No Sir, shut 'em only and your lips for ever, for we must trust
you as much as our women.

Hor. You know all vanity's kill'd in me, I have no occasion for talking. 15

La. Fid. Now Ladies, supposing we had drank each of us our two
Bottles, let us speak the truth of our hearts.

Dayn. and *Squeam.* Agreed.

La. Fid. By this brimmer, for truth is no where else to be found, [Not
in thy heart false man.   20

                                                    Aside to Hor.

Hor. You have found me a true man I'm sure.

                                                    Aside to Lady Fid.

La. Fid. Not every way –

                                                    Aside to Hor.

But let us sit and be merry.

                              Lady Fidget *sings.*

                                    1.

Why should our damn'd Tyrants oblige us to live
On the pittance of Pleasure which they only give.   25
    We must not rejoyce,
    With Wine and with noise.
In vaine we must wake in a dull bed alone,
Whilst to our warm Rival the Bottle, they're gone.
    Then lay aside charms,   30
    *And take up these arms.**

                                                    *The Glasses.

                                    2.

'Tis Wine only gives 'em their Courage and Wit,
Because we live sober to men we submit.
    If for Beauties you'd pass,
    Take a lick of the Glass.   35
'Twill mend your complexions, and when
    they are gone,
The best red we have is the red of the Grape.
    Then Sisters lay't on,
    And dam a good shape.   40

Dayn. Dear Brimmer, well in token of our openness and plain dealing, let us throw our Masques over our heads.

Hor. So 'twill come to the Glasses anon.

Squeam. Lovely Brimmer, let me enjoy him first.

La. Fid. No, I never part with a Gallant, till I've try'd him. Dear 45
Brimmer that mak'st our Husbands short sighted.

Dayn. And our bashful gallants bold.

Squeam. And for want of a Gallant, the Butler lovely in our eyes,
drink Eunuch.

La. Fid. Drink thou representative of a Husband, damn a Husband. 50

Dayn. And as it were a Husband, an old keeper.

Squeam. And an old Grandmother.

Hor. And an English Bawd, and a French Chirurgion.

La. Fid. Ay we have all reason to curse 'em.

Hor. For my sake Ladies. 55

La. Fid. No, for our own, for the first spoils all young gallants
industry.

Dayn. And the others art makes 'em bold only with common
women.

Squeam. And rather run the hazard of the vile distemper amongst 60
them, than of a denial amongst us.

Dayn. The filthy Toads chuse Mistresses now, as they do Stuffs, for
having been fancy'd and worn by others.

Squeam. For being common and cheap.

La. Fid. Whilst women of quality, like the richest Stuffs, lye 65
untumbled, and unask'd for.

Hor. Ay neat, and cheap, and new often they think best.

Dayn. No Sir, the Beasts will be known by a Mistriss longer than
by a suit.

Squeam. And 'tis not for cheapness neither. 70

La. Fid. No, for the vain fopps will take up Druggets, and embroider
'em, but I wonder at the depraved appetites of witty men, they use
to be out of the common road, and hate imitation, pray tell me
beast, when you were a man, why you rather chose to club with a
multitude in a common house, for an entertainment, than to be the 75
only guest at a good Table.

Hor. Why faith ceremony and expectation are unsufferable to those
that are sharp bent, people always eat with the best stomach at an
ordinary, where every man is snatching for the best bit.

La. Fid. Though he get a cut over the fingers – but I have heard 80
people eat most heartily of another man's meat, that is, what they
do not pay for.

Hor. When they are sure of their wellcome and freedome, for ceremony in love and eating, is as ridiculous as in fighting, falling on
briskly is all should be done in those occasions. 85

La. Fid. Well then let me tell you Sir, there is no where more
freedome than in our houses, and we take freedom from a
young person as a sign of good breeding, and a person may be

as free as he pleases with us, as frolick, as gamesome, as wild as he
will.   90

Hor. Han't I heard you all declaim against wild men.

La. Fid. Yes, but for all that, we think wildness in a man, as desireable
a quality, as in a Duck, or Rabbet; a tame man, foh.

Hor. I know not, but your Reputations frightned me, as much as your
Faces invited me.   95

La. Fid. Our Reputation, Lord! Why should you not think, that we
women make use of our Reputation, as you men of yours, only to
deceive the world with less suspicion; our virtue is like the State-
man's Religion, the Quakers Word, the Gamesters Oath, and the
Great Man's Honour, but to cheat those that trust us.   100

Squeam. And that Demureness, Coyness, and Modesty, that you see
in our Faces in the Boxes at Plays, is as much a sign of a kind
woman, as a Vizard-mask in the Pit.

Dayn. For I assure you, women are least mask'd, when they have the
Velvet Vizard on.   105

La. Fid. You wou'd have found us modest women in our denyals
only.

Squeam. Our bashfulness is only the reflection of the Men's.

Dayn. We blush, when they are shame-fac'd.

Hor. I beg your pardon Ladies, I was deceiv'd in you devilishly, but   110
why, that mighty pretence to Honour?

La. Fid. We have told you; but sometimes 'twas for the same reason
you men pretend business often, to avoid ill company, to enjoy the
better, and more privately those you love.

Hor. But why, wou'd you ne'er give a Friend a wink then?   115

La. Fid. Faith, your Reputation frightned us as much, as ours did
you, you were so notoriously lewd.

Hor. And you so seemingly honest.

La. Fid. Was that all that deterr'd you?

Hor. And so expensive – you allow freedom you say.   120

La. Fid. Ay, ay.

Hor. That I was afraid of losing my little money, as well as my little
time, both which my other pleasures required.

La. Fid. Money, foh – you talk like a little fellow now, do such as we
expect money?   125

Hor. I beg your pardon, Madam, I must confess, I have heard that
great Ladies, like great Merchants, set but the higher prizes upon
what they have, because they are not in necessity of taking the first
offer.

Dayn. Such as we, make sale of our hearts?   130

Squeam. We brib'd for our Love? Foh.

Hor. With your pardon, Ladies, I know, like great men in Offices, you
seem to exact flattery and attendance only from your Followers, but
you have receivers about you, and such fees to pay, a man is afraid to
pass your Grants; besides we must let you win at Cards, or we lose   135
your hearts; and if you make an assignation, 'tis at a Goldsmiths,

Jewellers, or China house, where for your Honour, you deposit to
him, he must pawn his, to the punctual Citt, and so paying for what
you take up, pays for what he takes up.

Dayn. Wou'd you not have us assur'd of our Gallants Love? 140

Squeam. For Love is better known by Liberality, than by Jealousie.

La. Fid. For one may be dissembled, the other not – but my Jealousie
can be no longer dissembled, and they are telling-ripe:

Aside.

Come here's to our Gallants in waiting, whom we must name, and
I'll begin, this is my false Rogue. 145

Claps him on the back.

Squeam. How!

Hor. So all will out now –

Squeam. Did you not tell me, 'twas for my sake only, you reported
your self no man?

Aside to Horner.

Dayn. Oh Wretch! did you not swear to me, 'twas for my Love, and 150
Honour, you pass'd for that thing you do?

Aside to Horner.

Hor. So, so.

La. Fid. Come, speak Ladies, this is my false Villain.

Squeam. And mine too.

Dayn. And mine. 155

Horn. Well then, you are all three my false Rogues too, and there's an
end on't.

La. Fid. Well then, there's no remedy, Sister Sharers, let us not fall out,
but have a care of our Honour; though we get no Presents, no Jewels
of him, we are savers of our Honour, the Jewel of most value and use, 160
which shines yet to the world unsuspected, though it be counterfeit.

Hor. Nay, and is e'en as good, as if it were true, provided the world
think so; for Honour, like Beauty now, only depends on the opinion
of others.

La. Fid. Well Harry Common, I hope you can be true to three, swear, 165
but 'tis no purpose, to require your Oath; for you are as often
forsworn, as you swear to new women.

Hor. Come, faith Madam, let us e'en pardon one another, for all the
difference I find betwixt we men, and you women, we forswear our
selves at the beginning of an Amour, you, as long as it lasts. 170

Enter Sir Jaspar Fidget, *and old Lady* Squeamish.

Sir Jas. Oh my Lady *Fidget*, was this your cunning, to come to Mr.
Horner without me; but you have been no where else I hope.

La. Fid. No, Sir *Jaspar.*

Old La. Squeam. And you came straight hither Biddy.

Squeam. Yes indeed, Lady Grandmother.   175
Sir Jas. 'Tis well, 'tis well, I knew when once they were thoroughly
   acquainted with poor *Horner*, they'd ne'er be from him; you may let
   her masquerade it with my Wife, and *Horner*, and I warrant her
   Reputation safe.

Enter Boy.

Boy. O Sir, here's the Gentleman come, whom you bid me not suffer   180
   to come up, without giving you notice, with a Lady too, and other
   Gentlemen –
Hor. Do you all go in there, whil'st I send 'em away, and Boy, do you
   desire 'em to stay below 'til I come, which shall be immediately.

> *Exeunt Sir* Jaspar, *Lad.* Squeam. *Lad.*
> Fidget, *Mistriss* Dainty, Squeamish.

Boy. Yes Sir.   185

> *Exit.*
> *Exit* Horner *at t'other door, and returns with*
> *Mistriss* Pinchwife.

Hor. You wou'd not take my advice to be gone home, before your
   Husband came back, he'll now discover all, yet pray my Dearest be
   perswaded to go home, and leave the rest to my management, I'll
   let you down the back way.
Mrs. Pin. I don't know the way home, so I don't.   190
Hor. My man shall wait upon you.
Mrs. Pin. No, don't you believe, that I'll go at all; what are you weary
   of me already?
Hor. No my life, 'tis that I may love you long, 'tis to secure my love,
   and your Reputation with your Husband, he'll never receive you   195
   again else.
Mrs. Pin. What care I, d'ye think to frighten me with that? I don't
   intend to go to him again; you shall be my Husband now.
Hor. I cannot be your Husband, Dearest, since you are married to
   him.   200
Mrs. Pin. O wou'd you make me believe that – don't I see every day at
   London here, women leave their first Husbands, and go, and live
   with other men as their Wives, pish, pshaw, you'd make me angry,
   but that I love you so mainly.
Hor. So, they are coming up – In again, in, I hear 'em: 205

> *Exit Mistriss* Pinchwife.

Well, a silly Mistriss, is like a weak place, soon got, soon lost, a man
has scarce time for plunder; she betrays her Husband, first to her
Gallant, and then her Gallant, to her Husband.

Enter Pinchwife, Alithea, Harcourt, Sparkish, Lucy, *and a Parson.*

Mr. Pin. Come Madam, 'tis not the sudden change of your dress, the confidence of your asseverations, and your false witness there, shall 210 perswade me, I did not bring you hither, just now; here's my witness, who cannot deny it, since you must be confronted – Mr. *Horner,* did not I bring this Lady to you just now?

Hor. Now must I wrong one woman for anothers sake, but that's no new thing with me; for in these cases I am still on the criminal's side, 215 against the innocent.

Aside.

Alith. Pray, speak Sir.

Hor. It must be so – I must be impudent, and try my luck, impudence uses to be too hard for truth.

Aside.

Mr. Pin. What, you are studying an evasion, or excuse for her, 220 speak Sir.

Hor. No faith, I am something backward only, to speak in womens affairs or disputes.

Mr. Pin. She bids you speak.

Alith. Ay, pray Sir do, pray satisfie him. 225

Hor. Then truly, you did bring that Lady to me just now.

Mr. Pin. O ho –

Alith. How Sir –

Har. How, *Horner!*

Alith. What mean you Sir, I always took you for a man of Honour? 230

Hor. Ay, so much a man of Honour, that I must save my Mistriss, I thank you, come what will on't.

Aside.

Spar. So if I had had her, she'd have made me believe, the Moon had been made of a Christmas pye.

Lucy. Now cou'd I speak, if I durst, and 'solve the Riddle, who am the 235 Author of it.

Aside.

Alith. O unfortunate Woman! a combination against my Honour, which most concerns me now, because you share in my disgrace, Sir, and it is your censure which I must now suffer, that troubles me, not theirs. 240

Har. Madam, then have no trouble, you shall now see 'tis possible for me to love too, without being jealous, I will not only believe your innocence my self, but make all the world believe it –

Horner I must now be concern'd for this Ladies Honour.

Apart to Horner.

Hor. And I must be concern'd for this Ladies Honour too.   245
Har. This Lady has her Honour, and I will protect it.
Hor. My Lady has her Honour, but has given it me to keep, and I will
    preserve it.
Har. I understand you not.
Hor. I wou'd not have you.   250
Mrs. Pin. What's the matter with 'em all.

                            Mistress Pinchwife *peeping in behind.*

Mr. Pin. Come, come, Mr. *Horner*, no more disputing, here's the
    Parson, I brought him not in vain.
Har. No Sir, I'll employ him, if this Lady please.
Mr. Pin. How, what d'ye mean?   255
Spark. Ay, what does he mean?
Hor. Why, I have resign'd your Sister to him, he has my consent.
Mr. Pin. But he has not mine Sir, a womans injur'd Honour, no more
    than a man's, can be repair'd or satisfied by any, but him that first
    wrong'd it; and you shall marry her presently, or –   260

                            Lays his hand on his Sword.

            Enter to them Mistress Pinchwife.

Mistriss Pin. O Lord, they'll kill poor Mr. *Horner*, besides he shan't
    marry her, whilest I stand by, and look on, I'll not lose my second
    Husband so.
Mr. Pin. What do I see?
Alith. My Sister in my cloaths!   265
Spark. Ha!
Mr. Pin. Nay, pray now don't quarrel about finding work for the
    Parson, he shall marry me to Mr. *Horner*, for now I believe, you
    have enough of me.

                            To Mr. Pinchwife.

Hor. Damn'd, damn'd loving Changeling.   270
Mrs. Pin. Pray Sister, pardon me for telling so many lyes of you.
Har. I suppose the Riddle is plain now.
Lucy. No, that must be my work, good Sir, hear me.

                    Kneels to Mr. Pinchwife, who stands doggedly,
                            with his hat over his eyes.

Mr. Pin. I will never hear woman again, but make 'em all silent, thus –

                            Offers to draw upon his Wife.

Hor. No, that must not be.   275
Mr. Pin. You then shall go first, 'tis all one to me.

                    Offers to draw on Hor. *stopt by* Harcourt.

Har. Hold –

Enter Sir Jaspar Fidget, *Lady* Fidget, *Lady* Squeamish,
Mrs. Dainty Fidget, *Mrs.* Squeamish.

Sir Jas. What's the matter, what's the matter, pray what's the matter
Sir, I beseech you communicate Sir.

Mr. Pin. Why my Wife has communicated Sir, as your Wife may have   280
done too Sir, if she knows him Sir –

Sir Jas. Pshaw, with him, ha, ha, he.

Mr. Pin. D'ye mock me Sir, a Cuckold is a kind of a wild Beast, have a
care Sir –

Sir Jas. No sure, you mock me Sir – he cuckold you! it can't be, ha,   285
ha, he, why, I'll tell you Sir.

Offers to whisper.

Mr. Pin. I tell you again, he has whor'd my Wife, and yours too, if he
knows her, and all the women he comes near; 'tis not his dissembling, his hypocrisie can wheedle me.

Sir Jas. How does he dissemble, is he a Hypocrite? nay then – how –   290
Wife – Sister is he an Hypocrite?

Old La. Squeam. An Hypocrite, a dissembler, speak young Harlotry,
speak how?

Sir Jas. Nay then – O my head too – O thou libidinous Lady!

Old La. Squeam. O thou Harloting, Harlotry, hast thou done't then?   295

Sir Jas. Speak good *Horner*, art thou a dissembler, a Rogue? hast thou –

Hor. Soh –

Lucy. I'll fetch you off, and her too, if she will but hold her tongue.

Apart to Hor.

Hor. Canst thou? I'll give thee –

Apart to Luc.

Lucy to Mr. Pin. Pray have but patience to hear me Sir, who am the   300
unfortunate cause of all this confusion, your Wife is innocent, I only
culpable; for I put her upon telling you all these lyes, concerning my
Mistress, in order to the breaking off the match, between Mr.
Sparkish and her, to make way for Mr. *Harcourt*.

Spark. Did you so eternal Rotten-tooth, then it seems my Mistress   305
was not false to me, I was only deceiv'd by you, brother that shou'd
have been, now man of conduct, who is a frank person now, to
bring your Wife to her Lover – ha –

Lucy. I assure you Sir, she came not to Mr. *Horner* out of love, for she
loves him no more –   310

Mrs. Pin. Hold, I told lyes for you, but you shall tell none for me, for
I do love Mr. *Horner* with all my soul, and no body shall say me nay;
pray don't you go to make poor Mr. *Horner* believe to the contrary,
'tis spitefully done of you, I'm sure.

Hor. Peace, Dear Ideot.   315

Aside to Mrs. Pin.

Mrs. Pin. Nay, I will not peace.

Mr. Pin. Not 'til I make you.

Enter Dorilant, Quack.

Dor. Horner, your Servant, I am the Doctors Guest, he must excuse our intrusion.

Quack. But what's the matter Gentlemen, for Heavens sake, what's   320
the matter?

Hor. Oh 'tis well you are come – 'tis a censorious world we live in, you may have brought me a reprieve, or else I had died for a crime, I never committed, and these innocent Ladies had suffer'd with me, therefore pray satisfie these worthy, honourable, jealous Gentlemen   325
– that –

Whispers.

Quack. O I understand you, is that all – Sir *Jasper*, by heavens and upon the word of a Physician Sir, –

Whispers to Sir Jasper.

Sir Jas. Nay I do believe you truly – pardon me my virtuous Lady, and dear of honour.   330

Old La. Squeam. What then all's right again.

Sir Jas. Ay, ay, and now let us satisfie him too.

They whisper with Mr. Pinch.

Mr. Pin. An Eunuch! pray no fooling with me.

Quack. I'le bring half the Chirurgions in Town to swear it.

Mr. Pin. They – they'l sweare a man that bled to death through his   335
wounds died of an Apoplexy.

Quack. Pray hear me Sir – why all the Town has heard the report of him.

Mr. Pin. But does all the Town believe it.

Quack. Pray inquire a little, and first of all these.   340

Mr. Pin. I'm sure when I left the Town he was the lewdest fellow in't.

Quack. I tell you Sir he has been in *France* since, pray ask but these Ladies and Gentlemen, your friend Mr. *Dorilant*, Gentlemen and Ladies, han't you all heard the late sad report of poor Mr. *Horner*.

All Lad. Ay, ay, ay.   345

Dor. Why thou jealous Fool do'st thou doubt it, he's an errant French Capon.

Mrs. Pin. 'Tis false Sir, you shall not disparage poor Mr. *Horner*, for to my certain knowledge –

Lucy. O hold –   350

Squeam. Stop her mouth –

Aside to Lucy.

La. Fid. Upon my honour Sir, 'tis as true.

To Pinch.

Dayn. D'y think we would have been seen in his company –

Squeam. Trust our unspotted reputations with him!

La. Fid. This you get, and we too, by trusting your secret to a fool –   355

Aside to Hor.

Hor. Peace Madam, – well Doctor is not this a good design that carryes a man on unsuspected, and brings him off safe. –

Aside to Quack.

Mr. Pin. Well, if this were true, but my Wife –

Aside
Dorilant *whispers with Mrs.* Pinch.

Ali. Come Brother your Wife is yet innocent you see, but have a care of too strong an imagination, least like an over-concern'd timerous   360 Gamester by fancying an unlucky cast it should come, Women and Fortune are truest still to those that trust 'em.

Lucy. And any wild thing grows but the more fierce and hungry for being kept up, and more dangerous to the Keeper.

Ali. There's doctrine for all Husbands Mr. *Harcourt.*   365

Har. I edifie Madam so much, that I am impatient till I am one.

Dor. And I edifie so much by example I will never be one.

Spar. And because I will not disparage my parts I'le ne're be one.

Hor. And I alass can't be one.

Mr. Pin. But I must be one – against my will to a Country-Wife, with   370 a Country-murrain to me.

Mrs. Pin. And I must be a Country Wife still too I find, for I can't like a City one, be rid of my musty Husband and doe what I list.

Aside.

Hor. Now Sir I must pronounce your Wife Innocent, though I blush whilst I do it, and I am the only man by her now expos'd to shame,   375 which I will straight drown in Wine, as you shall your suspition, and the Ladies troubles we'l divert with a Ballet, Doctor where are your Maskers.

Lucy. Indeed she's Innocent Sir, I am her witness, and her end of coming out was but to see her Sisters Wedding, and what she has   380 said to your face of her love to Mr. *Horner* was but the usual innocent revenge on a Husbands jealousie, was it not Madam speak –

Mrs. Pin. Since you'l have me tell more lyes –

Aside to Lucy *and* Horner.

Yes indeed Budd.

Mr. Pin. For my own sake fain I wou'd all believe. Cuckolds like   385 Lovers shou'd themselves deceive.

But –

Sighs.

His honour is least safe, (too late I find)
Who trusts it with a foolish Wife or Friend.

A Dance of Cuckolds.

Hor. Vain Fopps, but court, and dress, and keep a puther,   390
To pass for Womens men, with one another.
But he who aimes by women to be priz'd,
First by the men you see must be despis'd.

[FINIS.]

EPILOGUE SPOKEN BY MRS. KNEP

Now you the Vigorous, who dayly here ⎫
O're Vizard-Mask, in publick domineer, ⎬
And what you'd doe to her if in Place where; ⎭
Nay have the confidence, to cry come out,
Yet when she says lead on, you are not stout;   5
But to your well-drest Brother straight turn round
And cry, Pox on her Ned, she can't be sound:
Then slink away, a fresh one to ingage, ⎫
With so much seeming heat and loving Rage, ⎬
You'd frighten listning Actress on the Stage: ⎭   10
Till she at last has seen you huffing come, ⎫
And talk of keeping in the Tyreing-Room, ⎬
Yet cannot be provok'd to lead her home: ⎭
Next you Fallstaffs of fifty, who beset
Your Buckram Maidenheads, which your friends get;   15
And whilst to them, you of Atchievements boast,
They share the booty, and laugh at your cost.
In fine, you Essens't Boyes, both Old and Young, ⎫
Who wou'd be thought so eager, brisk, and strong, ⎬
Yet do the Ladies, not their Husbands, wrong: ⎭   20
Whose Purses for your manhood make excuse,
And keep your Flanders Mares for shew, not use;
Encourag'd by our Womans Man to day,
A Horners part may vainly think to Play,
And may Intreagues so bashfully disown   25
That they may doubted be by few or none,
May kiss the Cards at Picquet, Hombre, – Lu, ⎫
And so be thought to kiss the Lady too; ⎬
But Gallants, have a care faith, what you do. ⎭
The World, which to no man his due will give,   30
You by experience know you can deceive,
And men may still believe you Vigorous,
But then we Women, – there's no cous'ning us.

[FINIS.]

William Congreve
(1670–1729)

The Way of the World (1700)

Audire est Operæ pretium, procedere recte
Qui mœchis non vultis – Hor. Sat. 2. l. I.
– Metuat doti deprensa. –   *Ibid.*

To the Right Honourable Ralph Earl of Mountague, &c.

My Lord,

Whether the World will arraign me of Vanity, or not, that I have
presum'd to Dedicate this Comedy to your Lordship, I am yet in
doubt: Tho' it may be it is some degree of Vanity even to doubt of it.
One who has at any time had the Honour of your Lordship's Conversation, cannot be suppos'd to think very meanly of that which he   5
would prefer to your Perusal: Yet it were to incur the Imputation of
too much Sufficiency, to pretend to such a Merit as might abide the
Test of your Lordship's Censure.

Whatever Value may be wanting to this Play while yet it is mine,
will be sufficiently made up to it, when it is once become your   10
Lordship's; and it is my Security, that I cannot have overrated it
more by my Dedication, than your Lordship will dignifie it by your
Patronage.

That it succeeded on the Stage, was almost beyond my Expectation;
for but little of it was prepar'd for that general Taste which seems now   15
to be predominant in the Pallats of our Audience.

Those Characters which are meant to be ridiculous in most of our
Comedies, are of Fools so gross, that in my humble Opinion, they
should rather disturb than divert the well-natur'd and reflecting part
of an Audience; they are rather Objects of Charity than Contempt;   20
and instead of moving our Mirth, they ought very often to excite our
Compassion.

This Reflection mov'd me to design some Characters, which
should appear ridiculous not so much thro' a natural Folly (which
is incorrigible, and therefore not proper for the Stage) as thro' an   25
affected Wit; a Wit, which at the same time that it is affected is
also false. As there is some Difficulty in the formation of a Character
of this Nature, so there is some Hazard which attends the progress

of its Success, upon the Stage: For many come to a Play, so over-
charg'd with Criticism, that they very often let fly their Censure,   30
when through their rashness they have mistaken their Aim. This
I had occasion lately to observe: For this Play had been Acted
two or three Days, before some of these hasty Judges cou'd find the
leisure to distinguish betwixt the Character of a *Witwoud* and a
Truewit.   35

I must beg your Lordship's Pardon for this Digression from the
true Course of this Epistle; but that it may not seem altogether
impertinent, I beg, that I may plead the occasion of it, in part of
that Excuse of which I stand in need, for recommending this Comedy
to your Protection. It is only by the Countenance of your Lordship,   40
and the *Few* so qualified, that such who write with Care and Pains can
hope to be distinguish'd: For the Prostituted Name of *Poet* promiscu-
ously levels all that bear it.

Terence, the most correct Writer in the World, had a *Scipio* and a
Lelius if not to assist him, at least to support him in his Reputation: 45
And notwithstanding his extraordinary Merit, it may be, their Coun-
tenance was not more than necessary.

The Purity of his Stile, the Delicacy of his Turns, and the Justness of
his Characters, were all of them Beauties, which the greater part of his
Audience were incapable of Tasting: Some of the coarsest Strokes of   50
Plautus, so severely censured by *Horace*, were more likely to affect the
Multitude; such, who come with expectation to Laugh out the last
Act of a Play, and are better entertained with two or three unseason-
able Jests, than with the artful Solution of the *Fable*.

As *Terence* excell'd in his Performances, so had he great Advantages   55
to encourage his Undertakings; for he built most on the Foundations
of *Menander*. His Plots were generally modell'd, and his Characters
ready drawn to his Hand. He copied *Menander*, and *Menander* had no
less Light in the Formation of his Characters, from the Observations
of *Theophrastus*, of whom he was a Disciple; and *Theophrastus* it is   60
known was not only the Disciple, but the immediate Successor of
Aristotle, the first and greatest Judge of Poetry. These were great
Models to design by; and the further Advantage which *Terence* possess'd, towards giving his Plays the due Ornaments of Purity of Stile,
and Justness of Manners, was not less considerable, from the freedom   65
of Conversation, which was permitted him with *Lelius* and *Scipio*, two
of the greatest and most polite Men of his Age. And indeed, the
Privilege of such a Conversation, is the only certain Means of attaining
to the Perfection of Dialogue.

If it has hapned in any part of this Comedy, that I have gain'd a   70
Turn of Stile, or Expression more Correct, or at least more Corrigible
than in those which I have formerly written, I must, with equal Pride
and Gratitude, ascribe it to the Honour of your Lordship's admitting
me into your Conversation, and that of a Society where every-body
else was so well worthy of you, in your Retirement last Summer   75
from the Town: For it was immediately after, that this Comedy

was written. If I have fail'd in my Performance, it is only to be
regretted, where there were so many, not inferiour either to a *Scipio*
or a *Lelius*, that there should be one wanting equal to the Capacity of a
Terence.   80

If I am not mistaken, Poetry is almost the only Art, which has not yet
laid claim to your Lordship's Patronage. Architecture, and Painting, to
the great Honour of our Country, have flourish'd under your Influ-
ence and Protection. In the mean time, Poetry, the eldest Sister of all
Arts, and Parent of most, seems to have resign'd her Birthright, by   85
having neglected to pay her Duty to your Lordship; and by permitting
others of a later Extraction, to preposses that Place in your Esteem, to
which none can pretend a better Title. Poetry, in its Nature, is sacred to
the Good and Great; the relation between them is reciprocal, and they
are ever propitious to it. It is the Privilege of Poetry to address to them, 90
and it is their Prerogative alone to give it Protection.

This receiv'd Maxim is a general Apology for all Writers who Conse-
crate their Labours to great Men: But I could wish at this time, that this
Address were exempted from the common pretence of all Dedications;
and that as I can distinguish your Lordship even among the most   95
Deserving, so this Offering might become remarkable by some particular Instance of Respect, which shou'd assure your Lordship, that I
am, with all due Sense of your extream Worthiness and Humanity,

My LORD,

Your Lordship's most obedient and most oblig'd humble Servant,   100

Will. Congreve.

PROLOGUE, SPOKEN BY MR. BETTERTON

Of those few Fools, who with ill Stars are curs'd,
Sure scribbling Fools, call'd Poets, fare the worst.
For they're a sort of Fools which *Fortune* makes,
And after she has made 'em Fools, forsakes.
With *Nature*'s Oafs 'tis quite a diff'rent Case,   5
For *Fortune* favours all her *Idiot-Race*:
In her own Nest the *Cuckow-Eggs* we find,
O'er which she broods to hatch the *Changling-Kind*.
No Portion for her own she has to spare,
So much she doats on her adopted Care.

    Poets are Bubbles, by the Town drawn in,   10
Suffer'd at first some trifling Stakes to win:
But what unequal Hazards do they run!
Each time they write, they venture all they've won:
The 'Squire that's butter'd still, is sure to be undone.
This Author, heretofore, has found your Favour,   15
But pleads no Merit from his past Behaviour.
To build on that might prove a vain Presumption,
Should Grants to Poets made, admit Resumption:

And in *Parnassus* he must lose his Seat,   20
If that be found a forfeited Estate.
    He owns, with Toil, he wrought the following Scenes,
But if they're naught ne're spare him for his Pains:
Damn him the more; have no Commiseration
For Dulness on mature Deliberation.   25
He swears he'll not resent one hiss'd-off Scene, ⎤
Nor, like those peevish Wits, his Play maintain, ⎬
Who, to assert their Sense, your Taste arraign. ⎦
Some Plot we think he has, and some new Thought;
Some Humour too, no Farce; but that's a Fault.   30
Satire, he thinks, you ought not to expect,
For so Reform'd a Town, who dares Correct?
To please, this time, has been his sole Pretence,
He'll not instruct, lest it should give Offence.
Should he by chance a Knave or Fool expose,   35
That hurts none here, sure here are none of those.
In short, our Play, shall (with your leave to shew it)
Give you one Instance of a Passive Poet.
Who to your Judgments yields all Resignation;
So Save or Damn, after your own Discretion.   40

DRAMATIS PERSONÆ

MEN

Fainall, In Love with *Mrs. Marwood*	Mr. Betterton.
Mirabell, In Love with *Mrs. Millamant*	Mr. Verbrugen.
Witwoud, ⎤ Followers of	⎤ Mr. Bowen.
Petulant, ⎦ *Mrs. Millamant*	⎦ Mr. Bowman.
Sir Wilfull Witwoud, Half Brother to *Witwoud*, and Nephew to *Lady Wishfort*	Mr. Underhill.
Waitwell, Servant to *Mirabell*	Mr. Bright.

WOMEN

Lady Wishfort, Enemy to *Mirabell*, for having falsely pretended Love to her	Mrs. Leigh.
Mrs. Millamant, A fine Lady, Niece to *Lady Wishfort*, and loves *Mirabell*	Mrs. Bracegirdle.
Mrs. Marwood, Friend to *Mr. Fainall*, and likes *Mirabell*	Mrs. Barry.
Mrs. Fainall, Daughter to *Lady Wishfort*, and Wife to *Fainall*, formerly Friend to *Mirabell*	Mrs. Bowman.

Foible, Woman to *Lady Wishfort*   Mrs. Willis.
Mincing, Woman to *Mrs. Millamant*   Mrs. Prince.

Dancers, Footmen, *and* Attendants.

Scene, London.

The Time equal to that of the Presentation.

Act I

Scene I

A Chocolate-house.

Mirabell *and* Fainall *Rising from Cards.* Betty *waiting.*

Mirabell. You are a fortunate Man, Mr. *Fainall.*

Fainall. Have we done?

Mirabell. What you please. I'll play on to entertain you.

Fainall. No, I'll give you your Revenge another time, when you are
not so indifferent; you are thinking of something else now, and play 5
too negligently; the Coldness of a losing Gamester lessens the
Pleasure of the Winner: I'd no more play with a Man that slighted
his ill Fortune, than I'd make Love to a Woman who undervalu'd
the Loss of her Reputation.

Mirabell. You have a Taste extreamly delicate, and are for refining on 10
your Pleasures.

Fainall. Prithee, why so reserv'd? Something has put you out of
Humour.

Mirabell. Not at all: I happen to be grave to day; and you are gay;
that's all. 15

Fainall. Confess, *Millamant* and you quarrell'd last Night, after I left
you; my fair Cousin has some Humours, that wou'd tempt the
patience of a Stoick. What, some Coxcomb came in, and was well
receiv'd by her, while you were by.

Mirabell. *Witwoud* and *Petulant;* and what was worse, her Aunt, your 20
Wife's Mother, my evil Genius; or to sum up all in her own Name,
my old Lady *Wishfort* came in. –

Fainall. O there it is then – She has a lasting Passion for you, and with
Reason. – What, then my Wife was there?

Mirabell. Yes, and Mrs. *Marwood* and three or four more, whom I 25
never saw before; seeing me, they all put on their grave Faces,
whisper'd one another; then complain'd aloud of the Vapours,
and after fell into a profound Silence.

Fainall. They had a mind to be rid of you.

Mirabell. For which Reason I resolv'd not to stir. At last the good old 30
Lady broke thro' her painful Taciturnity, with an Invective against

long Visits. I would not have understood her, but *Millamant* joining in the Argument, I rose and with a constrain'd Smile told her, I thought nothing was so easie as to know when a Visit began to be troublesome; she redned and I withdrew, without expecting   35
her Reply.

Fainall. You were to blame to resent what she spoke only in Compliance with her Aunt.

Mirabell. She is more Mistress of her self, than to be under the necessity of such a resignation.   40

Fainall. What? tho' half her Fortune depends upon her marrying with my Lady's Approbation?

Mirabell. I was then in such a Humour, that I shou'd have been better pleas'd if she had been less discreet.

Fainall. Now I remember, I wonder not they were weary of you; last   45
Night was one of their Cabal-nights; they have 'em three times a Week, and meet by turns, at one another's Apartments, where they come together like the Coroner's Inquest, to sit upon the murder'd Reputations of the Week. You and I are excluded; and it was once propos'd that all the Male Sex shou'd be excepted; but somebody   50
mov'd that to avoid Scandal there might be one Man of the Community; upon which Motion *Witwoud* and *Petulant* were enroll'd Members.

Mirabell. And who may have been the Foundress of this Sect? My Lady *Wishfort*, I warrant, who publishes her Detestation of Man-   55
kind; and full of the Vigour of Fifty five, declares for a Friend and *Ratifia*; and let Posterity shift for it self, she'll breed no more.

Fainall. The discovery of your sham Addresses to her, to conceal your Love to her Niece, has provok'd this Separation: Had you dissembl'd better, Things might have continu'd in the state of Nature.   60

Mirabell. I did as much as Man cou'd, with any reasonable Conscience; I proceeded to the very last Act of Flattery with her, and was guilty of a Song in her Commendation: Nay, I got a Friend to put her into a Lampoon, and compliment her with the Imputation of an Affair with a young Fellow, which I carry'd so far, that I told   65
her the malicious Town took notice that she was grown fat of a suddain; and when she lay in of a Dropsie, persuaded her she was reported to be in Labour. The Devil's in't, if an old woman is to be flatter'd further, unless a Man shou'd endeavour downright personally to debauch her; and that my Virtue forbad me. But for the   70
discovery of that Amour, I am Indebted to your Friend, or your Wife's Friend, Mrs. *Marwood*.

Fainall. What should provoke her to be your Enemy, without she has made you Advances, which you have slighted? Women do not easily forgive Omissions of that Nature.   75

Mirabell. She was always civil to me, till of late; I confess I am not one of those Coxcombs who are apt to interpret a Woman's good Manners to her Prejudice; and think that she who does not refuse 'em every thing, can refuse 'em nothing.

Fainall. You are a gallant Man, *Mirabell*; and tho' you may have 80
 Cruelty enough, not to satisfie a Lady's longing; you have too
 much Generosity, not to be tender of her Honour. Yet you speak
 with an Indifference which seems to be affected; and confesses you
 are conscious of a Negligence.

Mirabell. You pursue the Argument with a distrust that seems to be 85
 unaffected, and confesses you are conscious of a Concern for which
 the Lady is more indebted to you, than your Wife.

Fainall. Fie, fie Friend, if you grow Censorious I must leave you; –
 I'll look upon the Gamesters in the next Room.

Mirabell. Who are they? 90

Fainall. Petulant and *Witwoud.* – Bring me some Chocolate.

Exit.

Mirabell. Betty, what says your Clock?

Betty. Turn'd of the last Canonical Hour, Sir.

Exit.

Mirabell. How pertinently the Jade answers me! Ha? almost One a
 Clock! (*Looking at his Watch*) O, y'are come – 95

Enter a Servant.

Well, is the grand Affair over? You have been something tedious.

Servant. Sir, there's such Coupling at *Pancras* that they stand behind
 one another, as 'twere in a Country Dance. Ours was the last
 Couple to lead up; and no hopes appearing of dispatch, besides,
 the Parson growing hoarse, we were afraid his Lungs would have 100
 fail'd before it came to our turn; so we drove round to *Duke's Place*;
 and there they were riveted in a trice.

Mirabell. So, so, you are sure they are Married.

Servant. Married and Bedded, Sir: I am Witness.

Mirabell. Have you the Certificate? 105

Servant. Here it is, Sir.

Mirabell. Has the Taylor brought *Waitwell's* Cloaths home, and the
 new Liveries?

Servant. Yes, Sir.

Mirabell. That's well. Do you go home again, d'ee hear, and adjourn 110
 the Consummation till farther Order; bid *Waitwell* shake his Ears,
 and Dame *Partlet* rustle up her Feathers, and meet me at One a
 Clock by *Rosamond's* Pond. That I may see her before she returns
 to her Lady; and as you tender your Ears be secret.

Exit Servant.

Re-Enter Fainall.

Fainall. Joy of your Success, *Mirabell*; you look pleas'd. 115

Mirabell. Ay; I have been engag'd in a Matter of some sort of Mirth,
 which is not yet ripe for discovery. I am glad this is not a Cabal-night.

I wonder, *Fainall*, that you who are Married, and of Consequence should be discreet, will suffer your Wife to be of such a Party.

Fainall. Faith, I am not Jealous. Besides, most who are engag'd are 120 Women and Relations; and for the Men, they are of a Kind too Contemptible to give Scandal.

Mirabell. I am of another Opinion. The greater the Coxcomb, always the more the Scandal: For a Woman who is not a Fool, can have but one Reason for associating with a Man that is. 125

Fainall. Are you Jealous as often as you see *Witwoud* entertain'd by *Millamant?*

Mirabell. Of her Understanding I am, if not of her Person.

Fainall. You do her wrong; for to give her her Due, she has Wit.

Mirabell. She has Beauty enough to make any Man think so; and 130 Complaisance enough not to contradict him who shall tell her so.

Fainall. For a passionate Lover, methinks you are a Man somewhat too discerning in the Failings of your Mistress.

Mirabell. And for a discerning Man, somewhat too passionate a Lover; for I like her with all her Faults; nay, like her for her Faults. 135 Her Follies are so natural, or so artful, that they become her; and those Affectations which in another Woman wou'd be odious, serve but to make her more agreeable. I'll tell thee, *Fainall*, she once us'd me with that Insolence, that in Revenge I took her to pieces; sifted her and separated her Failings; I study'd 'em, and got 'em by rote. 140 The Catalogue was so large, that I was not without hopes, one Day or other to hate her heartily: To which end I so us'd my self to think of 'em, that at length, contrary to my Design and Expectation, they gave me every Hour less and less disturbance; 'till in a few Days it became habitual to me, to remember 'em without being displeas'd. 145 They are now grown as familiar to me as my own Frailties; and in all probability in a little time longer I shall like 'em as well.

Fainall. Marry her, marry her; be half as well acquainted with her Charms, as you are with her Defects, and my Life on't, you are your own Man again. 150

Mirabell. Say you so?

Fainall. I, I, I have Experience: I have a Wife, and so forth.

Enter Messenger.

Messenger. Is one Squire *Witwoud* here?

Betty. Yes; what's your Business?

Messenger. I have a Letter for him, from his Brother Sir *Wilfull*, which 155 I am charg'd to deliver into his own Hands.

Betty. He's in the next Room, Friend – That way.

Exit Messenger.

Mirabell. What, is the Chief of that noble Family in Town, Sir *Wilfull Witwoud?*

Fainall. He is expected to Day. Do you know him? 160

Mirabell. I have seen him, he promises to be an extraordinary Person; I think you have the Honour to be related to him.

Fainall. Yes; he is half Brother to this *Witwoud* by a former Wife, who was Sister to my Lady *Wishfort*, my Wife's Mother. If you marry *Millamant* you must call Cousins too.   165

Mirabell. I had rather be his Relation than his Acquaintance.

Fainall. He comes to Town in order to Equip himself for Travel.

Mirabell. For Travel! Why the Man that I mean is above Forty.

Fainall. No matter for that; 'tis for the Honour of *England*, that all *Europe* should know we have Blockheads of all Ages.   170

Mirabell. I wonder there is not an Act of Parliament to save the Credit of the Nation, and prohibit the Exportation of Fools.

Fainall. By no means, 'tis better as 'tis; 'tis better to Trade with a little Loss, than to be quite eaten up, with being overstock'd.

Mirabell. Pray, are the Follies of this Knight-Errant, and those of the   175 Squire his Brother, any thing related?

Fainall. Not at all; *Witwoud* grows by the Knight, like a Medlar grafted on a Crab. One will melt in your Mouth, and t'other set your Teeth on edge; one is all Pulp, and the other all Core.

Mirabell. So one will be rotten before he be ripe, and the other will be   180 rotten without ever being ripe at all.

Fainall. Sir *Wilfull* is an odd mixture of Bashfulness and Obstinacy – But when he's drunk, he's as loving as the Monster in the Tempest; and much after the same manner. To give the t'other his due; he has something of good Nature, and does not always want Wit.   185

Mirabell. Not always; but as often as his Memory fails him, and his common place of Comparisons. He is a Fool with a good Memory, and some few Scraps of other Folks Wit. He is one whose Conversation can never be approv'd, yet it is now and then to be endur'd. He has indeed one good Quality, he is not Exceptious; for he so   190 passionately affects the Reputation of understanding Raillery; that he will construe an Affront into a Jest; and call downright Rudeness and ill Language, Satyr and Fire.

Fainall. If you have a mind to finish his Picture, you have an opportunity to do it at full length. Behold the Original.   195

Enter Witwoud.

Witwoud. Afford me your Compassion, my Dears; pity me, *Fainall*, *Mirabell*, pity me.

Mirabell. I do from my Soul.

Fainall. Why, what's the Matter?

Witwoud. No Letters for me, *Betty?*   200

Betty. Did not the Messenger bring you one but now, Sir?

Witwoud. Ay, but no other?

Betty. No, Sir.

Witwoud. That's hard, that's very hard; – A Messenger, a Mule, a Beast of Burden, he has brought me a Letter from the Fool my   205 Brother, as heavy as a Panegyrick in a Funeral Sermon, or a Copy of

Commendatory Verses from one Poet to another. And what's worse,
'tis as sure a forerunner of the Author, as an Epistle Dedicatory.

Mirabell. A Fool, and your Brother, *Witwoud*!

Witwoud. Ay, ay, my half Brother. My half Brother he is, no nearer,   210
upon Honour.

Mirabell. Then 'tis possible he may be but half a Fool.

Witwoud. Good, good *Mirabell, le Drole*! Good, good, hang him,
don't let's talk of him: – *Fainall*, how does your Lady? Gad, I say
any thing in the World to get this Fellow out of my Head. I beg   215
Pardon that I shou'd ask a Man of Pleasure, and the Town, a
Question at once so Foreign and Domestick. But I talk like an old
Maid at a Marriage, I don't know what I say: But she's the best
Woman in the World.

Fainall. 'Tis well you don't know what you say, or else your Com-   220
mendation wou'd go near to make me either Vain or Jealous.

Witwoud. No Man in Town lives well with a Wife but *Fainall*: Your
Judgment *Mirabell*.

Mirabell. You had better step and ask his Wife; if you wou'd be
credibly inform'd.   225

Witwoud. Mirabell.

Mirabell. Ay.

Witwoud. My Dear, I ask ten thousand Pardons; – Gad I have forgot
what I was going to say to you.

Mirabell. I thank you heartily, heartily.   230

Witwoud. No, but prithee excuse me, – my Memory is such a
Memory.

Mirabell. Have a care of such Apologies, *Witwoud*; – for I never knew
a Fool but he affected to complain, either of the Spleen or his
Memory.   235

Fainall. What have you done with *Petulant*?

Witwoud. He's reckoning his Mony, – my Mony it was, – I have no
Luck to Day.

Fainall. You may allow him to win of you at Play; – for you are sure to
be too hard for him at Repartee: since you monopolize the Wit that   240
is between you, the Fortune must be his of Course.

Mirabell. I don't find that *Petulant* confesses the Superiority of Wit
to be your Talent, *Witwoud*.

Witwoud. Come, come, you are malicious now, and wou'd breed
Debates. – *Petulant*'s my Friend, and a very honest Fellow, and a   245
very pretty Fellow, and has a smattering – Faith and Troth a pretty
deal of an odd sort of a small Wit: Nay, I'll do him Justice. I'm his
Friend, I won't wrong him neither – And if he had but any Judgment in the World, – he wou'd not be altogether contemptible.
Come come, don't detract from the Merits of my Friend.   250

Fainall. You don't take your Friend to be over-nicely bred.

Witwoud. No, no, hang him, the Rogue has no Manners at all, that I
must own – No more breeding than a Bum-baily, that I grant you, –
'Tis Pity faith; the Fellow has Fire and Life.

Mirabell. What, Courage? 255

Witwoud. Hum, faith I don't know as to that, – I can't say as to that. – Yes, Faith, in a Controversie he'll contradict any Body.

Mirabell. Tho' 'twere a Man whom he fear'd, or a Woman whom he lov'd.

Witwoud. Well, well, he does not always think before he speaks; – We 260 have all our Failings; you're too hard upon him, you are, faith. Let me excuse him; – I can defend most of his Faults, except one or two; one he has, that's the Truth on't, if he were my Brother, I cou'd not acquit him – That indeed I cou'd wish were otherwise.

Mirabell. Ay marry, what's that, *Witwoud*? 265

Witwoud. O pardon me – Expose the Infirmities of my Friend. – No, my Dear, excuse me there.

Fainall. What I warrant he's unsincere, or 'tis some such Trifle.

Witwoud. No, no, what if he be? 'Tis no matter for that, his Wit will excuse that: A Wit shou'd no more be sincere, than a Woman 270 constant; one argues a decay of Parts, as t'other of Beauty.

Mirabell. May be you think him too positive?

Witwoud. No, no, his being positive is an Incentive to Argument, and keeps up Conversation.

Fainall. Too Illiterate. 275

Witwoud. That! that's his Happiness – His want of Learning, gives him the more opportunities to shew his natural Parts.

Mirabell. He wants Words.

Witwoud. Ay; but I like him for that now; for his want of Words gives me the pleasure very often to explain his meaning. 280

Fainall. He's Impudent.

Witwoud. No; that's not it.

Mirabell. Vain.

Witwoud. No.

Mirabell. What, he speaks unseasonable Truths sometimes, because 285 he has not Wit enough to invent an Evasion.

Witwoud. Truths! Ha, ha, ha! No, no, since you will have it, – I mean he never speaks Truth at all, – that's all. He will lie like a Chamber-maid, or a Woman of Quality's Porter. Now that is a Fault.

Enter Coachman.

Coachman. Is Master *Petulant* here, Mistress? 290

Betty. Yes.

Coachman. Three Gentlewomen in the Coach would speak with him.

Fainall. O brave *Petulant*, three!

Betty. I'll tell him.

Coachman. You must bring two Dishes of Chocolate and a Glass of 295 Cinnamon-water.

Exit Betty, *and Coachman.*

Witwoud. That should be for two fasting Strumpets, and a Bawd troubl'd with Wind. Now you may know what the three are.

Mirabell. You are very free with your Friends Acquaintance.

Witwoud. Ay, ay, Friendship without Freedom is as dull as Love   300
without Enjoyment, or Wine without Toasting; but to tell you a
Secret, these are Trulls that he allows Coach-hire, and something
more by the Week, to call on him once a Day at publick Places.

Mirabell. How!

Witwoud. You shall see he won't go to 'em because there's no more   305
Company here to take notice of him – Why this is nothing to what
he us'd to do; – Before he found out this way, I have known him call
for himself –

Fainall. Call for himself? What dost thou mean?

Witwoud. Mean, why he wou'd slip you out of this Chocolate-house,   310
just when you had been talking to him – As soon as your Back was
turn'd – Whip he was gone; – Then trip to his Lodging, clap on a
Hood and Scarf, and Mask, slap into a Hackney-Coach, and drive
hither to the Door again in a trice; where he wou'd send in for
himself, that I mean, call for himself, wait for himself, nay and what's   315
more, not finding himself, sometimes leave a Letter for himself.

Mirabell. I confess this is something extraordinary – I believe he waits
for himself now, he is so long a coming; O I ask his Pardon.

Enter Petulant.

Betty. Sir, the Coach stays.

Petulant. Well, well; I come – Sbud a Man had as good be a profess'd   320
Midwife as a profest Whoremaster, at this rate; to be knock'd up and
rais'd at all Hours and in all Places. Pox on 'em I won't come. – Dee
hear, tell 'em I won't come. – Let 'em snivel and cry their Hearts out.

Fainall. You are very cruel, *Petulant.*

Petulant. All's one, let it pass – I have a Humour to be cruel.   325

Mirabell. I hope they are not Persons of Condition that you use at
this rate.

Petulant. Condition, Condition's a dry'd Fig, if I am not in Humour
– By this Hand, if they were your – a – a – your What-dee-call-'ems
themselves, they must wait or rub off, if I want Appetite.   330

Mirabell. What-dee-call-'ems! What are they, *Witwoud?*

Witwoud. Empresses, my Dear – By your What-dee-call-'ems he
means Sultana Queens.

Petulant. Ay, *Roxolana's.*

Mirabell. Cry you Mercy.   335

Fainall. Witwoud says they are –

Petulant. What does he say th' are?

Witwoud. I; fine Ladies I say.

Petulant. Pass on, *Witwoud* – Hearkee, by this Light his Relations –
Two Coheiresses his Cousins, and an old Aunt, that loves Catter-   340
wauling better than a Conventicle.

Witwoud. Ha, ha, ha; I had a Mind to see how the Rogue wou'd
come off – Ha, ha, ha; Gad I can't be angry with him; if he said they
were my Mother and my Sisters.

Mirabell. No!   345

Witwoud. No; the Rogue's Wit and Readiness of Invention charm
   me, dear *Petulant.*

Betty. They are gone Sir, in great Anger.

Petulant. Enough, let 'em trundle. Anger helps Complexion, saves
   Paint.   350

Fainall. This Continence is all dissembled; this is in order to have
   something to brag of the next time he makes Court to *Millamant,*
   and swear he has abandon'd the whole Sex for her Sake.

Mirabell. Have you not left off your impudent Pretensions there yet?
   I shall cut your Throat, sometime or other, *Petulant,* about that   355
   Business.

Petulant. Ay, ay, let that pass – There are other Throats to be cut –

Mirabell. Meaning mine, Sir?

Petulant. Not I – I mean no Body – I know nothing – But there are
   Uncles and Nephews in the World – And they may be Rivals – What   360
   then? All's one for that –

Mirabell. How! hearkee *Petulant,* come hither – Explain, or I shall
   call your Interpreter.

Petulant. Explain, I know nothing – Why you have an Uncle, have
   you not, lately come to Town, and lodges by my Lady *Wishfort's?*   365

Mirabell. True.

Petulant. Why that's enough – You and he are not Friends; and if he
   shou'd marry and have a Child, you may be disinherited, ha?

Mirabell. Where hast thou stumbled upon all this Truth?

Petulant. All's one for that; why then say I know something.   370

Mirabell. Come, thou art an honest Fellow, *Petulant,* and shalt make
   Love to my Mistress, thou sha't, Faith. What hast thou heard of my
   Uncle?

Petulant. I, nothing I. If Throats are to be cut, let Swords clash;
   snugs the Word, I shrug and am silent.   375

Mirabell. O Raillery, Raillery. Come, I know thou art in the Women's
   Secrets – What you're a Cabalist, I know you staid at *Millamant's*
   last Night, after I went. Was there any mention made of my Uncle,
   or me? Tell me; if thou hadst but good Nature equal to thy Wit
   Petulant, Tony Witwoud, who is now thy Competitor in Fame,   380
   wou'd shew as dim by thee as a dead Whiting's Eye, by a Pearl of
   Orient; he wou'd no more be seen by thee, then *Mercury* is by the
   Sun: Come, I'm sure thou wo't tell me.

Petulant. If I do, will you grant me common Sense then, for the
   future?   385

Mirabell. Faith I'll do what I can for thee; and I'll pray that Heav'n
   may grant it thee in the mean time.

Petulant. Well, hearkee.

Fainall. Petulant and you both will find *Mirabell* as warm a Rival as a
   Lover.   390

Witwoud. Pshaw, pshaw, that she laughs at *Petulant* is plain. And for
   my part – But that it is almost a Fashion to admire her, I shou'd –

Hearkee – To tell you a Secret, but let it go no further – Between
Friends, I shall never break my Heart for her.

Fainall. How! 395

Witwoud. She's handsome; but she's a sort of an uncertain Woman.

Fainall. I thought you had dy'd for her.

Witwoud. Umh – No –

Fainall. She has Wit.

Witwoud. 'Tis what she will hardly allow any Body else; – Now, 400
Demme, I shou'd hate that, if she were as handsome as *Cleopatra.*
Mirabell is not so sure of her as he thinks for.

Fainall. Why do you think so?

Witwoud. We staid pretty late there last Night; and heard something
of an Uncle to *Mirabell*, who is lately come to Town, – and is 405
between him and the best part of his Estate; *Mirabell* and he are
at some distance, as my Lady *Wishfort* has been told; and you know
she hates *Mirabell*, worse than a Quaker hates a Parrot, or than a
Fishmonger hates a hard Frost. Whether this Uncle has seen Mrs.
Millamant or not, I cannot say; but there were Items of such a 410
Treaty being in Embrio; and if it shou'd come to Life; poor *Mirabell*
wou'd be in some sort unfortunately fobb'd i'faith.

Fainall. 'Tis impossible *Millamant* should hearken to it.

Witwoud. Faith, my Dear, I can't tell; she's a Woman and a kind of a
Humorist. 415

Mirabell. And this is the Sum of what you cou'd collect last Night.

Petulant. The Quintessence. May be *Witwoud* knows more, he stay'd
longer – Besides they never mind him; they say any thing before him.

Mirabell. I thought you had been the greatest Favourite.

Petulant. Ay *teste a teste*; But not in publick, because I make Remarks. 420

Mirabell. Do you.

Petulant. Ay, ay, pox I'm malicious, Man. Now he's soft you know,
they are not in awe of him – The Fellow's well bred, he's what you
call a – What-dee-call-'em. A fine Gentleman, but he's silly withal.

Mirabell. I thank you, I know as much as my Curiosity requires. 425
Fainall, are you for the *Mall*?

Fainall. Ay, I'll take a turn before Dinner.

Witwoud. Ay, we'll all walk in the Park, the Ladies talk'd of being there.

Mirabell. I thought you were oblig'd to watch for your Brother Sir
Wilfull's arrival. 430

Witwoud. No, no, he comes to his Aunts, my Lady *Wishfort*; pox on
him, I shall be troubled with him too; what shall I do with the Fool?

Petulant. Beg him for his Estate; that I may beg you afterwards; and
so have but one Trouble with you both.

Witwoud. O rare *Petulant*; thou art as quick as a Fire in a frosty 435
Morning; thou shalt to the *Mall* with us; and we'll be very severe.

Petulant. Enough, I'm in a Humour to be severe.

Mirabell. Are you? Pray then walk by your selves, – Let not us be
accessary to your putting the Ladies out of Countenance, with your
senseless Ribaldry; which you roar out aloud as often as they pass by 440

you; and when you have made a handsome Woman blush, then you
think you have been severe.

Petulant. What, what? Then let 'em either shew their Innocence by
not understanding what they hear, or else shew their Discretion by
not hearing what they would not be thought to understand.   445

Mirabell. But hast not thou then Sense enough to know that thou
ought'st to be most asham'd thy Self, when thou hast put another
out of Countenance.

Petulant. Not I, by this Hand – I always take blushing either for a ·
Sign of Guilt, or ill Breeding.   450

Mirabell. I confess you ought to think so. You are in the right, that you
may plead the error of your Judgment in defence of your Practice.
Where Modesty's ill Manners, 'tis but fit
That Impudence and Malice, pass for Wit.

Exeunt.

Act II

Scene I

St. James's Park.

Enter Mrs. Fainall *and* Mrs. Marwood.

Mrs. Fainall. Ay, ay, dear *Marwood*, if we will be happy, we must find
the means in our selves, and among our selves. Men are ever in
Extreams; either doating or averse. While they are Lovers, if they
have Fire and Sense, their Jealousies are insupportable: And when
they cease to Love, (we ought to think at least) they loath; they look   5
upon us with Horror and Distaste; they meet us like the Ghosts of
what we were, and as such fly from us.

Mrs. Marwood. True, 'tis an unhappy Circumstance of Life, that Love
shou'd ever die before us; and that the Man so often shou'd out-live
the Lover. But say what you will, 'tis better to be left, than never to   10
have been lov'd. To pass our Youth in dull Indifference, to refuse
the Sweets of Life because they once must leave us; is as preposterous, as to wish to have been born Old, because we one Day must be
Old. For my part, my Youth may wear and waste, but it shall never
rust in my Possession.   15

Mrs. Fainall. Then it seems you dissemble an Aversion to Mankind,
only in compliance with my Mothers Humour.

Mrs. Marwood. Certainly. To be free; I have no Taste of those insipid
dry Discourses, with which our Sex of force must entertain themselves, apart from Men. We may affect Endearments to each other,   20
profess eternal Friendships, and seem to doat like Lovers; but 'tis not
in our Natures long to persevere. Love will resume his Empire in our
Breasts, and every Heart, or soon or late, receive and readmit him as
its lawful Tyrant.

Mrs. Fainall. Bless me, how have I been deceiv'd! Why you profess a   25
Libertine.

Mrs. Marwood. You see my Friendship by my Freedom. Come, be as
sincere, acknowledge that your Sentiments agree with mine.

Mrs. Fainall. Never.

Mrs. Marwood. You hate Mankind?   30

Mrs. Fainall. Heartily, Inveterately.

Mrs. Marwood. Your Husband?

Mrs. Fainall. Most transcendantly; ay, tho' I say it, meritoriously.

Mrs. Marwood. Give me your Hand upon it.

Mrs. Fainall. There.   35

Mrs. Marwood. I join with you; what I have said, has been to try
you.

Mrs. Fainall. Is it possible? Dost thou hate those Vipers Men?

Mrs. Marwood. I have done hating 'em; and am now come to despise
'em; the next thing I have to do, is eternally to forget 'em.   40

Mrs. Fainall. There spoke the Spirit of an *Amazon*, a *Penthesilea*.

Mrs. Marwood. And yet I am thinking sometimes, to carry my Aversion further.

Mrs. Fainall. How?

Mrs. Marwood. Faith by Marrying; if I cou'd but find one that lov'd   45
me very well, and would be throughly sensible of ill usage; I think I
shou'd do my self the violence of undergoing the Ceremony.

Mrs. Fainall. You would not make him a Cuckold?

Mrs. Marwood. No; but I'd make him believe I did, and that's as bad.

Mrs. Fainall. Why, had not you as good do it?   50

Mrs. Marwood. O if he shou'd ever discover it, he wou'd then know
the worst; and be out of his Pain; but I wou'd have him ever to
continue upon the Rack of Fear and Jealousy.

Mrs. Fainall. Ingenious Mischief! Wou'd thou wert married to *Mirabell.*   55

Mrs. Marwood. Wou'd I were.

Mrs. Fainall. You change Colour.

Mrs. Marwood. Because I hate him.

Mrs. Fainall. So do I; but I can hear him nam'd. But what Reason
have you to hate him in particular?   60

Mrs. Marwood. I never lov'd him; he is, and always was insufferably
proud.

Mrs. Fainall. By the Reason you give for your Aversion, one wou'd
think it dissembl'd; for you have laid a Fault to his Charge, of which
his Enemies must acquit him.   65

Mrs. Marwood. O then it seems you are one of his favourable Enemies. Methinks you look a little pale, and now you flush again.

Mrs. Fainall. Do I? I think I am a little sick o' the suddain.

Mrs. Marwood. What ails you?

Mrs. Fainall. My Husband. Don't you see him? He turn'd short   70
upon me unawares, and has almost overcome me.

Enter Fainall *and* Mirabell.

Mrs. Marwood. Ha, ha, ha; he comes opportunely for you.

Mrs. Fainall. For you, for he has brought *Mirabell* with him.

Fainall. My Dear.

Mrs. Fainall. My Soul.   75

Fainall. You don't look well to Day, Child.

Mrs. Fainall. Dee think so?

Mirabell. He is the only Man that do's, Madam.

Mrs. Fainall. The only Man that would tell me so at least; and the
    only Man from whom I could hear it without Mortification.   80

Fainall. O my Dear I am satisfy'd of your Tenderness; I know you
    cannot resent any thing from me; especially what is an effect of my
    Concern.

Mrs. Fainall. Mr. *Mirabell*; my Mother interrupted you in a pleasant
    Relation last Night: I wou'd fain hear it out.   85

Mirabell. The Persons concern'd in that Affair, have yet a tollerable
    Reputation – I am afraid Mr. *Fainall* will be Censorious.

Mrs. Fainall. He has a Humour more prevailing than his Curiosity,
    and will willingly dispence with the hearing of one scandalous Story,
    to avoid giving an occasion to make another by being seen to walk   90
    with his Wife. This way Mr. *Mirabell*, and I dare promise you will
    oblige us both.

Exeunt Mrs. Fainall *and* Mirabell.

Fainall. Excellent Creature! Well sure if I shou'd live to be rid of my
    Wife, I shou'd be a miserable Man.

Mrs. Marwood. Ay!   95

Fainall. For having only that one Hope, the accomplishment of it, of
    Consequence must put an end to all my hopes; and what a Wretch is
    he who must survive his hopes! Nothing remains when that Day
    comes, but to sit down and weep like *Alexander*, when he wanted
    other Worlds to conquer.   100

Mrs. Marwood. Will you not follow 'em?

Fainall. Faith, I think not.

Mrs. Marwood. Pray let us; I have a Reason.

Fainall. You are not Jealous?

Mrs. Marwood. Of whom?   105

Fainall. Of *Mirabell.*

Mrs. Marwood. If I am, is it inconsistent with my Love to you that I
    am tender of your Honour?

Fainall. You wou'd intimate then, as if there were a *fellow-feeling*
    between my Wife and Him.   110

Mrs. Marwood. I think she do's not hate him to that degree she
    wou'd be thought.

Fainall. But he, I fear, is too Insensible.

Mrs. Marwood. It may be you are deceiv'd.

Fainall. It may be so. I do now begin to apprehend it.   115

Mrs. Marwood. What?

Fainall. That I have been deceiv'd Madam, and you are false.

Mrs. Marwood. That I am false! What mean you?

Fainall. To let you know I see through all your little Arts – Come, you both love him; and both have equally dissembl'd your Aver-   120
sion. Your mutual Jealousies of one another, have made you clash till you have both struck Fire. I have seen the warm Confession red'ning on your Cheeks, and sparkling from your Eyes.

Mrs. Marwood. You do me wrong.

Fainall. I do not – 'Twas for my ease to oversee and wilfully neglect the   125
gross advances made him by my Wife; that by permitting her to be engag'd, I might continue unsuspected in my Pleasures; and take you oftner to my Arms in full Security. But cou'd you think because the nodding Husband would not wake, that e'er the watchful Lover slept!

Mrs. Marwood. And wherewithal can you reproach me?   130

Fainall. With Infidelity, with loving of another, with love of *Mirabell.*

Mrs. Marwood. 'Tis false. I challenge you to shew an Instance that can confirm your groundless Accusation. I hate him.

Fainall. And wherefore do you hate him? He is Insensible, and your Resentment follows his Neglect. An Instance? The Injuries you   135
have done him are a proof; Your interposing in his Love. What cause had you to make Discoveries of his pretended Passion? To undeceive the credulous Aunt, and be the officious Obstacle of his Match with *Millamant?*

Mrs. Marwood. My Obligations to my Lady urg'd me: I had profess'd   140
Friendship to her; and could not see her easie Nature so abus'd by that Dissembler.

Fainall. What, was it Conscience then! profess'd a Friendship! O the pious Friendships of the Female Sex!

Mrs. Marwood. More tender, more sincere, and more enduring, than   145
all the vain and empty Vows of Men, whether professing Love to us, or mutual Faith to one another.

Fainall. Ha, ha, ha; you are my Wife's Friend too.

Mrs. Marwood. Shame and Ingratitude! Do you reproach me? You, you upbraid me! Have I been false to her, thro' strict Fidelity to   150
you, and sacrific'd my Friendship to keep my Love inviolate? And have you the baseness to charge me with the Guilt, unmindful of the Merit! To you it shou'd be meritorious, that I have been vicious. And do you reflect that Guilt upon me, which should lie buried in your Bosom?   155

Fainall. You misinterpret my Reproof. I meant but to remind you of the slight Account you once could make of strictest Ties, when set in Competition with your Love to me.

Mrs. Marwood. 'Tis false, you urg'd it with deliberate Malice – 'Twas spoke in scorn, and I never will forgive it.   160

Fainall. Your Guilt, not your Resentment, begets your Rage. If yet you lov'd, you could forgive a Jealousy: But you are stung to find you are discover'd.

Mrs. Marwood. It shall be all discover'd. You too shall be discover'd; be sure you shall. I can but be expos'd – If I do it my self I shall   165
prevent your Baseness.

Fainall. Why, what will you do?

Mrs. Marwood. Disclose it to your Wife; own what has past between us.

Fainall. Frenzy!

Mrs. Marwood. By all my Wrongs I'll do't – I'll publish to the World   170
the Injuries you have done me, both in my Fame and Fortune: With
both I trusted you, you Bankrupt in Honour, as indigent of Wealth.

Fainall. Your Fame I have preserv'd. Your Fortune has been
bestow'd as the prodigality of your Love would have it, in Pleasures
which we both have shar'd. Yet had not you been false, I had e'er   175
this repaid it – 'Tis true – Had you permitted *Mirabell* with *Millamant* to have stoll'n their Marriage, my Lady had been incens'd
beyond all means of reconcilement: *Millamant* had forfeited the
Moiety of her Fortune; which then wou'd have descended to my
Wife; – And wherefore did I marry, but to make lawful Prize of a   180
rich Widow's Wealth, and squander it on Love and you?

Mrs. Marwood. Deceit and frivolous Pretence.

Fainall. Death, am I not married? what's pretence? Am I not Impri-
son'd, Fetter'd? Have I not a Wife? Nay a Wife that was a Widow, a
young Widow, a handsome Widow; and would be again a Widow,   185
but that I have a Heart of Proof, and something of a Constitution
to bustle thro' the ways of Wedlock and this World. Will you yet be
reconcil'd to Truth and me?

Mrs. Marwood. Impossible. Truth and you are inconsistent – I hate
you, and shall for ever.   190

Fainall. For loving you?

Mrs. Marwood. I loath the name of Love after such usage; and next to
the Guilt with which you wou'd asperse me, I scorn you most.
Farewell.

Fainall. Nay, we must not part thus.   195

Mrs. Marwood. Let me go.

Fainall. Come, I'm sorry.

Mrs. Marwood. I care not – Let me go – Break my Hands, do – I'd
leave 'em to get loose.

Fainall. I would not hurt you for the World. Have I no other Hold to   200
keep you here?

Mrs. Marwood. Well, I have deserv'd it all.

Fainall. You know I love you.

Mrs. Marwood. Poor dissembling! – O that – Well, it is not yet –

Fainall. What? what is it not? What is it not yet? It is not yet too late –   205

Mrs. Marwood. No, it is not yet too late – I have that Comfort.

Fainall. It is to love another.

Mrs. Marwood. But not to loath, detest, abhor Mankind, my self and
the whole treacherous World.

Fainall. Nay, this is Extravagance – Come I ask your Pardon – No   210
Tears – I was to blame, I cou'd not love you and be easie in my

Doubts – Pray forbear – I believe you; I'm convinc'd I've done you wrong; and any way, every way will make amends; – I'll hate my Wife yet more, Dam her, I'll part with her, rob her of all she's worth, and we'll retire somewhere, any where to another World. I'll marry thee   215
– Be pacify'd – 'Sdeath they come, hide your Face, your Tears – You have a Mask, wear it a Moment. This way, this way, be persuaded.

Exeunt.

Enter Mirabell *and* Mrs. Fainall.

Mrs. Fainall. They are here yet.
Mirabell. They are turning into the other Walk.
Mrs. Fainall. While I only hated my Husband, I could bear to see   220
him; but since I have despis'd him, he's too offensive.
Mirabell. O you should Hate with Prudence.
Mrs. Fainall. Yes, for I have Lov'd with Indiscretion.
Mirabell. You shou'd have just so much disgust for your Husband, as
may be sufficient to make you relish your Lover.   225
Mrs. Fainall. You have been the cause that I have lov'd without
Bounds, and wou'd you set Limits to that Aversion, of which you
have been the occasion? Why did you make me marry this Man?
Mirabell. Why do we daily commit disagreeable and dangerous
Actions? To save that Idol Reputation. If the familiarities of our   230
Loves had produc'd that Consequence, of which you were appre-
hensive, where could you have fix'd a Father's Name with Credit, but
on a Husband? I knew *Fainall* to be a Man lavish of his Morals, an
interested and professing Friend, a false and a designing Lover; yet
one whose Wit and outward fair Behaviour have gain'd a Reputation   235
with the Town, enough to make that Woman stand excus'd, who has
suffer'd herself to be won by his Addresses. A better Man ought not
to have been sacrific'd to the Occasion; a worse had not answer'd to
the Purpose. When you are weary of him, you know your Remedy.
Mrs. Fainall. I ought to stand in some degree of Credit with you,   240
Mirabell.
Mirabell. In Justice to you, I have made you privy to my whole
Design, and put it in your Power to ruin or advance my Fortune.
Mrs. Fainall. Whom have you instructed to represent your pretended
Uncle?   245
Mirabell. Waitwell, my Servant.
Mrs. Fainall. He is an humble Servant to *Foible* my Mothers Woman;
and may win her to your Interest.
Mirabell. Care is taken for that – She is won and worn by this time.
They were married this morning.   250
Mrs. Fainall. Who?
Mirabell. Waitwell and *Foible.* I wou'd not tempt my Servant to betray
me by trusting him too far. If your Mother, in hopes to ruin me,
shou'd consent to marry my pretended Uncle, he might like *Mosca*
in the *Fox,* stand upon Terms; so I made him sure beforehand.   255

Mrs. Fainall. So, if my poor Mother is caught in a Contract, you will discover the Imposture betimes; and release her by producing a Certificate of her Gallants former Marriage.

Mirabell. Yes, upon Condition she consent to my Marriage with her Niece, and surrender the Moiety of her Fortune in her Posses- 260 sion.

Mrs. Fainall. She talk'd last Night of endeavouring at a Match between *Millamant* and your Uncle.

Mirabell. That was by *Foible's* Direction, and my Instruction, that she might seem to carry it more privately. 265

Mrs. Fainall. Well, I have an Opinion of your Success; for I believe my Lady will do any thing to get a Husband; and when she has this, which you have provided for her, I suppose she will submit to any thing to get rid of him.

Mirabell. Yes, I think the good Lady wou'd marry any Thing that 270 resembl'd a Man, tho' 'twere no more than what a Butler cou'd pinch out of a Napkin.

Mrs. Fainall. Female Frailty! We must all come to it, if we live to be Old and feel the craving of a false Appetite when the true is decay'd. 275

Mirabell. An old Woman's Appetite is deprav'd like that of a Girl – 'Tis the Green Sickness of a second Childhood; and like the faint Offer of a latter Spring, serves but to usher in the Fall; and withers in an affected Bloom.

Mrs. Fainall. Here's your Mistress.

Enter Mrs. Millamant, Witwoud, *and* Mincing. 280

Mirabell. Here she comes i'faith full sail, with her Fan spread and her Streamers out, and a shoal of Fools for Tenders – Ha, no, I cry her Mercy.

Mrs. Fainall. I see but one poor empty Sculler; and he tows her Woman after him. 285

Mirabell. You seem to be unattended, Madam – You us'd to have the *Beau-mond* Throng after you; and a Flock of gay fine Perrukes hovering round you.

Witwoud. Like Moths about a Candle – I had like to have lost my Comparison for want of Breath. 290

Millamant. O I have deny'd my self Airs to Day. I have walk'd as fast through the Crowd –

Witwoud. As a Favourite in disgrace; and with as few Followers.

Millamant. Dear Mr. *Witwoud,* truce with your Similitudes: For I am as sick of 'em – 295

Witwoud. As a Phisician of a good Air – I cannot help it Madam, tho' 'tis against my self.

Millamant. Yet again! *Mincing,* stand between me and his Wit.

Witwoud. Do Mrs. *Mincing,* like a Skreen before a great Fire. I confess I do blaze to Day, I am too bright. 300

Mrs. Fainall. But dear *Millamant,* why were you so long?

Millamant. Long! Lord, have I not made violent haste? I have ask'd every living Thing I met for you; I have enquir'd after you, as after a new Fashion.

Witwoud. Madam, truce with your Similitudes – No, you met her 305
Husband and did not ask him for her.

Mirabell. By your leave *Witwoud*, that were like enquiring after an old Fashion, to ask a Husband for his Wife.

Witwoud. Hum, a hit, a hit, a palpable hit, I confess it.

Mrs. Fainall. You were dress'd before I came abroad. 310

Millamant. Ay, that's true – O but then I had – *Mincing* what had I? Why was I so long?

Mincing. O Mem, your Laship staid to peruse a Pecquet of Letters.

Millamant. O ay, Letters – I had Letters – I am persecuted with Letters – I hate Letters – No Body knows how to write Letters; 315
and yet one has 'em, one does not know why – They serve one to pin up one's Hair.

Witwoud. Is that the way? Pray Madam, do you pin up your Hair with all your Letters? I find I must keep Copies.

Millamant. Only with those in Verse, Mr. *Witwoud.* I never pin up 320
my Hair with Prose. I fancy ones Hair wou'd not curl if it were pinn'd up with Prose. I think I try'd once *Mincing.*

Mincing. O Mem, I shall never forget it.

Millamant. Ay, poor *Mincing* tift and tift all the morning.

Mincing. 'Till I had the Cremp in my Fingers I'll vow Mem. And all 325
to no purpose. But when your Laship pins it up with Poetry, it sits so pleasant the next Day as any Thing, and is so pure and so crips.

Witwoud. Indeed, so crips?

Mincing. You're such a Critick, Mr. *Witwoud.*

Millamant. Mirabell, Did not you take Exceptions last Night? O ay, 330
and went away – Now I think on't I'm angry – No, now I think on't I'm pleas'd – For I believe I gave you some Pain.

Mirabell. Do's that please you?

Millamant. Infinitely; I love to give Pain.

Mirabell. You wou'd affect a Cruelty which is not in your Nature; 335
your true Vanity is in the power of pleasing.

Millamant. O I ask your Pardon for that – One's Cruelty is one's Power, and when one parts with one's Cruelty, one parts with one's Power; and when one has parted with that, I fancy one's Old and Ugly.

Mirabell. Ay, ay, suffer your Cruelty to ruin the object of your Power, 340
to destroy your Lover – And then how vain how lost a Thing you'll be! Nay, 'tis true: You are no longer handsome when you've lost your Lover; your Beauty dies upon the Instant: For Beauty is the Lover's Gift; 'tis he bestows your Charms – Your Glass is all a Cheat. The Ugly and the Old, whom the Looking-glass mortifies, yet after 345
Commendation can be flatter'd by it, and discover Beauties in it: For that reflects our Praises, rather than your Face.

Millamant. O the Vanity of these Men! *Fainall*, dee hear him? If they did not commend us, we were not handsome! Now you must know

they could not commend one, if one was not handsome. Beauty the 350
Lover's Gift – Lord, what is a Lover, that it can give? Why one
makes Lovers as fast as one pleases, and they live as long as one
pleases, and they die as soon as one pleases: And then if one pleases,
one makes more.

Witwoud. Very pretty. Why you make no more of making of Lovers, 355
Madam, than of making so many Card-matches.

Millamant. One no more owes one's Beauty to a Lover, than one's
Wit to an Eccho: They can but reflect what we look and say; vain
empty Things if we are silent or unseen, and want a being.

Mirabell. Yet to those two vain empty Things, you owe two the 360
greatest Pleasures of your Life.

Millamant. How so?

Mirabell. To your Lover you owe the pleasure of hearing your selves
prais'd; and to an Eccho the pleasure of hearing your selves talk.

Witwoud. But I know a Lady that loves talking so incessantly, she 365
won't give an Eccho fair play; she has that everlasting Rotation of
Tongue, that an Eccho must wait till she dies, before it can catch her
last Words.

Millamant. O Fiction; *Fainall*, let us leave these Men.

Mirabell [*aside to* Mrs. Fainall]. Draw off *Witwoud*. 370

Mrs. Fainall. Immediately; I have a Word or two for Mr. *Witwoud*.

Mirabell. I wou'd beg a little private Audience too –

Exit Witwoud *and* Mrs. Fainall.

You had the Tyranny to deny me last Night; tho' you knew I came
to impart a Secret to you, that concern'd my Love.

Millamant. You saw I was engag'd. 375

Mirabell. Unkind. You had the leisure to entertain a Herd of Fools;
Things who visit you from their excessive Idleness; bestowing on
your easiness that time, which is the incumbrance of their Lives. How
can you find delight in such Society? It is impossible they should
admire you, they are not capable: Or if they were, it shou'd be to you 380
as a Mortification; for sure to please a Fool is some degree of Folly.

Millamant. I please my self – Besides sometimes to converse with
Fools, is for my Health.

Mirabell. Your Health! Is there a worse Disease than the Conversation of Fools? 385

Millamant. Yes, the Vapours; Fools are Physicks for it, next to *Assa-
fœtida*.

Mirabell. You are not in a Course of Fools?

Millamant. *Mirabell*, If you persist in this offensive Freedom – You'll
displease me – I think I must resolve after all, not to have you – We 390
shan't agree.

Mirabell. Not in our Physick it may be.

Millamant. And yet our Distemper in all likelihood will be the same;
for we shall be sick of one another. I shan't endure to be repri-
manded, nor instructed; 'tis so dull to act always by Advice, and so 395

tedious to be told of ones Faults – I can't bear it. Well, I won't have you *Mirabell* – I'm resolv'd – I think – You may go – Ha, ha, ha. What wou'd you give, that you cou'd help loving me?

Mirabell. I would give something that you did not know, I cou'd not help it.   400

Millamant. Come, don't look grave then. Well, what do you say to me?

Mirabell. I say that a Man may as soon make a Friend by his Wit, or a Fortune by his Honesty, as win a Woman with plain Dealing and Sincerity.   405

Millamant. Sententious *Mirabell!* Prithee don't look with that violent and inflexible wise Face, like *Solomon* at the dividing of the Child in an old Tapestry-hanging.

Mirabell. You are merry, Madam, but I wou'd perswade you for one Moment to be serious.   410

Millamant. What, with that Face? No, if you keep your Countenance, 'tis impossible I shou'd hold mine. Well, after all, there is something very moving in a love-sick Face. Ha, ha, ha – Well I won't laugh, don't be peevish – Heigho! Now I'll be melancholly, as melancholly as a Watch-light. Well *Mirabell*, If ever you will win me woe me now –   415
Nay, if you are so tedious, fare you well; – I see they are walking away.

Mirabell. Can you not find in the variety of your Disposition one Moment –

Millamant. To hear you tell me that *Foible's* married, and your Plot like to speed – No.   420

Mirabell. But how you came to know it –

Millamant. Unless by the help of the Devil you can't imagine; unless she shou'd tell me her self. Which of the two it may have been, I will leave you to consider; and when you have done thinking of that; think of me.   425

                                                                                          Exit.

Mirabell. I have something more – Gone – Think of you! To think of a Whirlwind, tho' 'twere in a Whirlwind, were a Case of more steady Contemplation; a very tranquility of Mind and Mansion. A Fellow that lives in a Windmill, has not a more whimsical Dwelling than the Heart of a Man that is lodg'd in a Woman. There is no Point of the   430
Compass to which they cannot turn, and by which they are not turn'd; and by one as well as another; for Motion not Method is their Occupation. To know this, and yet continue to be in Love, is to be made wise from the Dictates of Reason, and yet persevere to play the Fool by the force of Instinct – O here come my pair of   435
Turtles – What, billing so sweetly! Is not *Valentine's* Day over with you yet?

                              Enter Waitwell *and* Foible.

Sirrah, *Waitwell,* why sure you think you were married for your own Recreation, and not for my Conveniency.

Waitwell. Your Pardon, Sir. With Submission, we have indeed been 440
   solacing in lawful Delights; but still with an Eye to Business, Sir. I
   have instructed her as well as I cou'd. If she can take your Directions
   as readily as my Instructions, Sir, your Affairs are in a prosperous way.
Mirabell. Give you Joy, Mrs. *Foible.*
Foible. O las Sir, I'm so asham'd – I'm afraid my Lady has been in a 445
   thousand Inquietudes for me. But I protest, Sir, I made as much
   haste as I could.
Waitwell. That she did indeed, Sir. It was my Fault that she did not
   make more.
Mirabell. That I believe. 450
Foible. But I told my Lady as you instructed me, Sir. That I had a
   prospect of seeing Sir *Rowland* your Uncle; and that I wou'd put
   her Ladyship's Picture in my Pocket to shew him; which I'll be sure
   to say has made him so enamour'd of her Beauty, that he burns with
   Impatience to lie at her Ladyship's Feet and worship the Original. 455
Mirabell. Excellent *Foible*! Matrimony has made you eloquent in Love.
Waitwell. I think she has profited, Sir. I think so.
Foible. You have seen Madam *Millamant*, Sir?
Mirabell. Yes.
Foible. I told her Sir, because I did not know that you might find an 460
   Opportunity; she had so much Company last Night.
Mirabell. Your Diligence will merit more – In the mean time –

Gives Mony.

Foible. O dear Sir, your humble Servant.
Waitwell. Spouse.
Mirabell. Stand off Sir, not a Penny – Go on and prosper, *Foible* – The 465
   Lease shall be made good and the Farm stock'd, if we succeed.
Foible. I don't question your Generosity, Sir: And you need not doubt
   of Success. If you have no more Commands Sir, I'll be gone; I'm sure
   my Lady is at her Toilet, and can't dress till I come – [*Looking out.*] O
   Dear, I'm sure that was Mrs. *Marwood* that went by in a Mask; if she 470
   has seen me with you I'm sure she'll tell my Lady. I'll make haste
   home and prevent her. Your Servant Sir. B'w'y *Waitwell.*

Exit Foible.

Waitwell. Sir *Rowland* if you please. The Jade's so pert upon her
   Preferment she forgets her self.
Mirabell. Come Sir, will you endeavour to forget your self – And 475
   transform into Sir *Rowland.*
Waitwell. Why Sir; it will be impossible I shou'd remember my self –
   Married, Knighted and attended all in one Day! 'Tis enough to
   make any Man forget himself. The Difficulty will be how to recover
   my Acquaintance and Familiarity with my former self; and fall from 480
   my Transformation to a Reformation into *Waitwell.* Nay, I shan't
   be quite the same *Waitwell* neither – For now I remember me, I am
   married, and can't be my own Man again.

Ay there's the Grief; that's the sad change of Life; To lose my Title, and
yet keep my Wife.   485

Exeunt.

Act III

Scene I

A Room in Lady Wishfort's *House.*

Lady Wishfort *at her Toilet,* Peg *waiting.*

Lady Wishfort. Merciful, no News of *Foible* yet?
Peg. No, Madam.
Lady Wishfort. I have no more patience – If I have not fretted my self
    till I am pale again, there's no Veracity in me. Fetch me the Red –
    The Red, do you hear, Sweet-heart? An errant Ash colour, as I'm a   5
    Person. Look you how this Wench stirs! Why dost thou not fetch me
    a little Red? Did'st thou not hear me, Mopus?
Peg. The red *Ratifia* does your Ladyship mean, or the Cherry Brandy?
Lady Wishfort. *Ratifia*, Fool? No Fool. Not the *Ratifia* Fool – Grant
    me patience! I mean the *Spanish* Paper Idiot, Complexion Darling.   10
    Paint, Paint, Paint, dost thou understand that, Changeling, dangling
    thy Hands like Bobbins before thee. Why dost thou not stir Puppet?
    thou wooden Thing upon Wires.
Peg. Lord, Madam, your Ladyship is so impatient – I cannot come at
    the Paint, Madam; Mrs. *Foible* has lock'd it up, and carry'd the Key   15
    with her.
Lady Wishfort. A Pox take you both – Fetch me the Cherry-Brandy
    then – [*Exit* Peg]. I'm as pale and as faint, I look like Mrs. Qualmsick
    the Curate's Wife, that's always breeding – Wench, come, come,
    Wench, what art thou doing, Sipping? Tasting? Save thee, dost thou   20
    not know the Bottle?

Enter Peg with a Bottle and China-cup.

Peg. Madam, I was looking for a Cup.
Lady Wishfort. A Cup, save thee, and what a Cup hast thou brought!
    Dost thou take me for a *Fairy*, to drink out of an *Acorn*? Why didst
    thou not bring thy Thimble? Hast thou ne'er a Brass-Thimble   25
    clinking in thy Pocket with a bit of Nutmeg? I warrant thee.
    Come, fill, fill. – So – again See who that is – [*One knocks.*] Set
    down the Bottle first. Here, here, under the Table – What wou'dst
    thou go with the Bottle in thy Hand like a Tapster. As I'm a Person,
    this Wench has liv'd in an Inn upon the Road, before she came to   30
    me, like *Maritornes* the *Asturian* in *Don Quixote*. No *Foible* yet?
Peg. No Madam, Mrs. *Marwood.*
Lady Wishfort. O *Marwood*, let her come in. Come in good *Marwood.*

Enter Mrs. Marwood.

Mrs. Marwood. I'm surpriz'd to find your Ladyship in *dishabilie* at this time of day. 35

Lady Wishfort. *Foible's* a lost Thing; has been abroad since Morning, and never heard of since.

Mrs. Marwood. I saw her but now, as I came mask'd through the Park, in Conference with *Mirabell.*

Lady Wishfort. With *Mirabell!* You call my Blood into my Face, with 40 mentioning that Traytor. She durst not have the Confidence. I sent her to Negotiate an Affair, in which if I'm detected I'm undone. If that wheadling Villain has wrought upon *Foible* to detect me, I'm ruin'd. Oh my dear Friend, I'm a Wretch of Wretches if I'm detected.

Mrs. Marwood. O Madam, you cannot suspect Mrs. *Foible's* Integrity. 45

Lady Wishfort. O, he carries Poyson in his Tongue that wou'd corrupt Integrity it self. If she has given him an Opportunity, she has as good as put her Integrity into his Hands. Ah dear *Marwood,* what's Integrity to an Opportunity? – Hark! I hear her – Go you Thing and send her in. [*Exit* Peg.] Dear Friend retire into my Closet, that I 50 may examine her with more freedom – You'll pardon me dear Friend, I can make bold with you – There are Books over the Chimney – *Quarles* and *Pryn,* and the *Short View of the Stage,* with *Bunyan's* Works to entertain you.

Exit Marwood.

Enter Foible.

O *Foible,* where hast thou been? What hast thou been doing? 55

Foible. Madam, I have seen the Party.

Lady Wishfort. But what hast thou done?

Foible. Nay, 'tis your Ladyship has done, and are to do; I have only promis'd. But a Man so enamour'd – So transported! Well, here it is, all that is left; all that is not kiss'd away – Well, if worshipping of 60 Pictures be a Sin – Poor Sir *Rowland,* I say.

Lady Wishfort. The Miniature has been counted like – But hast thou not betray'd me, *Foible?* Hast thou not detected me to that faithless *Mirabell?* – What had'st thou to do with him in the Park? Answer me, has he got nothing out of thee? 65

Foible [aside]. So, the Devil has been before hand with me, what shall I say? – Alas, Madam, cou'd I help it, if I met that confident Thing? Was I in Fault? If you had heard how he us'd me, and all upon your Ladyship's Account, I'm sure you wou'd not suspect my Fidelity. Nay, if that had been the worst I cou'd have born: But he had a 70 Fling at your Ladyship too; and then I could not hold; But i'faith I gave him his own.

Lady Wishfort. Me? What did the filthy Fellow say?

Foible. O Madam; 'tis a shame to say what he said – With his Taunts and his Fleers, tossing up his Nose. Humh (says he) what you are a 75 hatching some Plot (says he) you are so early abroad, or Catering (says he) ferreting for some disbanded Officer I warrant – Half Pay is but thin Subsistance (says he) – Well, what Pension does your Lady propose? Let me see (says he) what she must come down pretty deep now, she's super-annuated (says he) and –   80

Lady Wishfort. Ods my Life, I'll have him, I'll have him murder'd. I'll have him poyson'd. Where does he eat? I'll marry a Drawer to have him poyson'd in his Wine. I'll send for *Robin* from *Lockets* – Immediately.

Foible. Poyson him? Poysoning's too good for him. Starve him   85
Madam, starve him, marry Sir *Rowland* and get him disinherited. O you would bless your self, to hear what he said.

Lady Wishfort. A Villain, superannuated!

Foible. Humh (says he) I hear you are laying Designs against me too (says he), and Mrs. *Millamant* is to marry my Uncle; (he does not   90
suspect a Word of your Ladyship;) but (says he) I'll fit you for that, I warrant you (says he) I'll hamper you for that (says he) you and your old Frippery too (says he) I'll handle you –

Lady Wishfort. Audacious Villain! handle me, wou'd he durst – Frip-pery? old Frippery! Was there ever such a foul-mouth'd Fellow? I'll   95
be married to Morrow, I'll be contracted to Night.

Foible. The sooner the better, Madam.

Lady Wishfort. Will Sir *Rowland* be here, say'st thou? when *Foible?*

Foible. Incontinently, Madam. No new Sheriff's Wife expects the return of her Husband after Knighthood, with that Impatience in   100
which Sir *Rowland* burns for the dear hour of kissing your Lady-ship's Hands after Dinner.

Lady Wishfort. Frippery? Superannuated Frippery! I'll Frippery the Villain; I'll reduce him to Frippery and Rags. A Tatterdemallion – I hope to see him hung with Tatters, like a long Lane Pent-house, or   105
a Gibbet-thief. A slander-mouth'd Railer: I warrant the Spendthrift Prodigal's in Debt as much as the Million Lottery, or the whole Court upon a Birth day. I'll spoil his Credit with his Taylor. Yes, he shall have my Niece with her Fortune, he shall.

Foible. He! I hope to see him lodge in *Ludgate* first, and Angle into   110
Black Friers for Brass Farthings, with an old Mitten.

Lady Wishfort. Ay dear *Foible*, thank thee for that dear *Foible*. He has put me out of all patience. I shall never recompose my Features, to receive Sir *Rowland* with any Oeconomy of Face. This Wretch has fretted me that I am absolutely decay'd. Look *Foible.*   115

Foible. Your Ladyship has frown'd a little too rashly, indeed Madam. There are some Cracks discernable in the white Vernish.

Lady Wishfort. Let me see the Glass – Cracks, say'st thou? Why I am arrantly flea'd – I look like an old peel'd Wall. Thou must repair me *Foible*, before Sir *Rowland* comes; or I shall never keep up to my   120
Picture.

Foible. I warrant you, Madam; a little Art once made your Picture like you; and now a little of the same Art, must make you like your Picture. Your Picture must sit for you, Madam.

Lady Wishfort. But art thou sure Sir *Rowland* will not fail to come? 125
Or will a not fail when he does come? Will he be Importunate
Foible, and push? For if he shou'd not be Importunate – I shall
never break Decorums – I shall die with Confusion, if I am forc'd to
advance – Oh no, I can never advance – I shall swoon if he shou'd
expect advances. No, I hope Sir *Rowland* is better bred, than to put 130
a Lady to the necessity of breaking her Forms. I won't be too coy
neither. – I won't give him despair – But a little Disdain is not amiss;
a little Scorn is alluring.

Foible. A little Scorn becomes your Ladyship.

Lady Wishfort. Yes, but Tenderness becomes me best – A sort of a 135
dyingness – You see that Picture has a sort of a – Ha *Foible*? A
swimminess in the Eyes – Yes, I'll look so – My Niece affects it; but
she wants Features. Is Sir *Rowland* handsome? Let, my Toilet be
remov'd – I'll dress above. I'll receive Sir *Rowland* here. Is he
handsome? Don't answer me. I won't know: I'll be surpriz'd. I'll 140
be taken by Surprize.

Foible. By Storm, Madam. Sir *Rowland's* a brisk Man.

Lady Wishfort. Is he! O then he'll Importune, if he's a brisk Man. I
shall save Decorums if Sir *Rowland* importunes. I have a mortal
Terror at the apprehension of offending against Decorums. Noth- 145
ing but Importunity can surmount Decorums. O I'm glad he's a
brisk Man. Let my Things be remov'd, good *Foible*.

Exit.

Enter Mrs. Fainall.

Mrs. Fainall. O *Foible*, I have been in a Fright, least I shou'd come
too late. That Devil *Marwood* saw you in the Park with *Mirabell*,
and I'm afraid will discover it to my Lady. 150

Foible. Discover what, Madam?

Mrs. Fainall. Nay, nay, put not on that strange Face. I am privy to the
whole Design, and know that *Waitwell*, to whom thou wert this
morning Married, is to personate *Mirabell's* Uncle and as such
winning my Lady, to involve her in those Difficulties, from which 155
Mirabell only must release her, by his making his Conditions to
have my Cousin and her Fortune left to her own disposal.

Foible. O dear Madam, I beg your Pardon. It was not my Confidence
in your Ladyship that was deficient; but I thought the former good
Correspondence between your Ladyship and Mr. *Mirabell*, might 160
have hinder'd his communicating this Secret.

Mrs. Fainall. Dear *Foible* forget that.

Foible. O dear Madam, Mr. *Mirabell* is such a sweet winning Gentleman – But your Ladyship is the Pattern of Generosity. – Sweet Lady,
to be so good! Mr. *Mirabell* cannot chuse but be grateful. I find your 165
Ladyship has his Heart still. Now, Madam, I can safely tell your
Ladyship our success, Mrs. *Marwood* had told my Lady; but I
warrant I manag'd my self. I turn'd it all for the better. I told my

Lady that Mr. *Mirabell* rail'd at her. I laid horrid Things to his
charge, I'll vow; and my Lady is so incens'd, that she'll be contracted   170
to Sir *Rowland* to Night, she says; – I warrant I work'd her up, that
he may have her for asking her, as they say of a *Welch* Maiden-head.
Mrs. Fainall. O rare *Foible*!
Foible. Madam, I beg your Ladyship to acquaint Mr. *Mirabell* of his
success. I wou'd be seen as little as possible to speak to him, –   175
besides, I believe Madam *Marwood* watches me. – She has a
Month's mind; but I know Mr. *Mirabell* can't abide her. – [*Enter
Footman.*] *John* – remove my Lady's Toilet, Madam your Servant.
My Lady is so impatient, I fear she'll come for me, if I stay.
Mrs. Fainall. I'll go with you up the back Stairs, lest I shou'd meet her.   180

Exeunt.

Enter Mrs. Marwood.

Mrs. Marwood. Indeed Mrs. Engine, is it thus with you? Are you
become a go-between of this Importance? Yes, I shall watch you.
Why this Wench is the *Pass-par-tout*, a very Master-Key to every
Bodies strong Box. My Friend *Fainall*, have you carried it so swim-
mingly? I thought there was something in it; but it seems it's over   185
with you. Your loathing is not from a want of Appetite then, but from
a Surfeit. Else you could never be so cool to fall from a Principal to be
an Assistant; to procure for him! A Pattern of Generosity, that I
confess. Well, Mr. *Fainall*, you have met with your Match. – O
Man, Man! Woman, Woman! The Devil's an Ass: If I were a Painter,   190
I wou'd draw him like an Idiot, a Driveler, with a Bib and Bells. Man
shou'd have his Head and Horns, and Woman the rest of him. Poor
simple Fiend! Madam *Marwood* has a Months Mind, but he can't
abide her – 'Twere better for him you had not been his Confessor in
that Affair; without you cou'd have kept his Counsel closer. I shall   195
not prove another Pattern of Generosity; and stalk for him, till he
takes his Stand to aim at a Fortune, he has not oblig'd me to that,
with those Excesses of himself; and now I'll have none of him. Here
comes the good Lady, panting ripe; with a Heart full of Hope, and a
Head full of Care, like any Chymist upon the Day of Projection.   200

Enter Lady Wishfort.

Lady Wishfort. O dear *Marwood* what shall I say, for this rude forgetfulness – But my dear Friend is all Goodness.
Mrs. Marwood. No Apologies, dear Madam. I have been very well
entertained.
Lady Wishfort. As I'm a Person I am in a very Chaos to think I shou'd   205
so forget my self – But I have such an Olio of Affairs really I know not
what to do – [*Calls*] – *Foible* – I expect my Nephew Sir *Wilfull* every
moment too – Why *Foible* – He means to Travel for Improvement.
Mrs. Marwood. Methinks Sir *Wilfull* should rather think of Marrying
than Travelling at his Years. I hear he is turn'd of Forty.   210

Lady Wishfort. O he's in less Danger of being spoil'd by his Travels – I
am against my Nephews marrying too young. It will be time
enough when he comes back, and has acquir'd Discretion to choose
for himself.

Mrs. Marwood. Methinks Mrs. *Millamant* and he wou'd make a very 215
fit Match. He may Travel afterwards. 'Tis a Thing very usual with
young Gentlemen.

Lady Wishfort. I promise you I have thought on't – And since 'tis
your Judgment, I'll think on't again. I assure you I will; I value your
Judgment extreamly. On my Word I'll propose it. 220

Enter Foible.

Come, come *Foible* – I had forgot my Nephew will be here before
Dinner – I must make haste.

Foible. Mr. *Witwoud* and Mr. *Petulant*, are come to Dine with your
Ladyship.

Lady Wishfort. O Dear, I can't appear till I'm dress'd. Dear *Marwood* 225
shall I be free with you again, and beg you to entertain 'em. I'll
make all imaginable haste. Dear Friend excuse me.

Exit Lady *and* Foible.

Enter Mrs. Millamant *and* Mincing.

Millamant. Sure never any thing was so Unbred as that odious Man –
Marwood, your Servant.

Mrs. Marwood. You have a Colour, what's the matter? 230

Millamant. That horrid Fellow *Petulant*, has provok'd me into a
Flame – I have broke my Fan – *Mincing*, lend me yours; – Is not
all the Powder out of my Hair?

Mrs. Marwood. No, What has he done?

Millamant. Nay, he has done nothing; he has only talk'd – Nay, he 235
has said nothing neither; but he has contradicted every Thing that
has been said. For my part, I thought *Witwoud* and he wou'd have
quarrell'd.

Mincing. I vow Mem, I thought once they wou'd have fit.

Millamant. Well, 'tis a lamentable thing I'll swear, that one has not the 240
liberty of choosing one's Acquaintance, as one does one's Cloaths.

Mrs. Marwood. If we had the liberty, we shou'd be as weary of one Set
of Acquaintance, tho' never so good, as we are of one Suit, tho'
never so fine. A Fool and a *Doily* Stuff wou'd now and then find
Days of Grace, and be worn for variety. 245

Millamant. I could consent to wear 'em, if they wou'd wear alike; but
Fools never wear out – they are such *Drap-du-berry* Things! without one cou'd give 'em to one's Chamber-maid after a day or two.

Mrs. Marwood. 'Twere better so indeed. Or what think you of the
Play-house? A fine gay glossy Fool, shou'd be given there, like a 250
new masking Habit, after the Masquerade is over, and we have done
with the Disguise. For a Fool's Visit is always a Disguise; and never

admitted by a Woman of Wit, but to blind her Affair with a Lover of
Sense. If you wou'd but appear bare fac'd now, and own *Mirabell*;
you might as easily put off *Petulant* and *Witwoud*, as your Hood   255
and Scarf. And indeed 'tis time, for the Town has found it: The
secret is grown too big for the Pretence: 'Tis like Mrs. *Primly's* great
Belly; she may lace it down before, but it burnishes on her Hips.
Indeed, *Millamant*, you can no more conceal it, than my Lady
Strammel can her Face, that goodly Face, which in defiance of her   260
Rhenish-wine Tea, will not be comprehended in a Mask.

Millamant. I'll take my Death, *Marwood*, you are more Censorious,
than a decay'd Beauty, or a discarded Tost; *Mincing*, tell the Men
they may come up. My Aunt is not dressing; their Folly is less
provoking than your Mallice, the Town has found it. [*Exit* Min-   265
cing.] What has it found? That *Mirabell* loves me is no more a
Secret, than it is a Secret that you discover'd it to my Aunt, or
than the Reason why you discover'd it is a Secret.

Mrs. Marwood. You are nettl'd.

Millamant. You're mistaken. Ridiculous!   270

Mrs. Marwood. Indeed my Dear, you'll tear another Fan, if you don't
mitigate those violent Airs.

Millamant. O silly! Ha, ha, ha. I cou'd laugh immoderately. Poor
Mirabell! his Constancy to me has quite destroy'd his Complaisance
for all the World beside. I swear, I never enjoin'd it him, to be so coy   275
– If I had the Vanity to think he wou'd obey me; I wou'd command
him to shew more Gallantry – 'Tis hardly well bred to be so
particular on one Hand, and so insensible on the other. But I
despair to prevail, and so let him follow his own way. Ha, ha, ha.
Pardon me, dear Creature, I must laugh, Ha, ha, ha; tho' I grant   280
you 'tis a little barbarous, Ha, ha, ha.

Mrs. Marwood. What pity 'tis, so much fine Raillery, and deliver'd with
so significant Gesture, shou'd be so unhappily directed to miscarry.

Millamant. Ha? Dear Creature I ask your Pardon – I swear I did not
mind you.   285

Mrs. Marwood. Mr. *Mirabell* and you both, may think it a Thing
impossible, when I shall tell him, by telling you –

Millamant. O Dear, what? for it is the same thing, if I hear it – Ha, ha,
ha.

Mrs. Marwood. That I detest him, hate him, Madam.   290

Millamant. O Madam, why so do I – And yet the Creature loves me,
Ha, ha, ha. How can one forbear laughing to think of it – I am a Sybil
if I am not amaz'd to think what he can see in me. I'll take my Death,
I think you are handsomer – And within a Year or two as young. – If
you cou'd but stay for me, I shou'd overtake you – But that cannot   295
be – Well, that Thought makes me Melancholly – Now I'll be sad.

Mrs. Marwood. Your merry Note may be chang'd sooner than you
think.

Millamant. Dee say so? Then I'm resolv'd I'll have a Song to keep up
my Spirits.   300

Enter Mincing.

Mincing. The Gentlemen stay but to Comb, Madam; and will wait on you.

Millamant. Desire Mrs. – that is in the next Room to sing the Song, I wou'd have learnt Yesterday. You shall hear it Madam – Not that there's any great matter in it – But 'tis agreeable to my Humour. 305

Set by Mr. John Eccles, *and Sung by* Mrs. Hodgson.

SONG.

I.

Love's but the frailty of the Mind,
When 'tis not with Ambition join'd;
A sickly Flame, which if not fed expires;
And feeding, wasts in Self-consuming Fires. 310

II.

'Tis not to wound a wanton Boy
Or am'rous Youth, that gives the Joy;
But 'tis the Glory to have pierc'd a Swain,
For whom inferior Beauties sigh'd in vain.

III.

Then I alone the Conquest prize 315
When I insult a Rival's Eyes:
If there's Delight in Love, 'tis when I see
That Heart which others bleed for, bleed for me.

Enter Petulant *and* Witwoud.

Millamant. Is your Animosity compos'd, Gentlemen?

Witwoud. Raillery, Raillery, Madam, we have no Animosity – We hit 320 off a little Wit now and then, but no Animosity – The falling out of Wits is like the falling out of Lovers – We agree in the main, like Treble and Base. Ha, *Petulant!*

Petulant. Ay in the main – But when I have a Humour to contradict.

Witwoud. Ay, when he has a Humour to contradict, then I contradict 325 too. What, I know my Cue. Then we contradict one another like two Battle-dores: For Contradictions beget one another like *Jews.*

Petulant. If he says Black's Black – If I have a Humour to say 'tis Blue – Let that pass – All's one for that. If I have a Humour to prove it, it must be granted. 330

Witwoud. Not positively must – But it may – It may.

Petulant. Yes, it positively must, upon Proof positive.

Witwoud. Ay, upon Proof positive it must; but upon Proof presumptive it only may. That's a Logical Distinction now, Madam.

Mrs. Marwood. I perceive your Debates are of Importance and very 335 learnedly handl'd.

Petulant. Importance is one Thing, and Learning's another; but a Debate's a Debate, that I assert.

Witwoud. *Petulant*'s an Enemy to Learning; he relies altogether on his Parts.   340

Petulant. No, I'm no Enemy to Learning; it hurts not me.

Mrs. Marwood. That's a Sign indeed it's no Enemy to you.

Petulant. No, no, it's no Enemy to any Body, but them that have it.

Millamant. Well, an illiterate Man's my Aversion. I wonder at the Impudence of any Illiterate Man, to offer to make Love.   345

Witwoud. That I confess I wonder at too.

Millamant. Ah! to marry an Ignorant! that can hardly Read or Write.

Petulant. Why shou'd a Man be ever the further from being married tho' he can't Read, any more than he is from being Hang'd. The Ordinary's paid for setting the *Psalm*, and the Parish-Priest for 350 reading the Ceremony. And for the rest which is to follow in both Cases, a Man may do it without Book – So all's one for that.

Millamant. Dee hear the Creature? Lord, here's Company, I'll be gone.

Exeunt Millamant *and* Mincing.

Witwoud. In the Name of *Bartlemew* and his Fair, what have we here? 355

Mrs. Marwood. 'Tis your Brother, I fancy. Don't you know him?

Witwoud. Not I – Yes, I think it is he – I've almost forgot him; I have not seen him since the Revolution.

Enter Sir Wilfull Witwoud *in a Country Riding Habit, and Servant to* Lady Wishfort.

Servant. Sir, my Lady's dressing. Here's Company; if you please to walk in, in the mean time.   360

Sir Wilfull. Dressing! What it's but Morning here I warrant with you in *London*; we shou'd count it towards Afternoon in our Parts, down in *Shropshire* – Why then belike my Aunt han't din'd yet – Ha, Friend?

Servant. Your Aunt, Sir?

Sir Wilfull. My Aunt Sir, yes my Aunt Sir, and your Lady Sir; your 365 Lady is my Aunt, Sir – Why, what do'st thou not know me, Friend? Why then send Somebody here that does. How long hast thou liv'd with thy Lady, Fellow, ha!

Servant. A Week, Sir; longer than any Body in the House, except my Lady's Woman.   370

Sir Wilfull. Why then belike thou dost not know thy Lady, if thou see'st her, ha Friend?

Servant. Why truly Sir, I cannot safely swear to her Face in a Morning, before she is dress'd. 'Tis like I may give a shrew'd guess at her by this time.   375

Sir Wilfull. Well prithee try what thou can'st do; if thou can'st not guess, enquire her out, do'st hear Fellow? And tell her, her Nephew, *Sir Wilfull Witwoud* is in the House.

Servant. I shall, Sir.

Sir Wilfull. Hold ye, hear me Friend; a Word with you in your Ear,   380
prithee who are these Gallants?
Servant. Really Sir, I can't tell; here come so many here, 'tis hard to
know 'em all.

Exit Servant.

Sir Wilfull. Oons this Fellow knows less than a Starling; I don't think
a' knows his own Name.   385
Mrs. Marwood. Mr. *Witwoud*, your Brother is not behind Hand in
forgetfulness – I fancy he has forgot you too.
Witwoud. I hope so – The Devil take him that remembers first, I say.
Sir Wilfull. Save you Gentlemen and Lady.
Mrs. Marwood. For shame Mr. *Witwoud*; why won't you speak to   390
him? – And you, Sir.
Witwoud. Petulant speak.
Petulant. And you, Sir.
Sir Wilfull. No Offence, I hope.

Salutes Mrs. Marwood.

Mrs. Marwood. No sure, Sir.   395
Witwoud. This is a vile Dog, I see that already. No Offence! Ha, ha,
ha, to him; to him *Petulant*, smoke him.
Petulant. It seems as if you had come a Journey, Sir; hem, hem.

Surveying him round.

Sir Wilfull. Very likely, Sir, that it may seem so.
Petulant. No Offence, I hope, Sir.   400
Witwoud. Smoke the Boots, the Boots; *Petulant*, the Boots; Ha, ha, ha.
Sir Wilfull. May be not, Sir; thereafter as 'tis meant, Sir.
Petulant. Sir, I presume upon the Information of your Boots.
Sir Wilfull. Why, 'tis like you may, Sir: If you are not satisfy'd with the
Information of my Boots, Sir, if you will step to the Stable, you may   405
enquire further of my Horse, Sir.
Petulant. Your Horse, Sir! Your Horse is an Ass, Sir!
Sir Wilfull. Do you speak by way of Offence, Sir?
Mrs. Marwood. The Gentleman's merry, that's all, Sir – S'life, we shall
have a Quarrel betwixt an Horse and an Ass, before they find one   410
another out. You must not take any Thing amiss from your Friends,
Sir. You are among your Friends here, tho' it may be you don't
know it – If I am not mistaken, you are Sir *Wilfull Witwoud*.
Sir Wilfull. Right Lady; I am Sir *Wilfull Witwoud*, so I write my self;
no offence to any Body, I hope; and Nephew to the Lady *Wishfort*,   415
of this Mansion.
Mrs. Marwood. Don't you know this Gentleman, Sir?
Sir Wilfull. Hum! What sure 'tis not – Yea by'r Lady, but 'tis – 'Sheart
I know not whether 'tis or no – Yea but 'tis, by the *Rekin*. Brother
Anthony! What *Tony* i'faith! What do'st thou not know me? By'r   420
Lady nor I thee, thou art so Becravated, and Beperriwig'd – 'Sheart
why do'st not speak? Art thou o'er-joy'd?

Witwoud. Odso Brother, is it you? Your Servant Brother.

Sir Wilfull. Your Servant! Why yours, Sir. Your Servant again – 'Sheart, and your Friend and Servant to that – And a – [*puff*] and   425
a flap Dragon for your Service, Sir: And a Hare's Foot, and a Hare's Scut for your Service, Sir; an you be so cold and so courtly!

Witwoud. No offence, I hope, Brother.

Sir Wilfull. 'Sheart, Sir, but there is, and much offence. – A pox, is this your Inns o' Court breeding, not to know your Friends and   430
your Relations, your Elders, and your Betters?

Witwoud. Why Brother *Wilfull* of *Salop*, you may be as short as a *Shrewsbury* Cake, if you please. But I tell you, 'tis not modish to know Relations in Town. You think you're in the Country, where great lubberly Brothers slabber and kiss one another when they   435
meet, like a Call of Serjeants – 'Tis not the fashion here; 'tis not indeed, dear Brother.

Sir Wilfull. The Fashion's a Fool; and you're a Fop, dear Brother. 'Sheart, I've suspected this – By'r Lady I conjectur'd you were a Fop, since you began to change the Stile of your Letters, and write   440
in a scrap of Paper gilt round the Edges, no broader than a *Subpœna*. I might expect this, when you left off Honour'd Brother; and hoping you are in good Health, and so forth – To begin with a Rat me, Knight, I'm so sick of a last Nights debauch – O'ds heart, and then tell a familiar Tale of a Cock and a Bull, and a Whore and a   445
Bottle, and so conclude – You cou'd write News before you were out of your Time, when you liv'd with honest *Pumple Nose* the Attorney of *Furnival's* Inn – You cou'd intreat to be remember'd then to your Friends round the *Rekin*. We cou'd have Gazetts then, and *Dawks's* Letter, and the weekly Bill 'till of late Days.   450

Petulant. S'life, *Witwoud*, were you ever an Attorney's Clerk? Of the Family of the *Furnivals.* Ha, ha, ha!

Witwoud. Ay, ay, but that was for a while. Not long, not long; pshaw, I was not in my own Power then. An Orphan, and this Fellow was my Guardian; ay, ay, I was glad to consent to that, Man, to come to   455
London. He had the disposal of me then. If I had not agreed to that, I might have been bound Prentice to a Felt maker in *Shrewsbury*; this Fellow wou'd have bound me to a Maker of Felts.

Sir Wilfull. 'Sheart, and better than to be bound to a Maker of Fops; where, I suppose, you have serv'd your Time; and now you may set   460
up for your self.

Mrs. Marwood. You intend to Travel, Sir, as I'm inform'd.

Sir Wilfull. Belike I may Madam. I may chance to sail upon the salt Seas, if my Mind hold.

Petulant. And the Wind serve.   465

Sir Wilfull. Serve or not serve, I shant ask License of you, Sir; nor the Weather-Cock your Companion. I direct my Discourse to the Lady, Sir: 'Tis like my Aunt may have told you, Madam – Yes, I have settl'd my Concerns, I may say now, and am minded to see Foreign Parts. If an how that the Peace holds, whereby that is, Taxes abate.   470

Mrs. Marwood. I thought you had design'd for *France* at all Adventures.

Sir Wilfull. I can't tell that; 'tis like I may, and 'tis like I may not. I am somewhat dainty in making a Resolution, – because when I make it I keep it. I don't stand shill I, shall I, then; if I say't, I'll do't: But I have 475 Thoughts to tarry a small matter in Town, to learn somewhat of your *Lingo* first, before I cross the Seas. I'd gladly have a spice of your *French* as they say, whereby to hold discourse in Foreign Countries.

Mrs. Marwood. Here is an Academy in Town for that use.

Sir Wilfull. There is? 'Tis like there may. 480

Mrs. Marwood. No doubt you will return very much improv'd.

Witwoud. Yes, refin'd, like a *Dutch* Skipper from a Whale-fishing.

Enter Lady Wishort *and* Fainall.

Lady Wishfort. Nephew, you are welcome.

Sir Wilfull. Aunt, your Servant.

Fainall. Sir *Wilfull,* your most faithful Servant. 485

Sir Wilfull. Cousin *Fainall,* give me your Hand.

Lady Wishfort. Cousin *Witwoud,* your Servant; Mr. *Petulant,* your Servant. – Nephew, you are welcome again. Will you drink any Thing after your Journey, Nephew, before you eat? Dinner's almost ready. 490

Sir Wilfull. I'm very well I thank you Aunt – However, I thank you for your courteous Offer. 'Sheart, I was afraid you wou'd have been in the fashion too, and have remember'd to have forgot your Relations. Here's your Cousin *Tony,* belike, I may'nt call him Brother for fear of offence. 495

Lady Wishfort. O he's a Rallier, Nephew – My Cousin's a Wit. And your great Wits always rally their best Friends to chuse. When you have been abroad, Nephew, you'll understand Raillery better.

Fainall *and* Mrs. Marwood *talk apart.*

Sir Wilfull. Why then let him hold his Tongue in the mean time; and rail when that day comes. 500

Enter Mincing.

Mincing. Mem, I come to acquaint your Layship that Dinner is impatient.

Sir Wilfull. Impatient? Why then belike it won't stay, 'till I pull off my Boots. Sweet-heart, can you help me to a pair of Slippers? – My Man's with his Horses, I warrant. 505

Lady Wishfort. Fie, fie, Nephew, you wou'd not pull off your Boots here – Go down into the Hall – Dinner shall stay for you – My Nephew's a little unbred, you'll pardon him, Madam – Gentlemen will you walk? *Marwood* –

Mrs. Marwood. I'll follow you, Madam – Before Sir *Wilfull* is ready. 510

Manent Mrs. Marwood *and* Fainall.

Fainall. Why then *Foible's* a Bawd, an Errant, Rank, Match-making
Bawd, And I it seems am a Husband, a Rank-Husband; and my
Wife a very Errant, Rank-Wife, – all in the Way of the *World*. 'S
death to be an Anticipated Cuckold, a Cuckold in Embrio? Sure I
was born with budding Antlers like a young Satyre, or a Citizens 515
Child. 'S death to be Out-Witted, to be Out-Jilted – Out-Matri-
mony'd, – If I had kept my speed like a Stag, 'twere somewhat, –
but to crawl after, with my Horns like a Snail, and out-strip'd by my
Wife – 'tis Scurvy Wedlock.

Mrs. Marwood. Then shake it off, You have often wish'd for an 520
opportunity to part; – and now you have it. But first prevent their
Plot, – the half of *Millamant's* Fortune is too Considerable to be
parted with, to a Foe, to *Mirabell*.

Fainall. Dam him, that had been mine – had you not made that fond
discovery – that had been forfeited, had they been Married. My 525
Wife had added Lustre to my Horns, by that Encrease of fortune, –
I cou'd have worn 'em tipt with Gold, tho' my forehead had been
furnish'd like a Deputy-Lieutenant's Hall.

Mrs. Marwood. They may prove a Cap of Maintenance to you still, if
you can away with your Wife. And she's no worse than when you had 530
her – I dare swear she had given up her Game, before she was Marry'd.

Fainall. Hum! That may be – She might throw up her Cards; but I'le
be hang'd if she did not put Pam in her Pocket.

Mrs. Marwood. You Married her to keep you; and if you can contrive
to have her keep you better than you expected; why should you not 535
keep her longer than you intended?

Fainall. The means, the means.

Mrs. Marwood. Discover to my Lady your Wife's conduct; threaten to
part with her – My Lady loves her, and will come to any Composition to save her reputation, take the opportunity of breaking it, just 540
upon the discovery of this imposture. My Lady will be enraged
beyond bounds, and Sacrifice Neice, and Fortune, and all at that
Conjuncture. And let me alone to keep her warm, if she should Flag
in her part, I will not fail to prompt her.

Fainall. Faith this has an appearance. 545

Mrs. Marwood. I'm sorry I hinted to my Lady to endeavour a match
between *Millamant* and Sir *Wilfull*, that may be an Obstacle.

Fainall. O, for that matter leave me to manage him; I'll disable him
for that, he will drink like a *Dane*: after dinner, I'll set his hand in.

Mrs. Marwood. Well, how do you stand affected towards your Lady? 550

Fainall. Why faith I'm thinking of it. – Let me see – I am married
already; so that's over, – my Wife has plaid the Jade with me – Well,
that's over too – I never lov'd her, or if I had, why that wou'd have
been over too by this time – Jealous of her I cannot be, for I am
certain; so there's an end of Jealousie. Weary of her, I am, and shall 555
be – No, there's no end of that; No, no, that were too much to
hope. Thus far concerning my repose. Now for my Reputation, – As
to my own, I married not for it; so that's out of the Question, – And

as to my part in my Wife's – Why she had parted with hers before; so
bringing none to me, she can take none from me, 'tis against all rule 560
of Play, that I should lose to one, who has not where-withal to stake.

Mrs. Marwood. Besides you forget, Marriage is honourable.

Fainall. Hum! Faith and that's well thought on; Marriage is honourable as you say; and if so, Wherefore should Cuckoldom be a
discredit, being deriv'd from so honourable a root? 565

Mrs. Marwood. Nay I know not; if the root be Honourable, why not
the Branches?

Fainall. So, so, why this point's clear, – Well how do we proceed?

Mrs. Marwood. I will contrive a Letter which shall be deliver'd to my
Lady at the time when that Rascal who is to act Sir *Rowland* is with 570
her. It shall come as from an unknown hand – for the less I appear to
know of the truth – the better I can play the Incendiary. Besides I
would not have *Foible* provok'd if I cou'd help it, – because you know
she knows some passages – Nay I expect all will come out – But let the
Mine be sprung first, and then I care not if I'm discover'd. 575

Fainall. If the worst come to the worst, – I'll turn my Wife to Grass –
I have already a deed of Settlement of the best part of her Estate;
which I wheadl'd out of her; And that you shall partake at least.

Mrs. Marwood. I hope you are convinc'd that I hate *Mirabell*, now
you'll be no more Jealous. 580

Fainall. Jealous no, – by this Kiss – let Husbands be Jealous; But let the
Lover still believe. Or if he doubt, let it be only to endear his pleasure,
and prepare the Joy that follows, when he proves his Mistress true;
but let Husbands doubts Convert to endless Jealousie; or if they have
belief, let it Corrupt to Superstition, and blind Credulity. I am single; 585
and will herd no more with 'em. True, I wear the badge; but I'll
disown the Order. And since I take my leave of 'em, I care not if I
leave 'em a common Motto, to their common Crest.

All Husbands must, or pain, or shame, endure;
The Wise too Jealous are, Fools too secure. 590

Exeunt.

Act IV

Scene I

Scene Continues.

Enter Lady Wishfort *and* Foible.

Lady Wishfort. Is Sir *Rowland* coming say'st thou, *Foible?* and are
things in Order?

Foible. Yes, *Madam.* I have put Wax-Lights in the Sconces; and plac'd
the Foot-men in a Row in the Hall, in their best Liveries, with the
Coach-man and Postilion to fill up the Equipage. 5

Lady Wishfort. Have you pullvill'd the Coachman and Postilion, that they may not stink of the Stable, when Sir *Rowland* comes by?

Foible. Yes, *Madam.*

Lady Wishfort. And are the Dancers and the Musick ready, that he   10
may be entertain'd in all points with Correspondence to his Passion?

Foible. All is ready, *Madam.*

Lady Wishfort. And – well – and how do I look, *Foible?*

Foible. Most killing well, *Madam.*

Lady Wishfort. Well, and how shall I receive him? In what figure shall I   15
give his Heart the first Impression? There is a great deal in the first Impression. Shall I sit? – No I won't sit – I'll walk – aye I'll walk from the door upon his entrance; and then turn full upon him – No, that will be too sudden. I'll lie – aye, I'll lie down – I'll receive him in my little dressing Room, there's a Couch – Yes, yes, I'll give the first   20
Impression on a Couch – I wont lie neither but loll and lean upon one Elbow; with one Foot a little dangling off, Jogging in a thoughtful way – Yes – and then as soon as he appears, start, ay, start and be surpriz'd, and rise to meet him in a pretty disorder – Yes – O, nothing is more alluring than a Levee from a Couch in some Confusion. – It   25
shows the Foot to advantage, and furnishes with Blushes, and re-composing Airs beyond Comparison. Hark! There's a Coach.

Foible. 'Tis he, *Madam.*

Lady Wishfort. O dear, has my *Nephew* made his Addresses to *Mill-amant?* I order'd him.   30

Foible. Sir *Wilfull* is set in to Drinking, *Madam*, in the Parlour.

Lady Wishfort. Ods my life, I'll send him to her. Call her down, *Foible*; bring her hither. I'll send him as I go – When they are together, then come to me *Foible*, that I may not be too long alone with Sir *Rowland.*

Exit.

Enter Mrs. Millamant, *and* Mrs. Fainall.

Foible. Madam, I stay'd here, to tell your Ladyship that Mr. *Mirabell*   35
has waited this half hour for an Opportunity to talk with you. Tho' my Lady's Orders were to leave you and Sir *Wilfull* together. Shall I tell Mr. *Mirabell* that you are at leisure?

Millamant. No – What would the Dear man have? I am thoughtfull and would amuse my self, – bid him come another time.   40

Repeating and Walking about.

> *There never yet was Woman made,*
> *Nor shall but to be curs'd.*

That's hard!

Mrs. Fainall. You are very fond of Sir *John Suckling* to day, *Mill-amant*, and the *Poets.*   45

Millamant. He? Ay, and filthy Verses – So I am.

Foible. Sir *Wilfull* is coming, *Madam*. Shall I send Mr. *Mirabell* away?

Millimant. Ay, if you please *Foible*, send him away, – Or send him
hither, – just as you will Dear *Foible*. – I think I'll see him – Shall I?
Ay, let the Wretch come.   50

> [*Repeating.*] *Thyrsis a Youth of the Inspir'd train –*

Dear *Fainall*, Entertain Sir *Wilfull* – Thou hast Philosophy to
undergo a Fool, thou art Married and hast Patience – I would
confer with my own Thoughts.

Mrs. Fainall. I am oblig'd to you, that you would make me your   55
Proxy in this Affair; but I have business of my own.

> *Enter* Sir Wilfull.

O *Sir Wilfull*, you are come at the Critical Instant. There's your
Mistress up to the Ears in Love and Contemplation, pursue your
Point, now or never.

Sir Wilfull. Yes; my Aunt would have it so, – I would gladly have been   60
encouraged with a Bottle or two, because I'm somewhat wary at
first, before I am acquainted; – But I hope after a time, I shall break
my mind – that is upon further acquaintance, – So for the present
Cozen, I'll take my leave – If so be you'll be so kind to make my
Excuse, I'll return to my Company –   65

> *This while* Millamant *walks about repeating to her self.*

Mrs. Fainall. O fie Sir *Wilfull!* What, you must not be Daunted.

Sir Wilfull. Daunted, No, that's not it, it is not so much for that – for
if so be that I set on't, I'll do't. But only for the present, 'tis
sufficient till further acquaintance, that's all – your Servant.

Mrs. Fainall. Nay, I'll swear you shall never lose so favourable an   70
opportunity, if I can help it. I'll leave you together and lock the Door.

> *Exit.*

Sir Wilfull. Nay, nay Cozen, – I have forgot my Gloves, – What dee
do? 'Shart a'has lock'd the Door indeed I think – Nay Cozen
Fainall, open the Door – Pshaw What a Vixon trick is this? – Nay,
now a'has seen me too – Cozen, I made bold to pass thro' as it were,   75
– I think this Door's inchanted –.

Millamant [*Repeating*].

> I prithee spare me gentle Boy,
> Press me no more for that slight Toy.

Sir Wilfull. Anan? Cozen, your Servant.   80

Millamant. – *That foolish trifle of a heart* – Sir *Wilfull*!

Sir Wilfull. Yes, – your Servant. No offence I hope, Cozen.

Millamant [*Repeating.*]

> I swear it will not do its part,
> Tho' thou do'st thine, employ'st the Power and Art.   85

Natural, easie *Suckling*!

Sir Wilfull. Anan? *Suckling?* No such Suckling neither, Cozen, nor
Stripling: I thank Heav'n, I'm no Minor.

Millamant. Ah Rustick! ruder than *Gothick.*

Sir Wilfull. Well, Well, I shall understand your *Lingo* one of these   90
days, Cozen, in the mean while, I must answer in plain *English.*

Millamant. Have you any business with me, Sir *Wilfull*?

Sir Wilfull. Not at present Cozen, – Yes, I made bold to see, to come
and know if that how you were dispos'd to fetch a walk this
Evening, if so be that I might not be troublesome, I wou'd have   95
sought a walk with you.

Millamant. A walk? What then?

Sir Wilfull. Nay nothing – Only for the walks sake, that's all –

Millamant. I Nauseate walking; 'tis a Country diversion, I loath the
Country and every thing that relates to it.   100

Sir Wilfull. Indeed! Hah! Look ye, look ye, you do? Nay, 'tis like you
may – Here are choice of Pastimes here in Town, as Plays and the
like that must be confess'd indeed.

Millamant. Ah l' etourdie! I hate the Town too.

Sir Wilfull. Dear Heart, that's much – Hah! that you shou'd hate 'em   105
both! Hah 'tis like you may; there are some can't relish the Town,
and others can't away with the Country, – 'tis like you may be one
of those, Cozen.

Millamant. Ha, ha, ha. Yes, 'tis like I may. – You have nothing further
to say to me?   110

Sir Wilfull. Not at present, Cozen. – 'tis like when I have an Oppor-
tunity to be more private, – I may break my mind in some measure,
– I conjecture you partly guess – However that's as time shall try, –
But spare to speak and spare to speed, as they say.

Millamant. If it is of no great Importance, Sir *Wilfull*, you will oblige   115
me to leave me: I have just now a little business. –

Sir Wilfull. Enough, enough, Cozen, Yes, yes, all a case – When
you're dispos'd, when you're dispos'd. Now's as well as another
time; and another time as well as now. All's one for that, – yes, yes, if
your Concerns call you, there's no hast; it will keep cold as they say,   120
– Cozen, your Servant – I think this door's lock'd.

Millamant. You may go this way Sir.

Sir Wilfull. Your Servant, then with your leave I'll return to my
Company.

Exit.

Millamant. Ay, ay, ha, ha, ha.   125
Like Phoebus *sung the no less am'rous Boy.*

Enter Mirabell.

Mirabell. – *Like* Daphne *she as lovely and as Coy.* Do you lock your self
up from me, to make my search more Curious? Or is this pretty
Artifice Contriv'd, to Signifie that here the Chase must end, and my
pursuit be Crown'd, for you can fly no further. –   130

Millamant. Vanity! No – I'll fly and be follow'd to the last moment,
tho' I am upon the very Verge of Martimony, I expect you shou'd

solicite me as much as if I were wavering at the grate of a Monastery, with one foot over the threshold. I'll be solicited to the very last, nay and afterwards.   135

Mirabell. What, after the last?

Millamant. O, I should think I was poor and had nothing to bestow, if I were reduc'd to an Inglorious ease; and free'd from the Agreeable fatigues of sollicitation.

Mirabell. But do not you know, that when favours are conferr'd upon   140
Instant and tedious Sollicitation, that they diminish in their value, and that both the giver loses the grace, and the receiver lessens his Pleasure?

Millamant. It may be in things of common Application; but never sure in Love. O, I hate a Lover, that can dare to think, he draws a   145
moments air, Independent on the Bounty of his Mistress. There is not so Impudent a thing in Nature, as the sawcy look of an assured man, Confident of Success. The Pedantick arrogance of a very Husband, has not so Pragmatical an Air. Ah! I'll never marry, unless I am first made sure of my will and pleasure.   150

Mirabell. Wou'd you have 'em both before Marriage? Or will you be contented with the first now, and stay for the other till after grace?

Millamant. Ah don't be Impertinent – My dear Liberty, shall I leave thee? My faithful Solitude, my darling Contemplation, must I bid you then Adieu? ay-h adieu. – my morning thoughts, agreeable   155
wakings, indolent slumbers, all ye *douceurs,* ye *Someils du Matin,* adieu – I can't do't, 'tis more than Impossible – positively *Mirabell,* I'll lie a Bed in a morning as long as I please.

Mirabell. Then I'll get up in a morning as early as I please.

Millamant. Ah! Idle Creature, get up when you will – and dee hear, I   160
won't be call'd names after I'm Married; positively I won't be call'd Names.

Mirabell. Names!

Millamant. Ay as Wife, Spouse, My dear, Joy, Jewel, Love, Sweet heart and the rest of that Nauseous Cant, in which Men and their   165
Wives are so fulsomely familiar, – I shall never bear that, – Good *Mirabell* don't let us be familiar or fond, nor kiss before folks, like my Lady *Fadler* and Sr. *Francis*: Nor goe to *Hide-Park* together the first *Sunday* in a New Chariot, to provoke Eyes and Whispers; And then never to be seen there together again; as if we were proud of   170
one another the first Week, and asham'd of one another for ever After. Let us never Visit together, nor go to a Play together, But let us be very strange and well bred: let us be as strange as if we had been married a great while; and as well bred as if we were not marri'd at all.

Mirabell. Have you any more Conditions to offer? Hitherto your   175
demands are pretty reasonable.

Millamant. Trifles, – As liberty to pay and receive visits to and from whom I please, to write and receive Letters, without Interrogatories or wry Faces on your part. To wear what I please; and choose Conversation with regard only to my own taste; to have no   180

obligation upon me to converse with Wits that I don't like, because
they are your acquaintance; or to be intimate with Fools, because
they may be your Relations. Come to Dinner when I please, dine in
my dressing room when I'm out of humour without giving a reason.
To have my Closet Inviolate; to be sole Empress of my Tea-table, 185
which you must never presume to approach without first asking
leave. And lastly, where ever I am, you shall always knock at the
door before you come in. These Articles subscrib'd, If I continue
to endure you a little longer, I may by degrees dwindle into a Wife.

Mirabell. Your bill of fare is something advanc'd in this latter account. 190
Well, have I Liberty to offer Conditions – that when you are dwindl'd
into a Wife, I may not be beyond Measure enlarg'd into a Husband?

Millamant. You have free leave; propose your utmost, speak and
spare not.

Mirabell. I thank you. *Inprimis* then, I Covenant that your acquaint- 195
ance be General; that you admit no sworn Confident, or Intimate of
your own Sex; No she friend to skreen her affairs under your
Countenance and tempt you to make tryal of a Mutual Secresie.
No Decoy-Duck to wheadle you a *fop – scrambling* to the Play in a
Mask – then bring you home in a pretended fright, when you think 200
you shall be found out. – And rail at me for missing the Play, and
disappointing the Frolick which you had to pick me up and prove
my Constancy.

Millamant. Detestable *Inprimis!* I go to the Play in a Mask!

Mirabell. *Item,* I Article, that you continue to like your own Face, as 205
long as I shall. And while it passes Current with me, that you
endeavour not to new Coin it. To which end, together with all
Vizards for the day, I prohibit all Masks for the Night, made of oil'd
skins and I know not what – Hog's-bones, Hare's-gall, Pig-water,
and the marrow of a roasted Cat. In short, I forbid all Commerce 210
with the Gentlewoman in *what-de-call-it*-Court. *Item,* I shut my
doors against all Bauds with Baskets, and penny-worths of *Muslin,*
China, Fans, Atlases, &c. – *Item* when you shall be Breeding –

Millamant. Ah! Name it not.

Mirabell. Which may be presum'd, with a blessing on our endeavours – 215

Millamant. Odious endeavours!

Mirabell. I denounce against all strait-Laceing, Squeezing for a
Shape, till you mold my boy's head like a Sugar-loaf; and instead
of a Man-child, make me the Father to a Crooked-billet. Lastly to
the Dominion of the *Tea-Table,* I submit. – But with *proviso,* that 220
you exceed not in your province; but restrain your self to Native and
Simple *Tea-Table* drinks, as *Tea, Chocolate* and *Coffee.* As likewise
to Genuine and, Authoriz'd *Tea-Table* talk, – such as mending of
Fashions, spoiling Reputations, railing at absent Friends, and so
forth – but that on no account you encroach upon the mens 225
prerogative, and presume to drink healths, or toste fellows; for
prevention of which; I banish all *Foreign Forces,* all Auxiliaries to
the *Tea-Table,* as *Orange-Brandy,* all *Anniseed, Cinamon, Citron*

and *Barbado's-Waters*, together with *Ratifa* and the most noble
Spirit of *Clary*, – but for *Couslip-Wine*, *Poppy-Water* and all *Dormi-*   230
tives, those I allow, – these *proviso's* admitted, in other things I may
prove a tractable and complying Husband.

Millamant. O horrid *proviso's*! filthy strong Waters! I toste fellows,
Odious Men! I hate your Odious proviso's.

Mirabell. Then wee're agreed. Shall I kiss your hand upon the Con-   235
tract? and here comes one to be a witness to the Sealing of the Deed.

Enter Mrs. Fainall.

Millamant. *Fainall*, what shall I do? shall I have him? I think I must
have him.

Mrs. Fainall. Ay, ay, take him, take him, what shou'd you do?

Millamant. Well then – I'll take my death I'm in a horrid fright –   240
Fainall, I shall never say it – well – I think – I'll endure you.

Mrs. Fainall. Fy, fy, have him, have him, and tell him so in plain
terms: For I am sure you have a mind to him.

Millamant. Are you? I think I have – and the horrid Man looks as if
he thought so too – Well, you ridiculous thing you, I'll have you, – I   245
won't be kiss'd, nor I won't be thank'd – here kiss my hand tho' –
so hold your tongue now, and don't say a word.

Mrs. Fainall. *Mirabell*, there's a Necessity for your obedience, – You
have neither time to talk nor stay. My Mother is coming; and in my
Conscience if she should see you, wou'd fall into fits, and maybe   250
not recover time enough to return to Sir *Rowland*, who as *Foible*
tells me is in a fair way to succeed. Therefore spare your Extacies for
another occasion, and slip down the back-stairs, where *Foible* waits
to consult you.

Millamant. Ay, go, go. In the mean time I suppose you have said   255
something to please me.

Mirabell. I am all Obedience.

Exit Mirabell.

Mrs. Fainall. Yonder Sir *Wilfull's* Drunk; and so noisy that my
Mother has been forc'd to leave Sir *Rowland* to appease him; But
he answers her only with Singing and Drinking – what they have   260
done by this time I know not. But *Petulant* and he were upon
quarrelling as I came by.

Millamant. Well, If *Mirabell* shou'd not make a good Husband, I am
a lost thing; – for I find I love him violently.

Mrs. Fainall. So it seems, when you mind not what's said to you, – If   265
you doubt him, you had best take up with Sir *Wilfull*.

Millamant. How can you name that super-annuated Lubber, foh!

Enter Witwoud *from drinking.*

Mrs. Fainall. So, Is the fray made up, that you have left 'em?

Witwoud. Left 'em? I cou'd stay no longer – I have laugh'd like ten
Christnings – I am tipsy with laughing – If I had staid any longer   270

I shou'd have burst, – I must have been let out and piec'd in the
sides like an unsiz'd Camlet, – Yes, yes the fray is compos'd; my
Lady came in like a *Noli prosequi* and stop't their proceedings.
Millamant. What was the dispute?
Witwoud. That's the Jest, there was no dispute, they cou'd neither of   275
'em speak for rage; And so fell a sputt'ring at one another like two
roasting Apples.

Enter Petulant *Drunk.*

Now *Petulant*, all's over, all's well; Gad my head begins to whim it
about – Why dost thou not speak? thou art both as drunk and as
mute as a Fish.   280
Petulant. Look you Mrs. *Millamant*, – If you can love me dear Nymph
– say it – and that's the Conclusion – pass on, or pass off, – that's all.
Witwoud. Thou hast utter'd *Volumes, Folio's*, in less than *Decimo
Sexto*, my Dear *Lacedemonian*, Sirrah *Petulant*, thou art an Epito-
mizer of words.   285
Petulant. Witwoud – You are an anihilator of sense.
Witwoud. Thou art a retailer of Phrases; and dost deal in Remnants of
Remnants, like a maker of Pincushions – thou art in truth (Meta-
phorically speaking) A speaker of short-hand.
Petulant. Thou art (without a figure) Just one half of an Ass; and   290
Baldwin yonder, thy half Brother is the rest – A *gemini* of Asses
split, would make just four of you.
Witwoud. Thou dost bite my dear Mustard-seed; kiss me for that.
Petulant. Stand off – I'll kiss no more Males, – I have kiss'd your *twin*
yonder in a humour of reconciliation, till he [*hiccup*] rises upon my   295
stomack like a Radish.
Millamant. Eh! filthy creature – what was the quarrel?
Petulant. There was no quarrel – there might have been a quarrel.
Witwoud. If there had been words enow between 'em to have
express'd provocation; they had gone together by the Ears like a   300
pair of Castanets.
Petulant. You were the Quarrel.
Millamant. Me!
Petulant. If I have a humour to Quarrel, I can make less matters
conclude Premises, – If you are not handsom, what then? If I have a   305
humour to prove it. – If I shall have my Reward, say so; if not, fight
for your Face the next time your self – I'll go sleep.
Witwoud. Do, rap thy self up like a *Wood-louse* and dream Revenge –
and hear me, if thou canst learn to write by to morrow Morning,
Pen me a Challenge – I'll carry it for thee.   310
Petulant. Carry your Mistresses *Monkey* a *Spider*, – go flea Dogs, and
read Romances – I'll go to bed to my Maid.

Exit.

Mrs. Fainall. He's horridly drunk – how came you all in this
pickle? –

Witwoud. A plot, a plot, to get rid of the Knight, – your Husband's 315
advice; but he sneak'd off.

       Enter Lady Wishfort *and* Sir Wilfull *drunk.*

Lady Wishfort. Out upon't, out upon't, at years of Discretion, and
Comport your self at this Rantipole rate.
Sir Wilfull. No Offence Aunt.
Lady Wishfort. Offence? As I'm a Person, I'm asham'd of you, – 320
Fogh! how you stink of Wine! Dee think my Neice will ever endure
such a *Borachio*! you're an absolute *Borachio.*
Sir Wilfull. *Borachio*!
Lady Wishfort. At a time when you shou'd commence an Amour and
put your best foot foremost –
Sir Wilfull. 'Sheart, an you grutch me your Liquor, make a Bill – Give 325
me more drink and take my Purse. [*Sings,*]

              Prithee fill me the Glass
              Till it laugh in my Face,
           With Ale that is Potent and Mellow; 330
              He that Whines for a Lass,
              Is an Ignorant Ass,
           For a *Bumper* has not its Fellow.

but if you wou'd have me Marry my Cozen, – say the Word, and I'll
do't – *Wilfull* will do't, that's the Word – *Wilfull* will do't, that's my 335
Crest – my Motto I have forgot.
Lady Wishfort. My Nephew's a little overtaken Cozen – but 'tis with
drinking your Health – O' my Word you are oblig'd to him.
Sir Wilfull. *In vino veritas* Aunt, – If I drunk your Health to day Cozen
– I am a *Borachio.* But if you have a mind to be Marry'd, say the 340
Word, and send for the Piper, *Wilfull* will do't. If not, dust it away,
and let's have tother round – *Tony,* Ods heart where's *Tony* – *Tony*'s an
honest fellow, but he spits after a Bumper, and that's a Fault.
[*Sings,*]

           We'll drink and we'll never ha' done Boys 345
             Put the glass then around with the Sun Boys;
          Let *Apollo*'s Example invite us;
             For he's drunk every Night,
          And that makes him so bright,
             That he's able next Morning to light us. 350

the Sun's a good Pimple, an honest Soaker, he has a Cellar at your
Antipodes. If I travel Aunt, I touch at your *Antipodes* – your *Antipo-*
des are a good rascally sort of topsy-turvy Fellows – If I had a
Bumper I'd stand upon my Head and drink a Health to 'em – A
Match or no Match, Cozen, with the hard Name, – Aunt, *Wilfull* 355
will do't, If she has her Maidenhead let her look to't, – if she has

not, let her keep her own Counsel in the mean time, and cry out at the nine Months end.

Millamant. Your Pardon Madam, I can stay no longer – Sir *Wilfull* grows very powerful, Egh! how he smells! I shall be overcome if I stay.   360

> *Exeunt* Millamant *and* Mrs. Fainall.

Come, Cozen.

Lady Wishfort. Smells! he would poison a Tallow-Chandler and his Family. Beastly Creature, I know not what to do with him – Travel quoth a; Ay travel, travel, get thee gone, get thee but far enough, to the *Saracens* or the *Tartars*, or the *Turks* – for thou are not fit to live   365 in a Christian Commonwealth, thou beastly Pagan.

Sir Wilfull. Turks, no; no *Turks*, Aunt: Your *Turks* are Infidels, and believe not in the Grape. Your *Mahometan*, your *Mussulman* is a dry Stinkard – No Offence, Aunt. My Map says that your *Turk* is not so honest a Man as your Christian – I cannot find by the Map that your   370 *Mufti* is Orthodox – Whereby it is a plain Case, that Orthodox is a hard Word, Aunt, and [*hiccup*] Greek for Claret.

[*Sings,*]

> To drink is a Christian Diversion,
> Unknown to the *Turk* and the *Persian*:   375
>   Let *Mahometan* Fools
>   Live by Heathenish Rules,
> And be damn'd over Tea-Cups and Coffee.
>   But let British Lads sing,
>   Crown a Health to the King,   380
> And a Fig for your *Sultan* and *Sophy*.

Ah *Tony*!

> *Enter* Foible, *and whispers* Lady Wishfort.

Lady Wishfort. Sir *Rowland* impatient? Good lack! what shall I do with this beastly Tumbril? – Go lie down and sleep, you Sot – Or as I'm a person, I'll have you bastinado'd with Broom-sticks. Call up   385 the Wenches.

> *Exit* Foible.

Sir Wilfull. Ahey! Wenches, where are the Wenches?

Lady Wishfort. Dear Cozen *Witwoud*, get him away, and you will bind me to you inviolably. I have an Affair of moment that invades me with some precipitation – You will oblige me to all Futurity.   390

Witwoud. Come Knight – Pox on him. I don't know what to say to him – will you go to a Cock-match?

Sir Wilfull. With a Wench, *Tony*? Is she a shake-bag Sirrah? let me bite your Cheek for that.

Witwoud. Horrible! He has a breath like a *Bagpipe* – ay, ay, come will   395 you March my *Salopian*?

Sir Wilfull. Lead on little *Tony* – I'll follow thee my *Anthony,* My *Tantony,* Sirrah thou sha't be my *Tantony,* and I'll be thy *Pig.*
– and a fig for your *Sultan* and *Sophy.*

Exit Singing with Witwoud.

Lady Wishfort. This will never do. It will never make a Match. – At 400
least before he has been abroad.

Enter Waitwell, *disguis'd as for* Sir Rowland.

Dear Sir *Rowland,* I am Confounded with Confusion at the Retro-
spection of my own rudeness, – I have more pardons to ask than the
Pope distributes in the Year of *Jubilee.* But I hope where there is
likely to be so near an alliance, – We may unbend the severity of 405
Decorum – and dispence with a little Ceremony.

Waitwell. My Impatience *Madam,* is the effect of my transport; – and
till I have the possession of your adoreable Person, I am tantaliz'd
on a rack; And do but hang *Madam,* on the tenter of Expectation.

Lady Wishfort. You have Excess of gallantry Sir *Rowland;* and press 410
things to a Conclusion, with a most prevailing Vehemence. – But a
day or two for decency of Marriage –

Waitwell. For decency of Funeral, *Madam.* The delay will break my
heart – or if that should fail, I shall be Poyson'd. My *Nephew* will get
an inkling of my Designs and Poison me, – and I wou'd willingly 415
starve him before I die – I wou'd gladly go out of the World with
that Satisfaction. – That wou'd be some Comfort to me, If I cou'd
but live so long as to be reveng'd on that Unnatural *Viper.*

Lady Wishfort. Is he so Unnatural say you? truely I wou'd Contribute
much both to the saving of your Life; and the accomplishment of 420
your revenge – Not that I respect my self; tho' he has been a
perfidious wretch to me.

Waitwell. Perfidious to you!

Lady Wishfort. O Sir *Rowland,* the hours that he has dy'd away at my
Feet, the Tears that he has shed, the Oaths that he has sworn, the 425
Palpitations that he has felt, the Trances, and the Tremblings, the
Ardors and the Ecstacies, the Kneelings and the Riseings, the Heart-
heavings, and the hand-Gripings, the Pangs and the Pathetick
Regards of his protesting Eyes! Oh no memory can Register.

Waitwell. What, my Rival! is the Rebell my Rival? a'dies. 430

Lady Wishfort. No, don't kill him at once Sir *Rowland,* starve him
gradually inch by inch.

Waitwell. I'll do't. In three weeks he shall be barefoot; in a month out
at knees with begging an *Alms,* – he shall starve upward and
upward, till he has nothing living but his head, and then go out in 435
a stink like a Candle's end upon a Save-all.

Lady Wishfort. Well, Sir *Rowland,* you have the way, – You are no
Novice in the Labyrinth of Love – You have the Clue – But as I am a
person, Sir *Rowland,* You must not attribute my yielding to any
sinister appetite, or Indigestion of Widdow-hood; Nor Impute my 440

Complacency, to any Lethargy of Continence – I hope you do not think me prone to any iteration of Nuptials. –

Waitwell. Far be it from me –

Lady Wishfort. If you do, I protest I must recede – or think that I have made a prostitution of decorums, but in the Vehemence of Com- 445 passion, and to save the life of a Person of so much Importance –

Waitwell. I esteem it so –

Lady Wishfort. Or else you wrong my Condescension –

Waitwell. I do not, I do not –

Lady Wishfort. Indeed you do. 450

Waitwell. I do not, fair shrine of Vertue.

Lady Wishfort. If you think the least scruple of Carnality was an Ingredient –

Waitwell. Dear *Madam*, no. You are all *Camphire* and *Frankincense*, all *Chastity* and *Odour*. 455

Lady Wishfort. Or that –

Enter Foible.

Foible. **Madam**, the Dancers are ready, and there's one with a Letter, who must deliver it into your own hands.

Lady Wishfort. Sir *Rowland*, will you give me leave? think favourably, Judge Candidly and conclude you have found a Person who wou'd 460 suffer racks in honour's cause, dear Sir *Rowland*, and will wait on you Incessantly.

Exit.

Waitwell. Fie, fie! – What a Slavery have I undergone; Spouse, hast thou any *Cordial* – I want *Spirits*.

Foible. What a washy Rogue art thou, to pant thus for a quarter of an 465 hours lying and swearing to a fine Lady?

Waitwell. O, she is the *Antidote* to desire. Spouse thou will't fare the worse for't – I shall have no appetite to iteration of Nuptials – this eight and fourty Hours – by this hand I'd rather be a *Chair-man* in the *Dog-days* – than Act Sir *Rowland*, till this time to morrow. 470

Enter Lady Wishfort *with a Letter.*

Lady Wishfort. Call in the *Dancers*, – Sir *Rowland*, we'll sit if you please, and see the Entertainment.

Dance.

Now with your permission Sir *Rowland* I will peruse my Letter – I wou'd open it in your presence, because I wou'd not make you Uneasie. If it shou'd make you Uneasie I wou'd burn it – speak if it 475 do's – but you may see by the Superscription it is like a Woman's hand.

Foible [*to him*]. By Heaven! Mrs. *Marwood's*, I know it, – my heart akes – get it from her –.

Waitwell. A Woman's hand? No *Madam*, that's no Woman's hand I see that already. That's some body whose throat must be cut. 480

Lady Wishfort. Nay Sir *Rowland*, since you give me a proof of your
Passion by your Jealousie, I promise you I'll make you a return, by a
frank Communication – You shall see it – we'll open it together –
look you here.
[*Reads*] – Madam, *tho' unknown to you* (Look you there 'tis from no   485
body that I know) – *I have that honour for your Character, that I
think my self oblig'd to let you know you are abus'd. He who pretends to
be Sir* Rowland *is a cheat and a Rascal.* –
Oh Heavens! what's this?

Foible. Unfortunate, all's ruin'd.   490

Waitwell. How, how, Let me see, let me see – [*reading*] *A Rascal and
disguis'd and subborn'd for that imposture*, – O villany, O villany! –
by the Contrivance of –

Lady Wishfort. I shall faint, I shall die, I shall die, oh!

Foible [*to him*]. Say 'tis your Nephew's hand. – quickly, his plot, swear,   495
swear it. –

Waitwell. Here's a Villain! *Madam*, don't you perceive it, don't you
see it?

Lady Wishfort. Too well, too well. I have seen too much.

Waitwell. I told you at first I knew the hand – A Womans hand? the   500
Rascal writes a sort of a large hand; your *Roman* hand – I saw there
was a throat to be cut presently. If he were my Son as he is my
Nephew I'd Pistoll him –

Foible. O Treachery! But are you sure Sir *Rowland*, it is his writing?

Waitwell. Sure? am I here? do I live? do I love this Pearl of *India*?   505
I have twenty Letters in my Pocket from him, in the same Character.

Lady Wishfort. How!

Foible. O what luck it is Sir *Rowland*, that you were present at this
Juncture! this was the business that brought Mr. *Mirabell* disguis'd   510
to *Madam Millamant* this Afternoon. I thought something was
contriving, when he stole by me and would have hid his face.

Lady Wishfort. How, how! – I heard the Villain was in the house
indeed, and now I remember, my *Niece* went away abruptly, when
Sir *Wilfull* was to have made his addresses.   515

Foible. Then, then *Madam*, Mr. *Mirabell* waited for her in her Chamber, but I wou'd not tell your Lady-ship to discompose you when
you were to receive Sir *Rowland*.

Waitwell. Enough, his date is short.

Foible. No, good Sir *Rowland*, don't incurr the Law.   520

Waitwell. Law? I care not for Law. I can but die, and 'tis in a good
cause – my Lady shall be satisfied of my Truth and Innocence, tho'
it cost me my life.

Lady Wishfort. No, dear Sir *Rowland*, don't fight, if you shou'd be
kill'd I must never shew my face; or hang'd, – O Consider my   525
Reputation Sir *Rowland* – No you shan't fight, – I'll go in and
Examine my *Niece*; I'll make her Confess. I conjure you Sir *Rowland* by all your love not to fight.

Waitwell. I am Charm'd *Madam*, I obey. But some proof you must
let me give you; – I'll go for a black box, which Contains the   530
Writings of my whole Estate, and deliver that into your hands.
Lady Wishfort. Ay dear Sir *Rowland*, that will be some Comfort;
bring the Black-box.
Waitwell. And may I presume to bring a Contract to be sign'd this
Night? May I hope so farr?   535
Lady Wishfort. Bring what you will; but come alive, pray come alive.
O this is a happy discovery.
Waitwell. Dead or Alive I'll come – and married we will be in spight
of treachery; Ay and get an Heir that shall defeat the last remaining
glimpse of hope in my abandon'd *Nephew*. Come my Buxom Wid-   540
dow.
Ere long you shall Substantial proof receive
That I'm an Arrant Knight –
Foible. Or arrant Knave.

Exeunt.

Act V

Scene I

Scene Continues.

Lady Wishfort *and* Foible.

Lady Wishfort. Out of my house, out of my house, thou *Viper*, thou
Serpent, that I have foster'd, thou bosome traytress, that I rais'd from
nothing – begon, begon, begon, go, go, – that I took from Washing of
old Gause and Weaving of dead Hair with a bleak blew Nose, over a
Chafeing-dish of starv'd Embers and Dining behind a Traverse Rag,   5
in a shop no bigger than a Bird-cage, – go, go, starve again, do, do.
Foible. Dear *Madam*, I'll beg pardon on my knees.
Lady Wishfort. Away, out, out, go set up for your self again – do, drive a
Trade, do, with your three penny-worth of small Ware, flaunting
upon a Packthread, under a Brandy-sellers Bulk, or against a dead   10
Wall by a Ballad-monger. Go hang out an old *Frisoneer-gonget* with a
yard of Yellow *Colberteen* again; do; an old gnaw'd *Mask*, two rowes of
Pins and a *Childs Fiddle; A Glass Necklace* with the Beads broken, and
a *Quilted Night-cap* with one Ear. Go, go, drive a trade, – these were
your *Commodities* you treacherous Trull, this was your *Merchandize*   15
you dealt in when I took you into my house, plac'd you next my self,
and made you Governante of my whole Family. You have forgot this,
have you, now you have feather'd your Nest?
Foible. No, no, dear *Madam*. Do but hear me, have but a Moment's
patience – I'll Confess all. Mr. *Mirabell* seduc'd me; I am not the   20
first that he has wheadl'd with his dissembling Tongue; Your Ladyship's own Wisdom has been deluded by him, then how shou'd I a

poor Ignorant, defend my self? O *Madam*, if you knew but what he
promis'd me; and how he assur'd me your Ladyship shou'd come to
no damage – Or else the Wealth of the *Indies* shou'd not have   25
brib'd me to conspire against so Good, so Sweet, so kind a Lady
as you have been to me.

Lady Wishfort. No damage? What to Betray me, to Marry me to a
Cast-serving-man; to make me a receptacle, an Hospital for a
decay'd Pimp? No damage? O thou frontless Impudence, more   30
than a big-Belly'd Actress.

Foible. Pray do but hear me *Madam*, he cou'd not marry your Ladyship, *Madam* – No indeed his Marriage was to have been void in
Law; for he was married to me first, to secure your Lady-ship. He
cou'd not have bedded your Lady-ship: for if he had Consummated   35
with your Ladyship, he must have run the risque of the Law, and
been put upon his *Clergy* – Yes indeed, I enquir'd of the Law in that
case before I wou'd meddle or make.

Lady Wishfort. What, then I have been your Property, have I? I have
been convenient to you it seems, – while you were Catering for   40
Mirabell; I have been broker for you? What, have you made a
passive Bawd of me? – this Exceeds all precedent; I am brought to
fine uses, to become a botcher of second hand Marriages, between
Abigails and *Andrews*! I'll couple you, Yes, I'll baste you together,
you and your *Philander*. I'll *Dukes-Place* you, as I'm a Person. Your   45
Turtle is in Custody already; You shall Coo in the same Cage, if
there be Constable or warrant in the Parish.

Exit.

Foible. O that ever I was Born, O that I was ever Married, – a Bride, ay
I shall be a *Bridewell*-Bride. Oh!

Enter Mrs. Fainall.

Mrs. Fainall. Poor *Foible*, what's the matter?   50

Foible. O *Madam*, my Lady's gone for a Constable; I shall be had to a
Justice, and put to *Bridewell* to beat Hemp, poor *Waitwell's* gone to
prison already.

Mrs. Fainall. Have a good heart *Foible, Mirabell's* gone to give security for him. This is all *Marwood's* and my Husband's doing.   55

Foible. Yes, yes; I know it *Madam*; she was in my Lady's Closet, and
over-heard all that you said to me before Dinner. She sent the
Letter to my Lady, and that missing Effect, Mr. *Fainall* laid this
Plot to arrest *Waitwell*, when he pretended to go for the Papers;
and in the mean time Mrs. *Marwood* declar'd all to my Lady.   60

Mrs. Fainall. Was there no mention made of me in the Letter? – My
Mother do's not suspect my being in the Confederacy? I fancy
Marwood has not told her, tho' she has told my husband.

Foible. Yes *Madam*; but my Lady did not see that part; We stifl'd the
Letter before she read so far. Has that mischeivous Devil told Mr.   65
Fainall of your Ladyship then?

Mrs. Fainall. Ay, all's out, My affair with *Mirabell*, every thing discover'd. This is the last day of our living together, that's my Comfort.

Foible. Indeed *Madam*, and so 'tis a Comfort if you knew all, – he has been even with your Ladyship; which I cou'd have told you-long 70 enough since, but I love to keep Peace and Quietness by my good will: I had rather bring friends together, than set 'em at distance. But Mrs. *Marwood* and He are nearer related than ever their Parents thought for.

Mrs. Fainall. Say'st thou so *Foible*? Canst thou prove this? 75

Foible. I can take my Oath of it *Madam*, so can Mrs. *Mincing*, we have had many a fair word from *Madam Marwood*, to conceal something that pass'd in our Chamber one Evening when you were at *Hide-Park*; – And we were thought to have gone a Walking: But we went up unawares, – tho' we were sworn to secresie too; *Madam Mar-* 80 *wood* took a Book and swore us upon it: But it was but a Book of Verses and Poems, – So as long as it was not a Bible-Oath, we may break it with a safe Conscience.

Mrs. Fainall. This discovery is the most opportune thing I cou'd wish. Now *Mincing*? 85

Enter Mincing.

Mincing. My Lady wou'd speak with Mrs. *Foible, Mem.* Mr. *Mirabell* is with her, he has set your Spouse at liberty Mrs. *Foible*; and wou'd have you hide your self in my Lady's Closet, till my old Lady's anger is abated. O, my old Lady is in a perilous passion, at something Mr. *Fainall* has said. He swears, and my old Lady cry's. There's a fearful 90 Hurricane I vow. He says *Mem*, how that he'll have my Lady's Fortune made over to him, or he'll be divorc'd.

Mrs. Fainall. Do's your Lady and *Mirabell* know that?

Mincing. Yes *Mem*, they have sent me to see if Sir *Wilfull* be sober, and to bring him to them. My Lady is resolv'd to have him I think, 95 rather than loose such a vast Summ as six thousand Pound. O, come Mrs. *Foible*, I hear my old Lady.

Mrs. Fainall. Foible, you must tell *Mincing*, that she must prepare to vouch when I call her.

Foible. Yes, yes *Madam*. 100

Mincing. O yes *Mem*, I'll vouch any thing for your Ladyship's service, be what it will.

Exeunt Mincing *and* Foible.

Enter Lady Wishfort *and* Marwood.

Lady Wishfort. O my dear Friend, how can I Enumerate the benefits that I have receiv'd from your goodness? To you I owe the timely discovery of the false vows of *Mirabell*; To you the Detection of the 105 Imposter Sir *Rowland*. And now you are become an Intercessor with my Son-in-Law, to save the Honour of my House, and Compound for the frailties of my Daughter. Well Friend, you are enough to reconcile me to the bad World, or else I wou'd retire to Desarts

and Solitudes; and feed harmless Sheep by *Groves* and *Purling* 110
Streams. Dear *Marwood*, let us leave the World, and retire by our
selves and be *Shepherdesses*.

Mrs. Marwood. Let us first dispatch the affair in hand *Madam*, we
shall have leisure to think of Retirement afterwards. Here is one
who is concern'd in the treaty. 115

Lady Wishfort. O Daughter, Daughter, Is it possible thou shoud'st be
my Child, Bone of my Bone, and Flesh of my Flesh, and as I may
say, another Me, and yet transgress the most minute Particle of
severe Vertue? Is it possible you should lean aside to Iniquity who
have been Cast in the direct Mold of Vertue? I have not only been a 120
Mold but a Pattern for you, and a Model for you, after you were
brought into the World.

Mrs. Fainall. I don't understand your Ladyship.

Lady Wishfort. Not understand? Why have you not been Naught?
Have you not been Sophisticated? Not understand? Here I am 125
ruin'd to Compound for your *Caprices* and your *Cuckoldomes*. I
must pawn my *Plate*, and my *Jewells* and ruine my *Neice*, and all
little enough –

Mrs. Fainall. I am wrong'd and abus'd, and so are you. 'Tis a false
accusation, as false as *Hell*, as false as your Friend there, ay or your 130
Friend's Friend, my false Husband.

Mrs. Marwood. My Friend, Mrs. *Fainall*? Your Husband my Friend,
what do you mean?

Mrs. Fainall. I know what I mean *Madam*, and so do you; and so
shall the World at a time Convenient. 135

Mrs. Marwood. I am sorry to see you so passionate, *Madam*. More
Temper wou'd look more like Innocence. But I have done. I am
sorry my Zeal to serve your Ladyship and Family, shou'd admit of
Misconstruction, or make me liable to affronts. You will pardon me,
Madam, If I meddle no more with an affair, in which I am not 140
Personally concern'd.

Lady Wishfort. O dear Friend; I am so asham'd that you should meet
with such returns; – you ought to ask Pardon on your Knees,
Ungratefull Creature; she deserves more from you than all your
life can accomplish – O don't leave me destitute in this Perplexity; – 145
No, stick to me my good Genius.

Mrs. Fainall. I tell you *Madam* you're abus'd – stick to you? ay, like a
Leach, to suck your best Blood – she'll drop off when she's full.
Madam you sha'not pawn a *Bodkin*, nor part with a *Brass Counter*
in Composition for me. I defie 'em all. Let 'em prove their asper- 150
sions: I know my own Innocence, and dare stand a tryall.

Exit.

Lady Wishfort. Why, If she shou'd be Innocent, If she shou'd be
wrong'd after all, ha? I don't know what to think, – and I promise
you, her Education has been unexceptionable – I may say it; for
I chiefly made it my own Care to Initiate her very Infancy in the 155

Rudiments of Vertue, and to Impress upon her tender Years, a
Young *Odium* and *Aversion* to the very sight of Men, – ay Friend,
she wou'd ha' shriek'd, If she had but seen a Man, till she was in her
Teens. As I'm a Person 'tis true – She was never suffer'd to play with
a Male-Child, tho' but in Coats; Nay her very Babies were of the   160
Feminine Gender, – O, she never look'd a Man in the Face but her
own Father, or the Chaplain, and him we made a shift to put upon
her for a Woman, by the help of his long Garments, and his Sleek-
face; till she was going in her fifteen.

Mrs. Marwood. Twas much she shou'd be deceiv'd so long.   165

Lady Wishfort. I warrant you, or she wou'd never have born to have
been Catechis'd by him; and have heard his long lectures, against
Singing and Dancing, and such Debaucheries; and going to filthy
Plays, and Profane *Musick-meetings*, where the Leud Trebles squeek
nothing but Bawdy, and the Bases roar *Blasphemy*. O, she wou'd   170
have swooned at the sight or name of an obscene Play-Book – and
can I think after all this, that my Daughter can be Naught? What, a
Whore? And thought it excommunication to set her foot within the
door of a Play-house. O my dear friend, I can't believe it, No, no; as
she says, let him prove it, let him prove it.   175

Mrs. Marwood. Prove it *Madam*? What, and have your name prostituted in a publick Court; Yours and your Daughters reputation
worry'd at the Barr by a pack of Bawling Lawyers? To be usherd
in with an *O Yez* of Scandal; and have your Case open'd by an old
fumbling Leacher in a Quoif like a Man Midwife to bring your   180
Daughter's Infamy to light, to be a Theme for legal Punsters, and
Quiblers by the Statute; and become a Jest, against a Rule of Court,
where there is no precedent for a Jest in any record; not even in
Dooms-day-Book: to discompose the gravity of the Bench, and provoke Naughty Interrogatories, in more Naughty *Law Latin*; while   185
the good Judge tickl'd with the proceeding, Simpers under a Grey
beard, and fidges off and on his Cushion as if he had swallow'd
Cantharides, or sat upon *Cow-Itch*.

Lady Wishfort. O, 'tis very hard!

Mrs. Marwood. And then to have my Young *Revellers* of the *Temple*,   190
take Notes like Prentices at a *Conventicle*; and after, talk it all over
again in Commons, or before Drawers in an *Eating-house*.

Lady Wishfort. Worse and Worse.

Mrs. Marwood. Nay this is nothing; if it wou'd end here, 'twere well.
But it must after this be consign'd by the Short-hand Writers to the   195
publick Press; and from thence be transferr'd to the hands, nay into
the Throats and Lungs of Hawkers, with Voices more Licentious
than the loud *Flounder-man's* or the *Woman* that crys *Grey-pease*;
and this you must hear till you are stunn'd; Nay you must hear
nothing else for some days.   200

Lady Wishfort. O, 'tis Insupportable. No, no, dear Friend make it, up,
make it up; ay, ay, I'll Compound. I'll give up all, my self and my all,
my *Neice* and her all, – any thing, everything for Composition.

Mrs. Marwood. Nay *Madam*, I advise nothing, I only lay before you as a Friend the Inconveniencies which perhaps you have Overseen. Here 205 comes Mr. *Fainall.* If he will be satisfi'd to huddle up all in Silence, I shall be glad. You must think I would rather Congratulate, than Condole with you.

Enter Fainall.

Lady Wishfort. Ay, ay, I do not doubt it, dear *Marwood*: No, no, I do not doubt it. 210

Fainall. Well Madam; I have suffer'd my self to be overcome by the Importunity of this Lady your Friend; and am content you shall enjoy your own proper Estate during Life; on condition you oblige your self never to Marry, under such penalty as I think convenient.

Lady Wishfort. Never to Marry? 215

Fainall. No more Sir *Rowlands*, – the next Imposture may not be so timely detected.

Mrs. Marwood. That condition I dare answer, my Lady will consent to, without difficulty; she has already but too much experienc'd the perfidiousness of Men. Besides Madam, when we retire to our 220 pastoral Solitude we shall bid adieu to all other Thoughts.

Lady Wishfort. Aye that's true; but in Case of Necessity; as of Health, or some such Emergency –

Fainall. O, if you are prescrib'd Marriage, you shall be consider'd; I will only reserve to my self the Power to chuse for you. If your Physick be 225 wholsome, it matters not who is your Apothecary. Next, my Wife shall settle on me the remainder of her Fortune, not made over already; And for her Maintenance depend entirely on my Discretion.

Lady Wishfort. This is most inhumanly Savage; exceeding the Barbarity of a *Muscovite* Husband. 230

Fainall. I learn'd it from his *Czarish* Majestie's Retinue, in a Winter Evenings Conference over Brandy and Pepper, amongst other secrets of Matrimony and Policy, as they are at present Practis'd in the *Northern* Hemisphere. But this must be agreed unto, and that positively. Lastly, I will be endow'd in right of my Wife, with that six 235 thousand Pound, which is the Moiety of Mrs. *Millamant's* Fortune in your Possession: And which she has forfeited (as will appear by the last Will and Testament of your deceas'd Husband Sir *Jonathan Wishfort*) by her disobedience in Contracting her self against your Consent or Knowledge; and by refusing the offer'd Match with Sir 240 *Wilfull Witwoud*, which you like a careful Aunt had provided for her.

Lady Wishfort. My Nephew was *non Compos*, and cou'd not make his Addresses.

Fainall. I come to make demands, – I'll hear no objections. 245

Lady Wishfort. You will grant me time to Consider.

Fainall. Yes, while the Instrument is drawing, to which you must set your Hand till more sufficient Deeds can be perfected, which I will take care shall be done with all possible speed. In the mean while,

I will go for the said Instrument, and till my return, you may   250
Ballance this Matter in your own Discretion.

Exit Fainall.

Lady Wishfort. This Insolence is beyond all Precedent, all Parallel,
must I be subject to this merciless Villain?

Mrs. Marwood. 'Tis severe indeed *Madam*, that you shou'd smart for
your Daughters wantonness.   255

Lady Wishfort. 'Twas against my Consent that she Married this Bar-
barian, But she wou'd have him, tho' her Year was not out. – Ah!
her first Husband my Son *Languish*, would not have carry'd it thus.
Well, that was my Choice, this is her's; she is match'd now with a
Witness – I shall be mad, Dear Friend is there no Comfort for me?   260
Must I live to be confiscated at this Rebel-rate? – Here come two
more of my *Egyptian* Plagues too.

Enter Millamant *and* Sir Wilfull.

Sir Wilfull. Aunt, your Servant.

Lady Wishfort. Out *Caterpillar*, Call not me Aunt, I know thee not.

Sir Wilfull. I confess I have been a little in disguise as they say, –   265
S'heart! and I'm sorry for't. What wou'd you have? I hope
I committed no Offence Aunt – and if I did I am willing to make
satisfaction; and what can a man say fairer? If I have broke any thing,
I'll pay for't, an it cost a Pound. And so let that content for what's
past, and make no more words. For what's to come to pleasure you   270
I'm willing to marry my Cozen. So pray lets all be Friends, she and
I are agreed upon the matter, before a Witness.

Lady Wishfort. How's this dear *Neice*? Have I any comfort? Can this
be true?

Millamant. I am content to be a Sacrifice to your repose *Madam*, and   275
to Convince you that I had no hand in the Plot, as you were
misinform'd; I have laid my commands on *Mirabell* to come in
Person, and be a Witness that I give my hand to this flower of
Knight-hood; and for the Contract that past between *Mirabell* and
me, I have oblig'd him to make a Resignation of it, in your Lady-   280
ship's presence; – He is without and waits your leave for admittance.

Lady Wishfort. Well, I'll swear I am something reviv'd at this Testimony
of your Obedience; but I cannot admit that Traytor, – I fear I cannot
fortifie my self to support his appearance. He is a terrible to me as a
Gorgon; if I see him, I fear I shall turn to Stone, petrifie Incessantly.   285

Millamant. If you disoblige him he may resent your refusal and insist
upon the contract still. Then 'tis the last time he will be offensive to
you.

Lady Wishfort. Are you sure it will be the last time? – if I were sure of
that – shall I never see him again?   290

Millamant. Sir *Wilfull*, you and he are to Travel together, are you not?

Sir Wilfull. 'Sheart the Gentleman's a civil Gentleman, Aunt, let him
come in; why we are sworn Brothers and fellow Travellers. – We are

to be *Pylades* and *Orestes*, he and I – He is to be my Interpreter in
foreign Parts. He has been Oversea's once already; and with proviso 295
that I Marry my Cozen, will cross 'em once again, only to bear me
Company, – 'Sheart, I'll call him in, – an I set on't once, he shall
come in; and see who'll hinder him.

Exit.

Mrs. Marwood. This is precious Fooling, if it wou'd pass, but I'll
know the bottom of it. 300
Lady Wishfort. O dear *Marwood*, you are not going?
Marwood. Not far Madam; I'll return immediately.

Exit.

Re-enter Sir Wilfull *and* Mirabell.

Sir Wilfull. Look up Man, I'll stand by you, 'sbud an she do frown,
she can't kill you; – besides – Hearkee she dare not frown desper-
ately, because her face is none of her own; 'Sheart an she shou'd her 305
forehead wou'd wrinkle like the Coat of a Cream-cheese, but mum
for that, fellow Traveller.
Mirabell. If a deep sense of the many Injuries I have offer'd to so
good a Lady, with a sincere remorse, and a hearty Contrition, can
but obtain the least glance of Compassion I am too Happy, – Ah 310
Madam, there was a time – but let it be forgotten – I confess I have
deservedly forfeited the high Place I once held, of sighing at your
Feet; nay kill me not, by turning from me in disdain, – I come not to
plead for favour; – Nay not for Pardon, I am a Suppliant only for
your pity – I am going where I never shall behold you more – 315
Sir Wilfull. How, fellow Traveller! – You shall go by your self then.
Mirabell. Let me be pitied first; and afterwards forgotten, – I ask no
more.
Sir Wilfull. By'r Lady a very reasonable request; and will cost you
nothing, Aunt – Come, come, Forgive and Forget Aunt, why you 320
must an you are a Christian.
Mirabell. Consider *Madam*, in reality; You cou'd not receive much
prejudice; it was an Innocent device; tho' I confess it had a Face of
guiltiness, – it was at most an Artifice which Love Contriv'd – and
errours which Love produces have ever been accounted *Venial*. At 325
least think it is Punishment enough, that I have lost what in my
heart I hold most dear, that to your cruel Indignation, I have
offer'd up this Beauty, and with her my Peace and Quiet; Nay all
my hopes of future Comfort.
Sir Wilfull. An he do's not move me, wou'd I might never be *O' the* 330
Quorum – an it were not as good a deed as to drink, to give her to
him again, – I wou'd I might never take Shipping – Aunt, if you
don't forgive quickly; I shall melt, I can tell you that. My contract
went no further than a little Mouth-Glew, and that's hardly dry; –
One dolefull Sigh more from my fellow Traveller and 'tis dissolv'd. 335

Lady Wishfort. Well *Nephew*, upon your account – ah, he has a false
Insinuating Tongue – Well Sir, I will stifle my just resentment at my
Nephew's request. – I will endeavour what I can to forget, – but on
proviso that you resign the Contract with my *Neice* Immediately.

Mirabell. It is in Writing and with Papers of Concern; but I have sent 340
my Servant for it, and will deliver it to you, with all acknowledg-
ments for your transcendent goodness.

Lady Wishfort [*apart*]. Oh, he has *Witch-craft* in his Eyes and
Tongue; – When I did not see him I cou'd have brib'd a Villain to
his Assassination; but his appearance rakes the *Embers* which have so 345
long layn smother'd in my Breast. –

Enter Fainall and Mrs. Marwood.

Fainall. Your date of deliberation *Madam*, is expir'd. Here is the
Instrument, are you prepar'd to sign?

Lady Wishfort. If I were prepar'd; I am not Impowr'd. My *Neice* exerts
a lawfull claim, having Match'd her self by my direction to Sir *Wilfull.* 350

Fainall. That sham is too gross to pass on me, – tho 'tis Impos'd on
you, *Madam.*

Millamant. Sir, I have given my consent.

Mirabell. And Sir, I have resign'd my pretensions.

Sir Wilfull. And Sir, I assert my right; and will maintain it in defiance 355
of you Sir, and of your Instrument. S'heart an you talk of an
Instrument Sir, I have an old *Fox* by my Thigh shall hack your
Instrument of *Ram Vellum* to shreds, Sir. It shall not be sufficient
for a *Mittimus* or a *Taylor's* measure; therefore withdraw your
Instrument Sir, or by'r Lady I shall draw mine. 360

Lady Wishfort. Hold *Nephew*, hold.

Millamant. Good Sir *Wilfull*, respite your valour.

Fainall. Indeed? are you provided of a Guard, with your single Beef-
eater there? but I'm prepar'd for you and Insist upon my first
proposal. You shall submit your own Estate to my management, 365
And absolutely make over my Wife's to my sole use; As pursuant to
the Purport and Tenor of this other Covenant, – I suppose *Madam*,
your Consent is not requisite in this Case; nor Mr. *Mirabell*, your
resignation; nor Sir *Wilfull*, your right – You may draw your *Fox* if
you please Sir, and make a *Bear-Garden* flourish somewhere else; For 370
here it will not avail. This, my Lady *Wishfort*, must be subscrib'd, or
your Darling Daughter's turn'd a drift, like a Leaky hulk to Sink or
Swim, as she and the Current of this Lewd Town can agree.

Lady Wishfort. Is there no means, no Remedy, to stop my ruine?
Ungrateful Wretch! dost thou not owe thy being, thy subsistance 375
to my Daughter's Fortune?

Fainall. I'll answer you when I have the rest of it in my possession.

Mirabell. But that you wou'd not accept of a Remedy from my hands
– I own I have not deserv'd you shou'd owe any Obligation to me;
or else perhaps I cou'd advise. – 380

Lady Wishfort. O what? what? to save me and my Child from Ruine, from Want, I'll forgive all that's past; Nay I'll consent to any thing to come, to be deliver'd from this Tyranny.

Mirabell. Ay *Madam*; but that is too late, my reward is intercepted. You have dispos'd of her, who only cou'd have made me a Compen-   385
sation for all my Services; – But be it as it may. I am resolv'd I'll serve you, you shall not be wrong'd in this *Savage* manner.

Lady Wishfort. How! dear Mr. *Mirabell*, can you be so generous at last! But it is not possible. *Hearkee*. I'll break my *Nephews* Match, you shall have my *Niece* yet, and all her fortune; if you can but save   390
me from this imminent danger.

Mirabell. Will you? I take you at your word. I ask no more. I must have leave for two Criminals to appear.

Lady Wishfort. Ay, ay, any Body, any body.

Mirabell. *Foible* is one and a Penitent.   395

Enter Mrs. Fainall, Foible, *and* Mincing.

Mrs. Marwood [*to* Fainall] O my shame! [Mirabell *and* Lady Wishfort *go to* Mrs. Fainall *and* Foible]. These Corrupt things are bought and brought hither to expose me –

Fainall. If it must all come out, why let 'em know it, 'tis but *the way of the World*. That shall not urge me to relinquish or abate one title   400
of my Terms, no, I will insist the more.

Foible. Yes indeed *Madam*; I'll take my Bible-oath of it.

Mincing. And so will I, *Mem*.

Lady Wishfort. O *Marwood, Marwood* art thou false? my friend deceive me? hast thou been a wicked accomplice with that profligate   405
man?

Mrs. Marwood. Have you so much Ingratitude and Injustice, to give credit against your Friend, to the Aspersions of two such Mercenary Truls?

Mincing. Mercenary, *Mem*? I scorn your words. 'Tis true we found   410
you and Mr. *Fainall* in the Blew garret; by the same token, you swore us to Secresie upon *Messalinas's* Poems. Mercenary? No, if we wou'd have been Mercenary, we shou'd have held our Tongues; You wou'd have brib'd us sufficiently.

Fainall. Go, you are an Insignificant thing, – Well, what are you the   415
better for this? Is this Mr. *Mirabell*'s Expedient? I'll be put off no longer – You thing that was a Wife, shall smart for this. I will not leave thee where-withall to hide thy Shame; Your Body shall be Naked as your Reputation.

Mrs. Fainall. I despise you and defie your Malice – You have aspers'd   420
me wrongfully – I have prov'd your falsehood – Go you and your treacherous – I will not name it, but starve together – perish.

Fainall. Not while you are worth a Groat, indeed my dear. *Madam*, I'll be fool'd no longer.

Lady Wishfort. Ah Mr. *Mirabell*, this is small comfort, the detection   425
of this affair.

Mirabell. O in good time – Your leave for the other Offender and Penitent to appear, *Madam.*

Enter Waitwell *with a Box of Writings.*

Lady Wishfort. O Sir *Rowland* – well Rascal.

Waitwell. What your Ladyship pleases. – I have brought the Black   430
box at last, *Madam.*

Mirabell. Give it me. *Madam*, you remember your promise.

Lady Wishfort. I, dear Sir!

Mirabell. Where are the Gentlemen?

Waitwell. At hand Sir, rubbing their Eyes, – Just risen from Sleep.   435

Fainall. S'death what's this to me? I'll not wait your private concerns.

Enter Petulant *and* Witwoud.

Petulant. How now? what's the matter? who's hand's out?

Witwoud. Hey day! what are you all got together like Players at the end of the last Act?

Mirabell. You may remember Gentlemen, I once requested your   440
hands as Witnesses to a certain Parchment.

Witwoud. Ay I do, my hand I remember – *Petulant* set his Mark.

Mirabell. You wrong him, his name is fairly written as shall appear – you do not remember Gentlemen, any thing of what that Parchment contain'd – [*undoing the Box.*]   445

Witwoud. No.

Petulant. Not I. I writ. I read nothing.

Mirabell. Very well, now you shall know – *Madam*, your promise.

Lady Wishfort. Ay, ay, Sir, upon my honour.

Mirabell. Mr. *Fainall*, it is now time that you shou'd know, that your   450
Lady while she was at her own disposal, and before you had by your Insinuations wheadl'd her out of a pretended Settlement of the greatest part of her fortune –

Fainall. Sir! pretended!

Mirabell. Yes Sir. I say that this Lady while a Widdow, having it seems   455
receiv'd some Cautions respecting your Inconstancy and Tyranny of temper, which from her own partial Opinion and fondness of you, she cou'd never have suspected – she did I say by the wholesome advice of Friends and of Sages learned in the Laws of this Land, deliver this same as her Act and Deed to me in trust, and to the uses within   460
mention'd. You may read if you please – [*holding out the Parchment*] tho perhaps what is inscrib'd on the back may serve your occasions.

Fainall. Very likely Sir, What's here? Damnation! [*Reads*] *A deed of Conveyance of the whole Estate real of* Arabella Languish *Widdow in trust to* Edward Mirabell. Confusion!   465

Mirabell. Even so Sir, 'tis *the way of the World*, Sir: of the Widdows of the World. I suppose this Deed may bear an Elder Date than what you have obtain'd from your Lady.

Fainall. Perfidious Fiend! then thus I'll be reveng'd. – [*offers to run at Mrs.* Fainall.]   470

Sir Wilfull. Hold Sir, now you may make your *Bear-Garden* flourish somewhere else Sir.

Fainall. Mirabell, You shall hear of this Sir, be sure you shall, let me pass *Oafe.*

Exit.

Mrs. Fainall. Madam, you seem to stifle your Resentment: You had 475
better give it Vent.

Mrs. Marwood. Yes it shall have Vent – and to your Confusion, or I'll perish in the attempt.

Exit.

Lady Wishfort. O Daughter, Daughter, 'tis plain thou hast inherited
thy Mother's prudence. 480

Mrs. Fainall. Thank Mr. *Mirabell,* a Cautious Friend, to whose advice all is owing.

Lady Wishfort. Well Mr. *Mirabell,* you have kept your promise, – and I must perform mine. – First I pardon for your sake, Sir *Rowland* there and *Foible,* – The next thing is to break the Matter to my 485
Nephew – and how to do that –

Mirabell. For that *Madam,* give your self no trouble – let me have your Consent – Sir *Wilfull* is my Friend; he has had compassion upon Lovers and generously engag'd a Volunteer in this Action, for our Service, and now designs to prosecute his Travells. 490

Sir Wilfull. S'heart Aunt, I have no mind to marry. My Cozen's a Fine Lady, and the Gentleman loves her and she loves him, and they deserve one another; my resolution is to see Foreign Parts – I have set on't – And when I'm set on't, I must do't. And if these two Gentlemen wou'd Travel too, I think they may be spar'd. 495

Petulant. For my part, I say little – I think things are best off or on.

Witwoud. I Gad I understand nothing of the matter, – I'm in a maze yet, like a *Dog* in a *Dancing School.*

Lady Wishfort. Well Sir, take her, and with her all the Joy I can give you.

Millamant. Why do's not the man take me? wou'd you have me give 500
my self to you over again.

Mirabell. Ay, and over and over again; for I wou'd have you as often as possibly I can. [*Kisses her hand*]. Well, heav'n grant I love you not too well, that's all my fear.

Sir Wilfull. S'heart you'll have him time enough to toy after you're 505
married; or if you will toy now; Let us have a Dance in the mean time, that we who are not Lovers, may have some other employ-ment, besides looking on.

Mirabell. With all my heart dear Sir *Wilfull,* what shall we do for Musick? 510

Foible. O Sir, Some that were provided for Sir *Rowland's* Entertain-ment are yet within Call.

A Dance.

Lady Wishfort. As I am a person I can hold out no longer; – I have wasted my spirits so to day already; that I am ready to sink under the fatigue; and I cannot but have some fears upon me yet, that my Son   515
Fainall will pursue some desperate Course.

Mirabell. **Madam,** disquiet not your self on that account, to my knowledge his Circumstances are such, he must of force comply. For my part I will Contribute all that in me lies to a Reunion, [*To Mrs.* Fainall] in the mean time, *Madam,* let me before these Witnesses, restore to   520
you this deed of trust. It may be a means well manag'd to make you live Easily together. From hence let those be warn'd, who mean to wed;
Lest mutual falsehood stain the Bridal-Bed:
For each deceiver to his cost may find,
That marriage frauds too oft are paid in kind.   525

Exeunt Omnes.

EPILOGUE SPOKEN BY MRS. BRACEGIRDLE

After our *Epilogue* this Crowd dismisses,
I'm thinking how this Play'll be pull'd to Pieces.
But pray consider, ere you doom its fall,
How hard a thing 'twould be, to please you all.
There are some Criticks so with Spleen diseas'd,   5
They scarcely come inclining to be Pleas'd:
And sure he must have more than mortal Skill,
Who pleases any one against his Will.
Then, all bad Poets we are sure are Foes,
And how their Number's swell'd the Town well knows: 10
In shoals, I've mark'd 'em judging in the Pit; ⎫
Tho' they're on no pretence for Judgment fit ⎬
But that they have been Damn'd for want of wit. ⎭
Since when, they by their own offences taught
Set up for Spys on Plays and finding Fault.   15
Others there are whose Malice we'd prevent; ⎫
Such, who watch Plays, with scurrilous intent ⎬
To mark out who by *Characters* are meant. ⎭
And tho' no perfect likeness they can Trace;
Yet each pretends to know the *Copy'd Face.*   20
These with false Glosses, feed their own Ill-nature,
And turn to *Libel,* what was meant a *Satire.*
May such malicious *Fops* this Fortune find,
To think themselves alone the *Fools* design'd:
If any are so arrogantly Vain,   ⎫   25
To think they *singly* can support a *Scene,* ⎬
And furnish *Fool* enough to entertain.   ⎭

For well the Learn'd and the Judicious know,⎫
That *Satire* scorns to stoop so meanly low, ⎬
As any *one abstracted Fop* to shew.   ⎭   30
For, as when Painters form a matchless Face,
They from each *Fair One* catch some different Grace,
And shining Features in one Portrait blend,
To which no single Beauty must pretend:
So Poets oft, do in one Piece expose   35
Whole *Belles Assemblées* of *Cocquetts* and *Beaux*.

[FINIS.]